IN A MANNER OF SPEAKING

IN A MANNER OF SPEAKING

SPEAKING

Phrases, Expressions, and Proverbs and
How We Use and Misuse Them

COLIN MCNAIRN

Skyhorse Publishing

"Comment," "Oscar Wilde," from DOROTHY PARKER: COMPLETE POEMS by Dorothy Parker, copyright (c) 1999 by The National Association for the Advancement of Colored People. Used by permission of Penguin, a division of Penguin Group (USA) LLC and by permission of Gerald Duckworth & Co. Ltd

"Reflections on Ice Breaking," "The Oyster," "Compliments of a Friend," "Everybody's Mind to Me a Kingdom is," "Seductive Reflection" and "Thought Thought While Waiting for a Pronouncement from a Doctor..." by Ogden Nash, copyright 1931; 1931; 1949; 1952; 1940 and 1942 by Ogden Nash. Reprinted by permission of Curtis Brown, Ltd. and by permission of Carlton Publishing Group

These and other permissions are noted in the Endnotes

Skyhorse Publishing books may be purchased in bulk at special discounts for sales promotion, corporate gifts, fund-raising, or educational purposes. Special editions can also be created to specifications. For details, contact the Special Sales Department, Skyhorse Publishing, 307 West 36th Street, 11th Floor, New York, NY 10018 or info@ skyhorsepublishing.com.

Skyhorse® and Skyhorse Publishing® are registered trademarks of Skyhorse Publishing, Inc.®, a Delaware corporation.

Visit our website at www.skyhorsepublishing.com.

10 9 8 7 6 5 4 3 2 1

Library of Congress Cataloging-in-Publication Data is available on file.

Cover design by Jane Sheppard

Print ISBN: 978-1-63220-520-9
Ebook ISBN: 978-1-63220-898-9

Printed in the United States of America

To Marian

TABLE OF CONTENTS

INTRODUCTION

This book is about expressions and about sayings, also called proverbs, and how we put them to work in our communications, both oral and written. The number of these pre-packaged aids to making ourselves understood, and enlivening what we have to say, is vast. There's no way that a single book could possibly cover the "whole kit and caboodle," "the whole shebang," "the whole megillah," "the whole enchilada," "the whole nine yards," "the whole box and dice," "the full Monty." And these are just a few of the expressions we might use to say the whole lot.

I have chosen, therefore, to zero in on those expressions and sayings, or their take-offs, that are funny, quirky or just plain folksy, or that are playfully dressed up in rhyme or alliteration. I single out others because they've "gone off the rails" for one reason or other. They may have become clichés, which are trite expressions that it's said, "tongue in cheek," should be "avoided like the plague." They may have been distorted "to all intensive purposes" through what is, "to all intents and purposes," a misunderstanding. They may have come to be regarded as politically incorrect, creating stains on their reputations "as black as the ace of spades," if you'll pardon an expression that's sometimes branded as racist. Still other expressions and sayings are "put under the spotlight" because they're shrouded in mystery and bear some explanation.

I've taken "the world as my oyster," but primarily the English-speaking part of that world, and drawn upon geographically widespread manners of speaking, especially those in the United States, the United Kingdom, Canada and Australia. Since all of these countries share a common linguistic heritage, as well as similar social and political customs, a good many expressions and sayings are the same or similar throughout the four nations. But others, such as local colloquialisms and the rhyming slang of Cockney or Australian origin, are "as different as chalk and cheese," as the Brits would say.

This book is unlike most others in the field, for it's not simply a compilation of expressions or sayings with meanings and origins. Rather, it spins a narrative that "runs the gamut" of the characteristics of both tools of communication, including their style, their use of various literary devices, including metaphors, similes and other figures of speech, their recurring patterns, their encryption as acronyms and the varieties of images they commonly draw upon—ranging from the world of animals to the human anatomy to the food and drink that we consume. The book is also different from its predecessors in that it brings expressions and sayings together "under one roof" and illuminates their similarities and differences.

Particular attention is paid to the extent to which expressions and sayings have developed from, or infiltrated, the worlds of literature, advertising, entertainment, sports, politics and the mass media. Illustrations are drawn from quotable quotes, song titles and lyrics, light verse and, mindful of the saying that "a picture is worth a thousand words," cartoons. Collectively, these examples demonstrate the extent to which expressions and sayings have permeated our popular culture.

The primary purpose of the book is to enrich our understanding of language through an entertaining look at expressions and sayings with special attention to the ways in which they've been used or manipulated in a humorous fashion. And so, "without further ado," I end this introduction with a quotation, from the hostess of a children's radio program, which became so popular in Britain that it now warrants an entry in the *Little Oxford Dictionary of Proverbs*: "Are you sitting comfortably? Then we'll begin."

1

EXPRESSIONS MADE MEMORABLE

Substance without style is like a face without a smile.

Anon.

Why is it that we remember certain expressions while others "go in one ear and out the other?" Are we seduced by style, particularly the use of alliteration or rhyme? In this chapter, we'll see that these two devices often help in "getting a foot in the door" and leaving a mental imprint of an expression. In fact, they may provide the only reason for the continuing popularity of a number of expressions that lack any real logic. In that case, it's clearly a matter of style over substance.

Rhyming expressions are particularly effective with children. A young child quickly learns what "yummy in the tummy" means and is "egged on," when he does something amusing, by the comment that he's being "a silly billy" or "a funny bunny." When he gets older and more restless, he comes to understand the much stranger diagnosis that he has "ants in his pants." He eventually learns to rebuke his playmates with juvenile jingles such as "liar, liar, pants on fire" and "I'm the king of the castle and you're the dirty rascal." Then, when old enough to be responsible for his own behavior, he becomes familiar with the threat "you're cruisin' for a bruisin'," when he acts up. Alternatively, he may be intimidated by the less common "you're achin' for a breakin'" or "you're aimin' for a maimin'." All three expressions are fast becoming obsolete, however, now that the corporal punishment of children is generally frowned upon.

There are many slang terms or expressions that are in the form of rhyming reduplications, for example, "higgledy piggledy," "fuzzy wuzzy," "mumbo jumbo" and "nitty gritty." Some rhyming reduplications, such as "the heebie jeebies," "the bees knees," "hocus pocus," "okay dokey," "helter skelter," "hanky panky" and "artsy fartsy," are light-hearted terms that came out of the roaring twenties before the dirty thirties turned everyone more serious. This kind of whimsical expression, from whatever era, is frequently written with a hyphen between the two words on the theory that it's a compound noun or a compound adjective.

Many of the words in these rhyming reduplications are simply made up and each of the words is matched up with another word in a nonsensical way, hence the alternative description of these combinations as nonsense pairings. Most of these pairings have, nonetheless, acquired a certain accepted meaning, which may be completely unrelated to the meaning, if any, of either of the component words. "Higgledy piggledy," for example, is generally used, in a no-nonsense way, to mean mixed together in a jumbled, confused or disorderly manner. The expression itself meets this definition, for the order of the "l" and the "e" in each word has to be reversed to come up with the proper pronunciation.

"Higgledy piggledy" seems to be used more for effect than to convey any particular meaning in the nursery rhyme that begins: "Higgledy piggledy, my black hen, she lays eggs for gentlemen," although some might argue that "higgledy piggledy" must be the name of the hen. "Fuzzy wuzzy" is clearly the inappropriate name of an animal in the old children's poem that goes like this:

Fuzzy wuzzy was a bear.
Fuzzy wuzzy had no hair.
Fuzzy wuzzy wasn't fuzzy, was he?

But the expression has also been used, most famously by the British poet Rudyard Kipling, to describe black people by allusion to their tight curly hair. In Kipling's poem "Fuzzy Wuzzy," they are members of a Sudanese fighting force for which he has much praise. Nonetheless, the term is now widely regarded as derogatory for its racial stereotyping.

The question, "do yo' hair be kinky?" was raised in the opening line of an ad on the popular country music show broadcast every Saturday night from the Grand Ole Opry in Nashville, Tennessee. Mimicking jive talk, this was the attention grabber for a short exposé on the straightening merits of a hairdressing pomade manufactured by one of the early sponsors of this long running radio program. Although something of a catchphrase in its day, it ultimately fell into disrepute, just as "fuzzy wuzzy" has done, hastened no doubt by the fact that "kinky" has an alternative meaning of sexually weird.

"Mumbo jumbo," like "fuzzy wuzzy," emerged from an African setting. It was the name given by the Mandingo people of West Africa to a protective ancestral figure who punished wives accused by their husbands of being troublesome in some way, particularly by getting into conflicts with their fellow wives. Behind every appearance of Mumbo Jumbo was a respected male tribesman, selected for the occasion, masquerading in a familiar bark cloth and long coat get-up. The punishment that Mumbo Jumbo would usually mete out, after a hasty finding of guilt, was a public beating of the offending spouse while she was tied naked to a post. This background would seem to bear little relationship to the current use of "mumbo jumbo" as referring to unintelligible language or gibberish. But the term also has a secondary meaning as a belief or behavior based on superstition, which provides a closer tie-in to the Mumbo Jumbo of West African tradition. Some have argued that "mumbo jumbo" is racist, given its likely origin in a cruel practice of a black ethnic group and the gullibility of the members of that group. This reaction may have been fueled by the fact that the parents in *The Story of Little Black Sambo*, published in 1899 and widely condemned as racist by today's standards, were named Black Mumbo and Black Jumbo.

"Mumbo jumbo" is likely to remain popular, however, as a good way to describe a jumble of verbal nonsense, particularly typical of "bureaucratese." That language of officialdom has no other recognized name that's nearly as appropriate as "mumbo jumbo" with its dose of resigned humor.

"Nitty gritty," which occurs in the larger expression "getting down to the nitty gritty," is closer to "the fuzzy line" (a term that's still acceptable) separating the politically correct from the politically incorrect. The expression simply means getting down to the basic essentials. However, it's thought by some to refer to the debris at the bottom of slave ships after they were unloaded and, therefore, as conjuring up nasty images of slavery. Yet there's no evidence that "nitty gritty" was understood to be associated in any way with the slave trade until those who are critical of it speculated upon a connection in recent times. To be on the safe side, it might be better to "get down to brass tacks," rather than the "nitty gritty," which would just as well convey the essential idea of getting down to the basics. Undeterred by the controversy, the folk-rock group, The Nitty Gritty Dirt Band, has "thrown caution to the wind," choosing to emphasize its country music roots through its name.

In a famous incident in February, 1971, Pierre Elliott Trudeau, then Prime Minister of Canada, coined a new rhyming reduplication "fuddle duddle" to describe something off-color that he may have said. At the time, he was accused by certain lip-reading Opposition members in Parliament of having mouthed a two-word obscenity directed at them across the floor of the House of Commons. When he was confronted by the press with that accusation, he engaged in a technical diversion by asking what "mouthed" meant. He never did admit that anything improper passed his lips, although the general public considered him guilty as charged by the Opposition. "Fuddle duddle" found its way, in due course, into the *Canadian Oxford Dictionary* as an oath meaning "go to hell" or "drop dead." Both of these meanings are very mild substitutes for what the PM likely "mouthed." A more accurate definition of "fuddle duddle" would be "a euphemistic rhyming cover-up for the 'f' word." As such, it's a minced oath or, in the popular jargon, an expletive-deletive.

A few rhyming duplications have a good deal of logic to them because the two words that make them up are suggestive of the meaning of the reduplication. This is true of "itsy bitsy" and "teenie weenie." These two reduplications are, perhaps, best known, in the adult world, for their combination in this line from a popular song of the 1960s: "She Wore an Itsy Bitsy Teenie Weenie Yellow Polka Dot Bikini." With this doubling up of reduplications to similar effect, who could possibly miss the bare fact that her bathing suit was very skimpy? According to the song, this swimming attire explained why, in those more modest times, she didn't want to come out of the change room and, after overcoming that hurdle, why she didn't want to get out of the water.

There are many rhyming expressions, besides the typical rhyming reduplications, that have little or no inherent logic and are remembered, in large part, because of their rhythmic quality. "Loose as a goose," for example, hardly seems a suitable description of someone who is relaxed, cool and indifferent given the aggressive behavior of geese, particularly those with goslings in tow. Yet, that's the way the expression is used. "Loosey goosey," a spin-off reduplication, is also a poor candidate for what it signifies, namely laid-back or imprecise. The only thing loose about a goose is its overactive bowels.

If someone is described as "drunk as a skunk," the analogy really doesn't help to call up an image of one who is seriously inebriated. As far as we know, skunks are teetotalers. While they may, at times, be high, it's because of their scent and not because they've been "into the sauce." The recognizable characteristics of many other animals provide a rich source for revealing similes: "sly as a fox," "happy as a lark," "strong as an ox," "proud as a peacock," "slow as a snail" and "quiet as a mouse." But "loose as a goose" and "drunk as a skunk" hardly have the same illustrative quality; they don't play upon a common stereotype of a particular creature. Rather, their attraction lies in their rhyming cadence.

In Australia, where there are no skunks, it may be more appropriate to go for alliteration, rather than rhyme, and say that someone is "wasted as a wallaby." While this is not an established expression, it could catch on as a result of a story that appeared, under the headline "Hopping Mad: Stoned Wallabies Make Crop Circles," in *The Sydney Morning Herald*. The newspaper reported that wallabies are getting high on Tasmanian opium crops causing disorientation and a propensity to hop around in circles, leaving a telltale imprint in the poppy fields. If this report is to be believed, there is now more empirical evidence to support "wasted as a wallaby" than there is to support "drunk as a skunk."

Another possible alliterative simile, "fried as a frustrated fruit fly," would also be a good candidate to replace "drunk as a skunk." A recent study reported by the magazine *Science* compared the drinking behavior of male fruit flies who had just had sex with virgin females to that of other male fruit flies who had been exposed to recently mated females and were spurned because the females were sexually sated. For their efforts, successful or otherwise, the members of both male groups were offered two kinds of liquid refreshment, one laced with alcohol and the other not. In their misery, the unsatisfied fruit flies drank heavily of the mixture spiked with alcohol; their experience with the females was, apparently, "enough to drive them to drink." In their euphoria, the satisfied fruit flies were more inclined to choose the non-alcoholic option. Therefore, "fried as a frustrated fruit fly" would make a lot of sense on scientific grounds although, like "wasted as a wallaby," it has yet to gain general acceptance.

"That's tough titty" is a sarcastic way of saying that's just too bad. This alliterative expression comes from a line of uncertain origin: "Tough titty said the kitty when the milk went dry." While this has the beauty of combining alliteration with a rhyme, the rhyme seems forced. It's much more likely that the nursing cat, rather than her deprived kitten, would utter the words "tough titty," to express callous indifference, should the mother's milk dry up.

Sometimes alliterative expressions, like some rhyming expressions, provide no useful frame of reference for the meaning they're meant to convey. While something or somebody may be "dead as a doornail" or "deader than a doornail," a door nail is no more lacking in life than any other inanimate object so as to justify its use as signifying "dead as dead can be." "Dead as a dodo" is a much more revealing alliterative expression, drawing as it does on the notion of the extinct as an emphatic representation of "dead and departed." Other alliterative expressions, such as "a war of words," "good as gold" and "come hell or high water," also do a good job of leading us to their meaning. So does "too pooped to pop," although some might jump to the wrong conclusion that it has something to do with being "loosey goosey."

Still other alliterative expressions that embody pairs of words or word couplings have been called Siamese twins because they're composed of two words, usually linked by "and" or "or," one of which has more or less the same meaning as the other or encompasses the other. This aptly describes "alas and alack," "hale and hearty," "slip and slide" and "vim and vigor." All of these pairs are taken to exhibit an acceptable redundancy in the interests of effect, clarity or emphasis.

The Italian-American expression "badaboom badabing," which can just as well be reversed or else shortened to "badabing," consists of a nonsense pairing in alliterative form. Neither of its two made-up words seems to make any sense but "badaboom badabing" nonetheless became popular, as an exclamation, after it was used by actor James Caan, playing the role of Sonny Corleone, in the original *Godfather* movie. Later, it featured in the TV series *The Sopranos*, as the name of a mob-owned strip club. It's been suggested that the word "badabing" is intended to reflect the sound of a drum roll used to punctuate a vaudeville show. In this situation, the sound of the drum plugged a gap and provided a diversion after a comedian had "laid an egg" with a punch line that had "fallen flat." This may explain why "badaboom badabing" came to be used, in the midst of a spoken narrative, as a filler between two happenings, indicating that "one thing led to another," without being specific, or simply *et voilà*, as the French would say. Sonny Corleone used the expression in *The Godfather* to describe the effortless nature and predictable outcome of an up-close mob shooting.

Rhyming expressions and alliterative expressions aren't always doublets; they may also be triplets. The best known example of a rhyming triplet is "snug as a bug in a rug," which is apparently another of the inventions from the lightning mind of Benjamin Franklin. The phrase "nattering nabobs of negativism" was coined by William Safire when acting as a speechwriter for U.S. Vice President Spiro T. Agnew. It soon became a popular expression, particularly among politicians who used it as a dismissive denunciation of a critical press.

"The fickle finger of fate" is used to describe the vagaries of chance or the caprices of destiny, which may foreshadow something quite ominous. The creators of *Laugh-In*, the popular television series of the late 1960s and early 1970s, added to the alliteration in this expression, turning it into a quad, when they instituted the Flying Fickle Finger of Fate Award. The award was presented, in each show, to recognize a dubious achievement by a famous person. The statuette emblematic of the award was known as the "Rigid Digit." One of the recipients was the conservative commentator, William F. Buckley. He was singled out for bastardizing a familiar saying when he advised: "Never clarify tomorrow what you can obscure today." Had he been alliteratively and lyrically inclined, he might have said: If your "bullshit baffles brains" today, don't later "stoop and scoop" the crap away.

2

DON'T TAKE THE EXPRESSION LITERALLY

When a middle-aged man says in a moment of weariness that he is half dead, he is telling the literal truth.

Elmer Davis, American News Reporter and Author

How much simpler life would be if all expressions were to be taken literally. Simpler yes, but much less interesting as we would miss out on the color and intrigue of idiomatic expressions and of expressions that use hyperbole, understatement or irony to make a point. These expressions all ignore the admonition that the March Hare gave Alice in Wonderland because they really don't say what they mean. As we shall see in this chapter, humorists have had a lot of fun with idiomatic expressions by using them in a way that suggests a literal meaning that they don't normally bear.

An idiomatic expression can challenge us because its individual words, taken at face value, don't lead us inevitably to the sense in which the expression is commonly used. A prime example is "kick the bucket," an idiomatic way of saying "die." Yet there's nothing in our usual understanding of "giving the boot to" a bucket, in a physical sense, that would be likely to equate it with someone's demise. The actual, figurative meaning of an idiomatic expression, such as this, is associative. It comes from the customary identification of a particular image with the words in the expression taken as a whole.

It's much easier to guess at the meaning of "hold your tongue" from the bare words of that idiomatic expression. The physical act of holding your tongue would result in a loss of the capacity to speak. Therefore, it's not a large leap in logic from holding your tongue to the notion of remaining silent, which is the figurative meaning of the expression. It helps, as a springboard in making the leap, that "tongue" serves as a metaphor for speaking when it pops up in several other words and phrases, such as "tongue-tied" and "having a silver tongue."

A phrase that makes up an idiomatic expression can often be used as well for its literal meaning. It's fairly clear, for example, that "kick the bucket" is intended to be taken literally in the following sentence: The cow managed to "kick the bucket" before the milkmaid had even begun to milk her and then returned, still engorged, to the pasture.

The literal meaning of a phrase that makes up an idiomatic expression may, however, be quite implausible in almost any context. If an individual is said to "have butterflies in his stomach," it's very unlikely that he has actually swallowed some of these flying insects. The more likely scenario is that the individual is being portrayed as having the same sort of sensation as would come from having "butterflies in his stomach," namely a queasy feeling. That's often attributable to a case of nerves, thus the figurative meaning of the expression, namely "nervous."

Idiomatic expressions can be particularly problematic for those who aren't very familiar with the English language. Imagine the reaction of a young child or an ESL (English as a Second Language) student when first told to "eat your heart out." He would immediately wonder why he should self-destruct in this odd way and, in any event, how such a feat could be physically accomplished. He would be particularly confused if he had been told, "don't lose heart" when facing the challenges of learning the language. He would certainly be unlikely to guess that "eat your heart out" was simply an invitation to envy. Or imagine an arriving foreign tourist, drawing upon the language learned from a Berlitz guide, trying to understand why his fellow airline passengers have broken out in laughter at the stewardess's final announcement before landing, thanking them all for their business and for allowing the crew "to take them for a ride."

The word "literally" can be usefully added when a phrase, known for its figurative meaning, is used in its literal sense and the context doesn't make that perfectly plain. If the airline stewardess wanted to "play it straight" and forego the opportunity to get a laugh out of her passengers, she might have said: Thank you for letting the crew take you for a ride, literally speaking. This would remove any suggestion that the passengers were deceived into taking a flight with the airline, which the figurative meaning of the phrase would convey.

"So far so good," but some people are in the unfortunate habit of using idiomatic expressions in conversation with the addition of the word "literally" for emphasis. Someone might say, in order to underline his astonishment at something, "it literally blew my mind." While it may have blown his mind in a figurative sense, it won't have done so in a literal sense. If it had, he wouldn't have had the wit left to express his astonishment. There are T-shirts available for purchase by anyone who is seriously bothered by this use of "literally" and wants to advertise his discomfort. They proclaim the message: "Misuse of literally makes me figuratively insane." It would probably be a mistake, however, to "get your shirt in a knot" over this common error.

Of course, one can always avoid a literal interpretation of a phrase by adding the disclaimer: "It's just an expression." Thus, "it blew my mind" followed by those magic words would make it clear that the speaker's mind didn't really explode but was still functioning, "thank you very much."

A popular formula for humorous quips is to take an idiomatic expression and then add something that exploits the literal meaning. Oscar Wilde applied this recipe in his line from *Lady Windermere's Fan*: "I like talking to a brick wall—it's the only thing in the world that never contradicts me!" Someone who obviously did face contradiction and got into a heated exchange, described the experience this way: "We went at it hammer and tongs…I won in the end though; I had the hammer." This line was part of a routine by the British comedians Eric Morecambe and Ernie Wise.

A peculiar form of humor known as the Wellerism will often treat an idiomatic expression as if it were to be taken literally. It does this, in the style of Sam Weller, a character in Charles Dickens' *Pickwick Papers*, through its description of the circumstances of an individual, an animal or an object reported to have used the expression. This can be illustrated by a few choice examples:

"I am dressed to kill" as the recruit said when he donned his uniform.
"I'll be a monkey's uncle" said the ape when he learned that his sister was pregnant.
"You'll break my heart" as the oak said to the hatchet.

The facetious question: "Would you 'give your right arm' to be ambidextrous?" also involves a play upon two different meanings, one of which could have dire consequences if you answered "yes." In that event, the literal meaning would entail cutting off your arm, which would spite your desire to be ambidextrous and leave you seriously disabled "into the bargain."

Expressions are sometimes used in jest in other situations in which they can carry both a figurative meaning and a literal meaning, each of which is perfectly plausible. Dorothy Parker, the American journalist and writer, famously wrote to a friend who had just given birth: "Congratulations. We all knew you had it in you." In a verse of a popular song on a Spike Jones recording of the 1940's, "Doodles" Weaver, uncle of the actress Sigourney Weaver, recounts his resolution for the current New Year that he wouldn't tell any more corny jokes. When interrupted towards the end of the song by a ringing telephone, he's heard to say into the phone; "Hello, what's that? The church burned down. Holy Smoke!" Consequently, his New Year's resolution also "went up in smoke," but of the secular variety.

This kind of double play, in which Dorothy Parker and "Doodles" Weaver were engaged, is sometimes used to commercial advantage. It makes its subtle appearance in this Snapper lawn mower slogan: "Anything less won't cut it" and in this advertising claim by a competitor that nothing "makes the cut" like a genuine Honda lawn mower. It's also evident in this ad for a used musical instrument: "Guitar for sale...cheap...no strings attached," and in this driving school sign: "If your wife wants to drive, don't stand in her way."

Newspaper headline writers are particularly adept at using common expressions in a way that carries two possible meanings, figurative and literal. A story in a Canadian newspaper, *The Globe and Mail,* reported on an agreement between a distiller and the U.S. Virgin Islands that would provide incentives for distilling operations on those islands to the inevitable detriment of distillers in nearby Puerto Rico. The headline: "Rum maker's pact with Virgin Islands leaves Puerto Rico in poor spirits." Another Caribbean nation, Cuba, was apparently determined to rally against a dispiriting decline in the market for its major export, cigars. Its plan was to take aim at the neglected female cigar smoker by introducing a milder tobacco product. That initiative prompted this headline in the same newspaper: "Poor Cigar Sales Drive Cuba to Turn Over a New Leaf."

A sports story in the *Toronto Star* about England's tie with the United States in their first-round match in the 2010 World Cup described the English team members' solidarity with their goalkeeper who had stopped a shot only to let the ball trickle out of his hands and crawl across the goal line, allowing the Americans to tie the match. The headline: "Teammates Stand Behind Keeper (Not a Bad Idea)." The same newspaper ran a story about Misjudgment Day, May 21, 2011, when the Apocalypse publicly predicted by pastor Harold Camping failed to materialize. The caption: "So I screwed up. It's not the end of the world."

A British tabloid, the *Daily Mail,* seems to have abandoned the figurative meaning of a modern expression, in favor of a literal meaning, by running the headline "Bog standard: Brussels demands the same toilet flush across the Continent after discovering Brits use the most water." The British expression "bog standard" ordinarily means perfectly ordinary, but the shorter flush called for by the European Commission, based in the Belgian capital, would be extraordinary for the average Brit, who is still wedded to Thomas Crapper's inefficient version of the flush toilet.

Sometimes, a headline writer will use an idiomatic expression in a completely inappropriate situation given the palpable risk that it could be interpreted literally. The Louisville *Courier-Journal* once carried this headline, memorable for its potentially disheartening message: "Chef throws his heart into helping feed needy." Talk about self sacrifice in aid of the less fortunate!

Idiomatic expressions are sometimes extended, to humorous effect, by adding an elaboration or qualification that builds upon both the literal and the figurative meaning of the expression. The warning, "if you get too big for your britches, you'll be exposed in the end" fits this description. So does the observation that "no matter how much you push the envelope, it'll still be stationery (stationary)." This line is better heard than read for its double meaning is driven by a pair of homophones. They sound the same but have quite different meanings, which color the preceding clause.

"She was Pure as Snow but she Drifted" is a *faux* country music title that follows the same pattern. The teasing question, "If I Said You Have a Beautiful Body, Would You Hold it Against Me?" is the real title of a country music hit released by the Bellamy Brothers duo in 1979. The title question was borrowed from comedian Groucho Marx, who used it, in a politically incorrect era, as a come-on to attractive female guests who appeared on his long-running TV show *You Bet Your Life*.

The expression "the cream of the crop" is used to describe the best, usually amongst a group of people. It involves a mixed metaphor because it combines two words that symbolize different notions that don't sit well together. "Cream" refers to something that rises to the top as in the process of milk separation. A "crop" refers to a group appearing or produced at the same time, just as a growing crop generally matures more or less at one time. When the two words are linked, as they are in the idiomatic expression "the cream of the crop," there's a distinct disconnect. The comparable French expression, *crème de la crème*, which is often used as a highbrow substitute, avoids any such dissonance.

Mixed metaphors are generally frowned upon. As it's sometimes put, "It's as plain as the egg on your face" that you should avoid mixed metaphors. The first part of that advice marries up the idiomatic expressions "as plain as the nose on your face" and "to have egg on your face," with their different metaphors, in a mixed idiom or an idiom blend. The only logic to a mixed idiom is that some literal elements of the expressions are related. The following additional examples make little sense but they carry a touch of humor in their inherent incongruity:

> to beat [someone] over the head with a dead horse (combining "to beat [someone] over the head" and "to flog a dead horse")
> as much fun as shooting monkeys in a barrel (combining "funnier than a barrel of monkeys" and "like shooting fish in a barrel")
> to take to [something] like a fish out of water (combining "to take to [something] like a duck to water" and "like a fish out of water")
> to bite more off the bullet than you can chew (combining "to bite off more than you can chew" and "to bite the bullet")

Sometimes mixed idioms are made up from idiomatic expressions that carry similar figurative meanings. "Don't rock the apple cart" has its genesis in "don't rock the boat" and "don't upset the apple cart," two expressions that come close to one another in the nature of their warnings against "making waves" and against disturbing a stable situation. "To step up to the plate" and "to grab the bull by the horns," both signifying decisive action, are combined in "to step up to the plate and grab the bull by the horns." "To eat humble crow" is the result of collapsing the expressions "to eat humble pie" and "to eat crow," which are alike in that they both signify humiliation when someone is shown to be wrong about something. The expression "to eat humble pie with a side of crow" is, obviously, derived from the same two sources.

In another twist, two or more idiomatic expressions that convey essentially the same figurative meaning may be put together in sequence for their combined impact and entertainment value. The prolific Scottish writer Alexander McCall Smith proved to be a master at this, in one of his 44 Scotland Street series of novels, through his description of the results of an engaged woman having just agreed, in a weak moment, to go sailing with her former boyfriend: "She had ruined everything. Rubicons had been crossed, boats burned, gooses cooked—and metaphors mixed with all the enthusiasm with which Betty Crocker or Jamie Oliver might throw together the ingredients of a cake."

Expressions can also be appended to construct mock proverbs, which simply sound like wise sayings. We might advise that "if someone 'sells you down the river', just 'go with the flow'." This means, in a figurative sense, that in the face of a betrayal you should swallow hard, while "keeping your head above water," and accept the situation or, in biblical terms, "turn the other cheek."

These mixed idioms have all been deliberately contrived for their humor, but there is also an accidental variety. It's more likely to come out in the spoken word than the written word. George W. Bush, who is famous for his lapses in language, which came to be known as "Bushisms," was once asked, at a press conference, what his biggest mistake was as U.S. president. In response, he complained that he hadn't been given the question in writing ahead of time, saying "you just put me under the spot here," mixing the notions of being "put under the spotlight" and being "put on the spot." But perhaps he knew full well that he was coining a new expression for, as he observed on another occasion, people were inclined to "misunderestimate" him.

It's not surprising that George W. Bush was often dubbed, in a cleverly calculated mixed idiom, as "born with a silver foot in his mouth," which said something about the privilege of his heritage as well as his propensity for malapropisms. That same idiom had been famously applied to his father, George H.W. Bush, by Ann Richards in a speech to the Democratic National Convention in 1988. This was before she became Governor of Texas, an office that she would lose in her first re-election bid, through a kind of poetic justice, to George W. Bush, who was an even better candidate than his father to wear the mantle of her mixed idiom.

Idiomatic expressions serve as important ingredients for Tom Swiftys, successors to Wellerisms, which were particularly popular in the 1960s. They take their name from the fictional hero in a series of books published by an American syndicate. Unlike most Bushisms, they aren't the result of misspeaking but are cunningly conceived. They follow a sentence structure that, typically, involves adding to a familiar statement the words "said Tom," together with an adverb that describes the manner in which Tom purportedly spoke. The adverb echoes, or hints at, some aspect of the statement. Here are some of the better examples:

"My mind's a clean slate," said Tom blandly.
"This is the calm before the storm," said Tom placidly.
"You sure took a haircut on that one," said Tom barbarously.
"His bark is worse than his bite," said Tom doggedly.
"You're sharp as a tack," said Tom pointedly but tactfully.

In all of these examples, an adverb plays upon the literal meaning of an idiomatic expression in the body of the statement.

While the purported quotations in the Tom Swifty format are generally unambiguous and quite respectable, this is not so for statements that are identified with the expression "as the actress said to the bishop" or "as the bishop said to the actress." This expression, in either form, is used in the U.K. to signal that something said has a double meaning and that one of the two meanings is quite lewd. It demands attention to the least respectable interpretation lest it be overlooked.

The expression was often used by Simon Templar, alias the Saint, in a series of mysteries by British writer Leslie Charteris. In *The Saint Goes On*, Templar adds "as the bishop said to the actress" immediately after using another expression, "make a clean breast of it," which in its usual figurative sense means making a full or heartfelt confession. However, Templar is making sure that he gets credit for using the expression in full awareness of the literal meaning, which takes the word "breast" as a description of a woman's bosom. If this dialogue had been set in our contemporary world, he might have said "nudge nudge wink wink" as a knowing way of drawing attention to the sexual innuendo.

It's not so obvious that the verb "to know" can have a sexual meaning. But the translators who prepared the King James Version of the

Bible clearly had such a meaning in mind when they settled on this passage in the Book of Genesis: "And Adam knew Eve his wife; and she conceived, and bare Cain." This explains why the phrase "in the biblical sense," added after the word "know," has come to be used as a humorous way of signifying that "know" is to be taken as a euphemistic reference to carnal knowledge.

Some expressions involve hyperbole, that is to say an exaggeration or overstatement for rhetorical effect, which means that they aren't to be taken literally. The American author and columnist, William Safire, pretended to admonish someone who resorted to this literary device with this line: "If I've told you once, I've told you a thousand times, resist hyperbole," nicely illustrating the sin he was supposedly railing against.

The hyperbole is painfully obvious when I say that I would "give my right arm" or "give my eye teeth" for something, If I were to say that I would "die for the chance" to do something, it's also pretty clear that I would be "stretching a point" in order to make a point. No one would take me to be seriously indicating that I'd be prepared to make the ultimate sacrifice.

We sometimes speculate that something would be "a fate worse than death." This also involves hyperbole for it's commonly used to describe something that would be unfortunate but would fall far short of outranking death in its cataclysmic proportions. It would usually be a fatal mistake to take the expression literally. On the other hand, a criminal convicted of a capital offence might react to the prospect of life imprisonment, rather than the death penalty, by expressing the opinion that a life sentence would be "a fate worse than death," fully expecting to be taken literally. If he wanted to make that expectation perfectly clear, he might put his position this way: "It's no exaggeration to say" that a life sentence would be "a fate worse than death." The opening expression in that sentence would serve to "set the record straight." By comparison, George W. Bush provided no such clarity with his use of the expression in this comment on expected voter behavior: "'It's no exaggeration to say' that the undecideds could go one way or another."

If we want to highlight the fact that something is unlikely to happen, the expression "if pigs could fly" comes in handy. It carries the notion of extreme skepticism about something ever coming to pass, particularly something that's promised or intended by another. It's sometimes used, with an appropriate sarcastic tone, in the form "when pigs fly," effectively characterizing something as "pie in the sky."

The celebrated American novelist John Steinbeck adopted the motto *ad astra per alia porci* (to the stars on the wings of a pig), which he used with a sketch of a winged pig that he called Pigasus after its equine counterpart, Pegasus. A story that has circulated widely on the Internet attributes Steinbeck's affinity for this motto to an experience as a student when one of his professors told him that he would be an author "when pigs fly."

The Walrus in Lewis Carroll's poem "The Walrus and the Carpenter" was not prepared to "dismiss out of hand" the possibility of pigs taking flight when he set out these talking points for the assembled Oysters:

"The time has come," the Walrus said,
"To talk of many things:
Of shoes—and ships—and sealing wax –
Of cabbages—and kings –
And why the sea is boiling hot –
And whether pigs have wings."

It's just as well that the Walrus's last question can now be answered, definitively, in the negative, for the flight of pigs could have a fallout like that of the flight of cows, to which we were alerted in this old schoolyard ditty:

Birdy, birdy in the sky
Dropped some whitewash in my eye
But I don't worry, I don't cry
I'm just glad that cows don't fly.

We'd "get in a real flap" if cows could fly and wouldn't get off much easier if pigs could fly. On the other hand, there's much to be said for flying frogs, for "if frogs had wings, they wouldn't bump their asses every time they jumped." That expression is meant to remind us that it's useless to wish for impossible things; we can't always expect smooth landings in life.

The more puzzling expression "in a pig's eye" also represents something that's "only in your dreams." It shouldn't be mistaken as referring to something that's to be found in Pig's Eye, Minnesota. That community is now more commonly referred to as St. Paul, which is more fitting to its status as state capital than was the nickname of its first settler, the French-Canadian bootlegger, Pierre "Pig's Eye" Parrant, by which it was originally known.

If the odds of something happening are very remote, you can bet "dollars to doughnuts" that it won't happen. But if you're not a betting person, you might simply express the probability of that something ever happening at an impossibly low level by using any of these infernal expressions; "not a hope in hell," "a snowball's chance in hell," "as much chance as a wax cat in hell," "when hell freezes over" or "it'll be a frosty Friday in hell before...," if none of the pig expressions "catches your eye."

The English mystery writer Simon Brett has taken it to an even lower level, as if that were possible, with this expanded expression; "till hell freezes over and they hold the Winter Olympics there." "Till hell freezes over" may also be used to express, in an emphatic way, a high degree of dogged determination. There's no mistaking this in the assertion made by a multinational oil company of the lengths to which it would go to contest a decision that an Ecuadorian court had rendered against it: "We will fight until hell freezes over and then fight it out on the ice," as if hell had, indeed, become a Winter Olympic hockey venue. An adverse judgment in the amount of eighteen billion dollars will "stiffen the backbone" every time! An Ontario judge declined to enforce that judgment or entertain a challenge to it, declaring in a bit of uncharacteristic judicial humor that "while Ontario enjoys a bountiful supply of ice for part of the year," it was not the place for the threatened fight.

The device of hyperbole is evident in humorous put-downs that tend to overstate an individual's shortcomings. Someone might be cuttingly described in any one of the following ways:

"having no more backbone than a chocolate éclair"
"not knowing his head from a hole in the ground"
"not knowing his ass from his elbow"
"not knowing if he's punched or bored"
"being unable to walk and chew gum at the same time"
"being unable to hit the broad side of a barn door"
"being unable to go two rounds with a revolving door"
"being unable to fight his way out of a wet paper bag"

In the same style, the Australian politician and one-time prime minister, Billy "the Little Digger" Hughes, said of Prime Minister Robert Menzies, on the eve of the Second World War, that "he couldn't lead a flock of homing pigeons," which must rank as one of the most telling expressions of political scorn. More recently, *New York Times* columnist Maureen Dowd has popularized the line: "If brains were elastic, he wouldn't have enough to make suspenders for a parakeet." She has characterized this as a paraphrase of something from the pen of Raymond Chandler, thereby giving it respectable credentials. It's not clear, however, that the American mystery writer ever wrote, or said, anything of the kind. Dowd has applied the line to several politicians she considered deserving, including Texas Governor Rick Perry, who campaigned for the 2012 Republican Party nomination for president. Her creative characterization owes something to a long established put-down: "If brains were gunpowder, he wouldn't have enough to blow his nose."

The American actor Robert Blake has recently popularized a description of another extreme condition when he has repeatedly said of himself, in his current indigent state: "I couldn't buy spats for a hummingbird." Were he biblically inclined, he might have said that he was "broker than the ten commandments" or "poor as Job's turkey," which draws upon the straitened circumstances of the central figure in the Book of Job, who was stripped of all his livestock and other worldly goods in order to test his faith in God.

Another form of humorous exaggeration follows the pattern "he's so ___ that…" The blank is often filled in with the word "mean" as in these Australian expressions; "he's so mean that he wouldn't give you a wave if he owned the ocean," "he's so mean that he wouldn't give you the time of day if he owned Big Ben" and "he's so mean that he wouldn't give you a light for your pipe at a bushfire." In the same cold blooded vein, Rudy Giuliani, the one time mayor of New York City, was once described as "so mean he wouldn't spit in your ear if your brains were on fire."

These exaggerated descriptions, framed as put-downs, are similar to insult jokes, which attribute an undesirable characteristic to an individual followed by an illustration or a statement of the consequence, as in:

> He's so dumb he looks into the mirror to see if his eyes are open.
> He's so ugly when he looks into a mirror his reflection ducks.
> He's so skinny he's only got one stripe on his PJ's.
> "He's so tight if you were to shove a lump of coal up his ass, in two weeks you'd have a diamond," per Ferris Bueller in the movie, *Ferris Bueller's Day Off*.
> They're so poor their dog gets nervous at Thanksgiving.

Sometimes, these are constructed as maternal insults, in which case they're known as "yo mamma jokes." A couple of these incorporate familiar idiomatic expressions in a context that suggests that they are to be taken literally, in particular: "Yo mama's so poor she can't even 'put her two cents in' to a conversation," and "Yo mama's so fat I need two buses and a train 'to get on her good side.'"

In the American south, any strong insult can be used without embarrassment by adding, as a saving grace, the genteel expression "bless your heart." This has the effect, in those parts, of detracting from the rudeness of the insult and softening its blow.

Like many of these insults, popular curses are often "over the top." "May the fleas of a thousand camels infest your armpits," was a favorite expression of Johnny Carson, one-time host of *The Tonight Show*. He used it in his recurring role as Carnac the Magnificent, a so-called "mystic from the east." The expression is sometimes supplemented by the clause, "and may your arms be too short to scratch."

The Irish are responsible for this even more long-winded condemnation: "May the curse of Mary Malone and her nine blind illegitimate children chase you so far over the hills of Damnation that the Lord himself can't find you with a telescope." Who could truthfully say in the face of such a powerful verbal assault that "sticks and stones will break my bones but words will never hurt me?" As for those who utter nasty oaths like this, they would do well to keep in mind the saying, "curses, like chickens, come home to roost."

Considerable misfortune is intended to be invoked by the classic Australian curse: "May your chooks [chickens] turn into emus and kick your dunny down." For those who aren't familiar with dunnies, the opening verses of an Ode to a Dunny, by an unknown author, will fill the gap:

They were funny looking buildings, that were once a way of life,
If you couldn't sprint the distance, then you really were in strife.
They were nailed, they were wired, but were mostly falling down,
There was one in every yard, in every house, in every town.

They were given many names, some were even funny,
But to most of us, we knew them as the outhouse or the dunny.
I've seen some of them all gussied up, with painted doors
and all,
But it really made no difference, they were just a port of call.

Not surprisingly, the old seafaring saying "any port in a storm" was often applied to a visit to the outhouse or the dunny.

Some expressions take the form of understatements that are used, ironically, to express an affirmative by negating the contrary or to express a negative by discounting an affirmative. For example, "not to do things by halves" means to do things, usually wholeheartedly, in a complete and thorough way. "Not too shabby" means nice or well done and if you're "not too fussy" about something, you really don't like it. "We are not amused" is said in order to indicate, politely but firmly, that we are annoyed. Queen Victoria is thought to have been the first to express displeasure in this way, which explains the use of the pronoun "we" which, for her, was the royal "we."

Similarly, many conversational expressions bear a meaning that is the opposite of what the literal interpretation would suggest and are used, typically, in a sarcastic manner. "Well that's just grand" is an exclamatory way of signaling that something isn't so great and, indeed, may amount to "a fine kettle of fish," which isn't so fine. But if "that's just grand" is used without an initial "well," the expression may be fraught with sarcasm and irony or with sincerity. Only context and inflection will reveal the true intent. But even a declared intention to be ironic can lead to confusion as this short poem by Bruce Bennett shows:

> I mean the opposite of what I say
> You've got it now? No, it's the other way.

The rhetorical question "isn't life grand?" can be cynical or sincere, although more often than not it's the former. It's pretty clear that Dorothy Parker, known for her caustic wit, was being cynical about the constancy of love, if not life itself, when she wrote:

> Oh, life is a glorious cycle of song,
> A medley of contemporanea:
> And love is a thing that can never go wrong;
> And I am Marie of Romania.

Marie was Princess Marie of Edinburgh, one of Queen Victoria's grandchildren, who became Queen of Romania when Prince Ferdinand, her husband in a largely loveless marriage, ascended to the Romanian throne in 1914. Thanks to Dorothy Parker, "I am Marie of Romania" became a popular way of expressing disbelief.

If someone reacts to what another person has said with "that's a likely story" or "in your humble opinion," he's effectively saying that the story is unlikely to be true or that the opinion is lacking in "humbility," to use a malapropism made popular by Hercule Poirot, Agatha Christie's fictional Belgian detective. If someone says, "tell me about it" he probably doesn't want to hear about it because he's already fully informed. And if he's told about it in any event, he might well ask "so what else is new?" as if to say it's not new. Finally, "fat chance" actually means slim chance and "same difference" means two things aren't different at all.

When we introduce a statement with "it goes without saying," we really don't mean it because we then go on to say the very thing that doesn't have to be said. The expression works in the same perverse way as the common assertion by a master of ceremonies that a guest speaker "needs no introduction," which is almost always the cue for the start of a none-too-succinct introduction. "That goes without saying," used as a comment on what someone else has just said, makes more sense. In this case, the unnecessary words have already been spoken and the expression, in this form, is just an observation that the words needn't have been spoken, for they simply conveyed what was self-evident.

Several other expressions bear a meaning that is quite inconsistent with what is suggested by the apparent literal meaning. Much like "eat your heart out," "knock yourself out" and "break a leg" seem to invoke the prospect of self inflicted bodily harm. "Knock yourself out" can have all kinds of nuances but, at its core, it means get on with something; it isn't really proposing that you should render yourself unconscious in the process. When it's turned around, as it often is, in the form "don't knock yourself out," the actual sense comes much closer to the literal. This negative exhortation conveys the notion that you shouldn't overexert yourself, in getting on with something, for it's "not worth the candle" but it can also be a cynical suggestion that you aren't making a real effort.

"Break a leg" is used to wish an actor good luck when he mounts the stage and "treads the boards." Yet, good luck is far removed from what the literal meaning would suggest. The expression is ironic in nature. Like many other expressions, it's part of the argot or jargon associated with a particular group, activity or way of life, in this case actors and acting, but it's now used, more widely, to wish someone good luck in other endeavors.

While the bad is really good in "break a leg," the good is really bad in "that takes the cake" or "he takes the cake." The logical conclusion to be taken from the cake expressions is that something positive, worthy of commendation, has happened since cakes were traditionally awarded as prizes. But these expressions are normally used to indicate, ironically, that something or somebody's conduct is particularly shocking or annoying and quite unworthy of favorable recognition. The British expressions "that takes the biscuit" and "he takes the biscuit" carry similar meanings.

Irony isn't always easy to recognize in these expressions. It's also quite obscure in the expression "may you live in interesting times," which is thought to come from ancient China. It sounds as if this wish is the sort of message that might be imbedded in a fortune cookie to foretell good luck. But it's not normally a blessing but a curse, for it assumes, cynically, that interesting times are likely to be marked by turbulent events that are unsettling. Much better to live in uninteresting but tranquil times!

The irony is much easier to spot in ironic similes. They set up an expectation with an adjective or a verb, which is immediately dashed with the comparison that follows. When we say that something is "as clear as mud"' or "as subtle as a sledgehammer," we are really saying that it's the furthest thing from clear or subtle. If we "need [something] like a hole in the head," we would be much better off without it. If someone is "as popular as a skunk at a garden party," he's extremely unpopular, at least in a North American setting where skunks are, frequently, unwelcome intruders upon human activities. The commonly offered comfort that a skunk will never release its offensive spray, except as a last ditch defense when provoked, is about "as reliable as a politician's promise" and, therefore, shouldn't persuade anyone to stick around and party with an intruding skunk "in the wings."

The detective writer Raymond Chandler was responsible for a fine ironic twist playing off the adjective "inconspicuous." In his novel *Farewell, My Lovely*, he provided this description of the flashily dressed gangster Moose Malloy; "...he looked about as inconspicuous as a tarantula on a slice of angel food."

Some of the most graphic ironic similes involve a comedown from the adjective "useful." Something may be described as being "as useful as an ashtray on a motorcycle," "as useful as a balsa wood anchor," "as useful as a screen door on a submarine," "as useful as a stripper in a nudist colony," "as useful as a chocolate teapot" or "as useful as a concrete canoe." The last of these expressions has lost a lot of its impact ever since the American Society of Civil Engineers began running its National Concrete Canoe Contest. In this competition, engineering students make the seemingly unfloatable float and "race" for the honor of winning what has been called, grandiosely, the America's Cup of Civil Engineering. If this plodding competition would "bore you out of your gourd," you might proclaim it to be "about as exciting as watching paint dry."

3

WHAT DO YOU MEAN BY THAT EXPRESSION?

What you don't understand you can make mean anything.

Chuck Palahniuk from his novel *Diary*

Many expressions seem to "pass all understanding" or, at least, to require a good deal of effort to get at what's meant. The reason for the opaqueness of an expression may be that it's illogical, absurd, incomplete, upended, archaic, ambiguous or simply a conversational set piece. The purpose of this chapter is to try to "cast light on" such expressions and uncover a sensible meaning or a sensible rationale for an accepted meaning. In some cases, it's concluded that this is "an exercise in futility" and that it's best to heed the "tried and true" advice: "Don't try to understand everything because sometimes it is not meant to be understood but to be accepted."

Several expressions take a large leap from the logical, thus inviting questions about their true meaning. Someone may be said to have "fallen head over heels" in a literal physical sense, or in a figurative sense as when he has fallen deeply in love. However, this juxtaposition of body parts reflects the natural state of standing up. When someone takes a serious tumble, he's more likely to reverse the norm and go heels over head. "Going ass over teakettle," a substitute for this wrongheaded expression, doesn't make any more sense but is sometimes favored for its brashness. Another synonymous expression, "going base over apex" is much more logical as it involves a clear reversal of the norm as represented by the usual position of a typical triangle.

The American expression "as phony as a two dollar bill" is used to describe something that's fake or a sham. But, in fact, two dollar bills are legal tender in the U.S., although they are now "as scarce as hens' teeth." Indeed, they've been in circulation from 1862 to the present day with only a ten-year gap. The alternative expression "as phony as a three dollar bill" is, therefore, much more sensible as this denomination of bill was never official U.S. currency. Joseph Smith, the prophet and founder of the Mormon Church, issued three dollar bills among the notes that he printed to pay for his U.S. presidential campaign of 1844, but all of his notes were suspect, not just the three dollar ones.

"I could care less" is another expression that doesn't stand up to logical analysis. This expression started out as "I couldn't care less," and still persists in that form as well. It's used for the purpose of making it perfectly clear that the speaker couldn't be more uninterested in, or unconcerned about, something. However, when the original expression migrated across the Atlantic to North America, it was inverted to "I could care less" without any apparent change in the original meaning. But, taken logically, "I could care less" indicates that the speaker could, in fact, be even less interested or concerned than he actually is. That's a far different state of affairs than is conveyed by the negative statement "I couldn't care less." Of course, the distinction between the literal senses of the two forms of the expression is probably something about which most people "couldn't care less." Therefore, they'd be quite happy with either form.

"Cheap at half the price," which may have originated as a cry from London street vendors, ranks up there with "I could care less" as an illogical or uninformative observation. Some use it to say that something is expensive; others use it to say that something is cheap. But if it's cheap at half the price, it could still be cheap at the full price or it could be expensive at the full price. If the expression is meant to indicate that something is very cheap, as any street traders would have wanted to suggest, it should take the form "cheap at twice the price."

"Starting from ground zero" is generally used to mean "going back to square one" or "starting from scratch." "Ground zero" originated as a term for the point on the earth's surface at which a nuclear explosion has occurred and from which the radius of its damage can be plotted. It later took on a broader meaning as the central point of anything.

With capitalized first letters, it also came to signify the site of the World Trade Center in Lower Manhattan, New York City, after the Center was destroyed on 9/11 (September 11, 2001). However, the expression "starting from ground zero," in the way it's normally used, assumes, wrongly, that "ground zero" has a different meaning yet again, namely a new beginning or an original starting point. The expression, therefore, builds on a misunderstanding.

There's really no excuse for the fairly common distortion of another modern expression "doing a 180," which denotes a reversal of position on something. One often hears people say that they have "done a 360" when they want to indicate that they have done an about face. But "a 360" is a complete rotation through all the degrees of a circle that would return them back to their starting positions, facing the way they did originally. Those who would double up on the 180 of the original expression, to a full 360, are either "doing a number on us" or, more likely, they have "come up short" on their knowledge of basic geometry.

When we speak of "the tail wagging the dog," "putting the cart before the horse" or "pushing on a string," we are deliberately playing upon the incongruous. The image called up by each of these expressions reflects the absurd or the improbable, much like the image drawn by "if pigs could fly."

Some absurd images carry an overtone of mockery. When we describe someone as "busier than a one-armed paper-hanger" or "busier than a one-legged man at an ass kicking contest," we risk giving offence. Because they draw attention to the limitations resulting from certain physical disabilities, these expressions are sometimes viewed as politically incorrect and, therefore, to be avoided. If they do slip out "without malice aforethought," the penitential plea "if you'll pardon the expression" can be quickly added. It's well to bear in mind, as a suitable substitute, the alternative expression, "busier than a two-headed cat in a creamery."

Some expressions are short-hand versions of longer expressions that have "fallen by the wayside." While the abbreviated forms sometimes make little sense, a certain logic often emerges if we know the longer expressions from which they are derived.

"Happy as a clam" is a well seasoned American expression. However, it's hard to imagine what signs of happiness are typically exhibited by clams. These bivalves certainly don't frolic about in an upbeat sort of way or emit joyful sounds that would demonstrate that they're "happy as larks" and they're not known to let smiles crease the lips of their shells. In fact, you would think that the prospect of becoming the main ingredient of a chowder would be unlikely to inspire any sort of positive attitude. However, the original version of the expression, "happy as a clam at high tide," provides a clue to its good sense. At high tide, clams are submerged and safe from the predations of clam diggers. Therefore, they're likely to be in a particularly good frame of mind at high water, certainly compared to what they would be feeling at low water. So much depends on time and place. But, why then would a clam also be happy when served up as a meal, as suggested by another expression, "happy as a clam in butter sauce?" Perhaps it's because buttering up can lead to a good deal of self-deception.

The "hair of the dog" is sometimes used to describe the singularly odd hangover remedy of having another drink the morning after overindulging. That would seem to be "like adding fuel to the fire," although, it could be argued that it's "fighting fire with fire," or, more precisely, "fighting firewater with firewater" in this case. The more common remedy for a hangover, also known as "the wrath of grapes," is to take some Bromoseltzer in a glass of water. But that's hardly as appealing; the comedian Joe E. Lewis once said that he would adopt this remedy except that he found the fizzing noise to be absolutely deafening.

The original expression, "hair of the dog that bit you," which has been shortened to "hair of the dog," helps us begin to understand the meaning of the more concise expression. A bit of research establishes that the traditional treatment for a canine bite that was doggedly followed in earlier times was to rub hairs of the offending cur into the wound, which was thought to promote healing. The more modern saying "the drunkard's cure is drink again" has little to do with "hitting the bottle" on the pretext of a hangover remedy and more to do with a cynical observation on the behavior of alcoholics, sometimes described, euphemistically, as "problem drinkers."

A heavy drinker of alcoholic beverages is said to "drink like a fish." Fish certainly take in lots of water, through their mouths, but they are not, of course, drinking the water because it's immediately expelled through their gills, enabling the fish to breathe. The concept of drinking like a fish should, therefore, carry the notion of taking in water to get a breath of air, but that's hardly consistent with the meaning the expression is used to convey. An unidentified wisecracker has compounded the seeming senselessness of the expression by coming up with this description of a combination of bad habits; "smoke like a fish, drink like a chimney."

If a drunk himself was asked to describe his condition, he might well say, in his inebriated state, that he was "under the affluence of incohol." This mangled expression is an example of a Spoonerism, named for the Reverend William Spooner, a warden of New College, Oxford, who had the habit of altering a phrase or a sentence through the interchange of sounds or words. It was never clear whether his transpositions were the result of a "slip of the tongue" or, to use an oxymoron, "accidentally on purpose." Perhaps the most famous Spoonerism to come from the master himself was the "queer old dean," said in reference to dear old Queen Victoria, who might have reacted with her own expression, "we are not amused," had Spooner's description come to her attention.

In the best of the Spooner tradition, the poet Ogden Nash turned around a common expression when he wrote: "I am a conscientious man, when I throw rocks at seabirds, I leave no tern unstoned." "In the same bent," he added, "I am a meticulous man and when I portray baboons I leave no stern untoned," suggesting that he was careful to redden the rear ends of his baboons. Nash's clever manipulation "just shows to go you" that an expression can, sometimes, be upended in more ways than one.

Spoonerisms have been used to contrive expressions that serve as a humorous, but imperfect, disguise for swearing. "Bass ackwards" is, perhaps, the best known of these inventive creations. Other Spoonerisms, such as "it just shows to go you," are used primarily for their nonsense effect. Thus, "the thick plottens" is sometimes substituted in fun for "the plot thickens," which is to say, in either version, that things are getting more complicated. "Nook and cranny" has also been turned around, with a like motive, to become "crook and nanny." This socio-political comment makes good use of that Spoonerism, coupling it with the expression from which it's derived:

> For the currency of the lives of most of us, the fashion in the business of the state has been to expand farther and farther into every nook and cranny, seeking the welfare of every crook and nanny.

This sentence was penned by Gordon Gibson, a senior fellow at a conservative Canadian think tank.

An expression may become completely inverted by the interchange of words. "Snatching victory from the jaws of defeat" means pulling off a win at the last minute against all odds. Not surprisingly, this has spawned a reverse expression, "snatching defeat from the jaws of victory," to describe the act of blowing a sure thing at the last minute. This was applied by many political commentators to the feat that Senator John Kerry pulled off as a candidate in the U.S. presidential election of 2004. In his "thirst for victory," he should have had in mind the old saying that "there's many a slip 'twixt the cup and the lip." But Kerry wasn't the first presidential candidate to "snatch defeat from the jaws of victory." That description was originally applied to New York Governor Thomas E, Dewey who lost out in the U.S. presidential election of 1948. The *Chicago Daily Tribune* was so convinced of his imminent victory that it ran the now famous headline, DEWEY DEFEATS TRUMAN, the morning after the election but before the final result was in.

Many seasoned expressions are mysterious because they allude to situations, events or practices that have fallen into obscurity, such as the traditional treatment for dog bites, which influenced the "hair of the dog." This is true of "mad as a hatter." The conventional wisdom is that the expression came about because mercury nitrate, which was once commonly used in treating fur for the making of felt hats, would damage the nervous systems of the hat makers. They would then exhibit certain signs of insanity that we now associate with mercury poisoning. One of these signs was labelled the Danbury Shakes, so called because they were prevalent among the citizens of Danbury, Connecticut, the hat-making capital of the world in the nineteenth century. The expression "mad as a hatter" likely provided some of the inspiration for Lewis Carroll's creation of the Hatter, one of the characters in *Alice's Adventures in Wonderland*, who appeared, along with the March Hare, at a mad tea-party. He, therefore, became known as the mad Hatter, although Carroll never called him that.

"Mad as a hatter" continues its association with toxicity as part of an expression-filled aid to health-care professionals in helping them recognize the symptoms of a drug overdose:

"blind as a bat," "mad as a hatter," "red as a beet," "hot as Hades," "dry as a bone," "the bowel and bladder lose their tone," and "the heart runs alone."

This mnemonic reminder signifies dilated pupils, delirium, a flushed complexion, hypothermia, dry skin, bladder retention and tachycardia.

If a particular rule is more often broken than not, we might say, in the words of Hamlet, that it is "more honored in the breach than in the observance." This common expression, to describe the effect of a particular rule, also makes little sense given that the verb "to honor" means "to respect." One can hardly be said to respect a rule by breaking it. The conundrum is resolved if we appreciate that the words Shakespeare put in the mouth of his protagonist have been taken out of context. They were used in relation to a custom, rather than a rule. In this case, the Danish people, following the example of their king, had adopted the habit of heavy drinking. This was a practice that the abstemious Hamlet found more honor in breaching that in observing. He was saying, in effect, that this customary practice was, like bad promises, "better broken than kept."

Another old custom—that of taking suckling pigs to market in a sack—gave rise to the expression "buying a pig in a poke." In this day and age, we would normally think of a poke as a jab, a push or a prod. But it also means a sack, from *poche*, the French word for a bag or a pocket. This provides the starting point for getting at the origin of the expression "buying a pig in a poke," which is used to describe the acquisition of something of uncertain value or usefulness. Unscrupulous farmers were known to substitute a worthless item for their pig, such as a cat, and then try to sell the poke and its contents to an unsuspecting purchaser, who thought he was buying a pig and paid accordingly. If the purchaser, guided by the maxim *caveat emptor* (buyer beware), were to examine the contents of the poke, before concluding the deal, he would "let the cat out of the bag," thus revealing the fraud and providing the stimulus for another expression used to describe the act of disclosing something that was meant to be concealed.

In a modern rendition of "a pig in a poke," George Clooney, playing the role of Jimmy "Dodge" Connelly in the movie *Leatherheads*, used that term as if it were the name of a trick football play in which a player with the "pigskin," a slang word for the football, hides it under his jersey and runs away from the play action, hopefully unnoticed by the opposing team but making for that team's goal line. Clooney, who apparently wrote this particular bit of dialogue for his character, was likely "poking fun" but we don't know for sure since he never "let the cat out of the bag."

The meaning of many expressions is obscured by the inclusion of archaic or fossil words that are no longer used in our language except as part of the surviving expressions. You might say that someone whose actions backfired on him was "hoist with his own petard," without having any idea that a "petard" was a primitive explosive device that was attached to a castle wall or gate to blow out a hole for attackers to enter. You could say that the word "petard" and the *materiel* that it represents are a "blast from the past." A petard was dangerous to handle for it would often detonate prematurely, hoisting the poor chap who was attempting to plant it and injuring him or, worst case scenario, "blasting him to smithereens." This last, graphic description also uses an unfamiliar word, in this case an Anglicized version of the Irish term *smiderin*, meaning a small fragment.

A single expression may carry more than one message if it contains a key word that has two or more meanings. "Getting your mojo working" or "getting your mojo back" (apparently it's easily lost) trade on several possible meanings of "mojo." Popularized by blues singer Muddy Waters in his 1957 recording, "Got My Mojo Working, I'm Your Hoochie Goochie Man," "mojo" was the term for a charm worn, for its magic properties, by adherents of voodoo, a form of religious witchcraft practiced by some black communities in the Americas. Quite naturally, it came to be used as a portent of magic or charm and as a substitute for the term "self-confidence" or "getting into the groove," especially after some debilitating setback. The word "mojo" also has a couple of slang meanings, namely prohibited narcotic drugs and male sexual potency. Austin Powers, a comic character modelled on James Bond and played by Mike Myers in the 1999 movie *The Spy Who Shagged Me*, demonstrated this last form of mojo "in spades." "Getting your mojo working" or getting it back can, therefore, refer to several different things; one illegal, one sexually excessive and, thankfully, one redemptive.

"It's all downhill from here" can take on two different meanings that are "polar opposites" driven by the fact that "downhill" is a Janus word, so named after the two-headed Roman god whose image faced both inwards and outwards at the temple gate. When it's used as a metaphor, "downhill" signifies progressively better, for instance when "you've got your mojo back," or progressively worse. Consider the birthday greeting: "Happy 65th. 'It's all downhill from here.'" This could mean that life will now get easier, say because of retirement and seniors benefits kicking in, or it could mean that life will get tougher as deteriorating health starts to take its toll. Walt Kelly's cartoon character, Pogo, hinted at the ambiguity in the expression with his enigmatic phrases "from here on up it's all downhill" and "from here on down it's all uphill."

The question "is the glass half empty of half full?" is generally thought to distinguish those with a pessimistic view of things from those with an optimistic view, depending on which of the two perceptions they have about the glass and its contents. However, the comedian George Carlin brought to light another possibility: "Some say the glass is half full, some say the glass is half empty. I say the glass is too big." Fellow comedian Bill Cosby also had an unconventional take on the expression, noting that the answer "depends on whether you're pouring or drinking." For the parched cynic, the perspectives of the optimist and the pessimist are of little concern, for he simply wonders who drank the other half.

The instruction "shake well before using" is quite familiar because it appears regularly on bottles of medicines, or containers of other products, that are in the form of a liquid suspension and need to be "shaken but not stirred," as James Bond said of his martinis. But does the instruction mean that the bottle or container must be "shaken well," in the sense of shaken vigorously, just before the product is used, or does it mean that the required shaking must take place "well before" use, in the sense of well in advance of use? While most of us have come to know that the first meaning is the intended one, how would a novice at the English language react to the instruction? Probably with a good deal of confusion. For him, the perverted proverb "if at first you don't succeed, try reading the instructions," would not be helpful as that's what caused confusion in the first place.

An expression that's obviously ambiguous should generally be avoided for it doesn't make for clarity of communication. However, there are some situations in which a degree of comfort can be found in using such an expression. The British economist John Maynard Keynes was plagued by economics students who sent him their theses asking that he read them and provide his comments. His standard response to each such request was that he would "lose no time" in reading the thesis, suggesting that he would read it right away. However, he was really saying that he wouldn't be wasting any of his time reading the thesis, which he didn't want to admit in so many words.

There are a lot of expressions that can only be understood as conversational formulae "if you get my drift" as the blowing snow said to the snow fence, thus expanding one such formula into a Wellcrism. If you don't get my drift, that's your cue to interrupt and call for an explanation. "I'm easy" can be inserted into an oral exchange to telegraph the idea that I have no definite opinion when it comes to a proposed course of action or no clear preference when it comes to choosing among two or more options. It's not usually meant to give the impression that I have loose morals. If you ask me a question that I can't answer, I might reply "you've got me there," but if I offer up an answer on which I decide to equivocate, I might add "but then again," followed by another possible answer.

Some conversational expressions take the form of rhetorical questions. "Is the Pope Catholic?" doesn't call for an answer because there can only be one response. The same thing can be said about the question: "Does a bear 'do his thing' in the woods?" or the more common, unsanitized version "Does a bear shit in the woods?" The recognition factor of this expression and its undeniable truth prompted a recent advertising campaign for Charmin toilet paper that features bears in the woods enjoying the ultra softness of this product. "Does a bear like honey?" and "Does a duck swim?" are also meant to make the point, in a saucy sort of way, that something is self-evident. There's really no room for a person who has heard any of these various questions to claim neutrality by saying "you've got me there" or by saying "yes" coupled with the immediate qualification, "but then again..."

An unqualified "yes" can also be the only answer to the strange greeting "Sure it's not yourself, is it?" typically spoken by an Irishman upon running into an acquaintance. Even in a case of mistaken identity, the answer would still have to be "Yes."

4

CODED EXPRESSIONS

Simply stated, it is sagacious to eschew obfuscation.

Norman R. Augustine, American
Business Executive & Author

If you don't know the code, just click here and expressions will be revealed for what they really mean. The fact is that several kinds of expressions—those that are euphemistic, dysphemistic, cynical or set in rhyming slang—serve as covers for what is really being said. Other expressions may be quite revealing but have been dressed down as acronyms, providing a cloak of camouflage that can flummox the unwitting. This chapter is all about these seductive expressions. They may involve a deliberate cover-up, convenience of communication, or entertainment value "pure and simple."

Euphemistic expressions make some situation or fact sound better, by a turn of phrase, than it really is. They avoid "calling a spade a spade." Dysphemistic expressions are the opposite of euphemistic expressions. They make some situation or fact sound worse than it really is, usually by employing direct, graphic or, sometimes, coarse language. While often degrading, they may be either hurtful or humorous in their deprecating tone.

Sometimes, a single expression is capable of being used either in a euphemistic way or a dysphemistic way. The expression "pushing up daisies" would take on a euphemistic tone if I were to say that I would expect to be "pushing up daisies" before my favorite baseball team won the World Series. But if I were to console someone who had lost a loved one by expressing my sorrow over the fact that her spouse was now "pushing up daisies," my attempt at a light hearted take on death would likely be misplaced, making matters worse rather than easing the pain of bereavement.

Like the expression "pushing up daisies," the folk ballad "Clementine," set in the California Gold Rush of 1849, touches upon the floral effect of interment. Clementine suffered a fatal fall "into the foaming brine" when running through the canyon where her father was "excavating for a mine." Her burial led to this prolific result:

> In a churchyard, near the canyon, where the myrtle doth entwine,
> There grow roses and other posies fertilized by Clementine.

Much better to be described as "pushing up daisies," or fertilizing roses or other posies, than to be described as going "from ashes to ashes, from dust to dust," which fails to emphasize any positive value in passing except for that of recycling.

There are lots of other options for whitewashing the blackness of death. Someone who has died may be said, by those who believe in an afterlife, to have been "called to higher service" or to have "gone to his eternal reward," "gone to meet his maker," "gone to join his ancestors" or "gone to a better place." These euphemistic expressions certainly follow the advice of the old song to "accentuate the positive, decentuate the negative" and assume the truth of the saying that "everyone wants to go to heaven but nobody wants to die."

Other evasions of the "bitter gall of death" involve the notion that someone has simply "bought the farm," "cashed in his chips," "popped his clogs" or, in dry mathematical terms, "reached actuarial maturity." Substitutes for the verb "to die" include "to kick the bucket," "to bite the dust," "to go the way of all flesh" or, in flowery literary terms, "to shuffle off this mortal coil," as Shakespeare's Hamlet put it, using "mortal coil" to refer to the turmoil of life. These expressions are generally used in a euphemistic way.

A very recent form of euphemism involves the description of many unappealing physical and mental characteristics of humans as "challenges" of one kind or another. Someone who is dead is said to be "metabolically challenged," someone who is mentally disabled to be "cerebrally challenged" and someone who is bald to be "follicly challenged." Someone who is "knee-high to a grasshopper," or short of stature by some other standard, is said to be "vertically challenged." A challenge is, of course, something that, through determination, can be met and overcome. Death, insanity, baldness and shortness are poor candidates for conquest "by dint of human effort." The creative descriptions of these conditions, as simply exposures to challenges, are really a spoof on the use of politically correct terminology.

The expressions used to describe the cerebrally challenged generally avoid a lot of the nasty old words like "mad," "nuts," "batty" and "insane," the exceptions being "mad as a hatter," "nuttier than a fruitcake" and having "bats in the belfry." Many alternative expressions carry a tone that is much less blunt but they are not always very sympathetic to those who are "not all there" or, more formally, *non compos mentis,* to dress it up in Latin. These individuals are painted, variously, as "one brick short of a load," "one French fry short of a Happy Meal," "a sandwich short of a picnic," "a stubbie short of a six pack," "having a screw loose," "not playing with a full deck," "not firing on all four cylinders" and "not the sharpest knife in the drawer," while their behavior may be ascribed to the fact that "the lights are on but nobody is home," they have "lost their marbles," they are "off their rocker," "the lift doesn't go to the top floor" or there are "kangaroos loose on the upper paddock." A couple of these expressions have provided fodder for the daft mixed idiom, "he's not the sharpest marble in the drawer."

Termination from employment is, undoubtedly, a traumatic event for the affected employee. It's not surprising, therefore, that several euphemistic expressions are used, often by the employer to ease his conscience, in order to avoid the harshness of describing someone as fired or, colloquially speaking, canned. Instead, the employee may be said to have been "made redundant," "written out of the script," "put out to grass" or "to pasture," "given his cards" or "a pink slip," "shown the gate" or "the door," "given the sack" or "involuntarily leisured," the most politically correct of all the options. One recent mass layoff was described, by an employer, as the result of adoption of "a synergy related headcount adjustment goal" and another as the consequence of "a targeted restructuring to better align the company with its core competencies." These rationalizations lack the luster and the pithy character of the more popular euphemistic expressions but they certainly avoid giving any hint about the reality for the affected employees.

Someone who is drunk may be variously described as "having taken a drop too much," "being well into his cups," "being half cut," "feeling no pain" or "being tight as a tick." It's fairly obvious, despite the apparent soft pedaling, why these expressions are taken to mean intoxicated. Another euphemistic description of drunkenness, "three sheets to the wind," is likely to be fully appreciated only by nautical types who "know the ropes." The sheets referred to here are neither bed linen nor sails but the lines that hold sails in place on a boat or a ship. If the lines on a sailing sloop were to become loose in the wind, the sails would luff, or flap, and the vessel would career out of control, as if a drunken sailor were at the helm. Nowadays, a drunk is more likely to be described, in a dig at political correctness, as "spatially perplexed" or as an "anti-sobriety activist," drawing on the social sciences rather than seafaring lore.

Cynicism, like euphemism, may color the meaning of an expression. It's the very purpose for inserting some expressions opening with the word "don't" into our daily speech. "Don't strain yourself" implies that you aren't "putting your shoulder to the wheel" or "pulling your weight" as you should be, although it appears to be a simple caution "to take it easy." "Don't mind me" is meant to suggest that another person is not giving me appropriate consideration, even though it seems to express a desire "to fade into the woodwork." The expression is sometimes expanded to "don't mind me, my kids don't."

"Don't hold your breath" indicates a degree of skepticism about whether something promised or expected will happen soon or at all. The idea is that if you were to hold your breath in anticipation, ignoring the advice, you'd probably expire before that something came to pass. "That'll be the day" likewise raises serious doubts about something ever happening.

In a subtle attempt at cynical humor, an expression may be described as an oxymoron when it's not really an example of that figure of speech at all. Applying the label "oxymoron" implies that the expression involves a contradiction in terms. Thus, "bureaucratic efficiencies," "reasonable attorney's fees," "business ethics" and "airline meals," when described as oxymorons or oxymora, carry the cynical assumption that the bureaucracy is incapable of acting efficiently, that attorneys' accounts are never reasonable, that business is never conducted on an ethical basis and that airline food can't possibly qualify as a meal. Only then can the expressions be considered contradictory in the manner of oxymora.

Sometimes, it's necessary to recognize a pun or double meaning before the supposed contradiction becomes apparent. For example, although "military intelligence" is sometimes described as an oxymoron, it only involves a possible contradiction if "intelligence" is taken to mean intellect rather than information gathering. The cynical reaction, invited by the person who calls it an oxymoron, is therefore that the expression is "off base" because the military is incapable of exhibiting any collective intellect.

Other expressions are true oxymora, such as "accidentally on purpose," "to damn with faint praise," "same difference" and "conspicuous by his absence." No cynical bent nor any search for a double meaning is required in order to be able to recognize a contradiction in these expressions.

Some expressions have been "reduced to the bare bones" through representation by acronym, providing a form of encoding in this way. MIA, the shortened form of "missing in action," is one of the many acronyms to come out of wartime. Breaking free from its origins, the expression it represents has evolved to describe someone whose whereabouts are unknown, whether the individual disappeared "in the heat of battle" or otherwise. Another military acronym SNAFU, which translates, in polite form, as "situation normal all fouled up," has been so widely used in civilian life that it has morphed into the word "snafu," meaning a situation marked by utter confusion.

"Not in my back yard," which is commonly represented by the acronym NIMBY, is a pejorative expression. It's implicitly critical of those who, for apparently selfish reasons, oppose a development, such as a new road or a wind farm, that would serve the public good but might adversely affect the opponents because of its proximity to their homes. The acronym NIMBY is so well recognized that it's often written, like many other popular acronyms, such as SNAFU, without capitals as if it were an ordinary word. Some "nimbies" who have taken "nimbyism" to the extreme are said to have adopted the BANANA credo, which means that their position has become "build absolutely nothing anywhere near anything." With a huge increase in the reports of back yards claimed to be off limits, NIMBY or "nimby," "if you will," has become something of a cliché. "By the way," or BTW, it joins at least two other ubiquitous acronyms with this distinction, namely BFF, for "best friends forever," and YOLO, for "you only live once."

Certain slang expressions are encrypted as acronyms in order to avoid explicit use of their crude language. Thus "cover your ass" may be portrayed through the short-hand CYA, "shit out of luck" through SOL and "sweet 'f' all" through SFA.

Many modern abbreviations are likely to drive the novice to an Internet slang dictionary, suitably available on-line. If a person has no idea what a particular acronym in a message stands for, he might simply reply BTSOOM. When pronounced, that acronym sounds suspiciously like a slang term for a woman's breasts. But, in fact, it's a cryptic version of "beats the stuffing [or shizzle] out of me," although it can be taken to represent the much less polite "beats the shit out of me."

"Netspeak," the Internet slang that is often used in computer-mediated communication, is heavily stocked with acronyms. This popular lingo with its indispensable short forms has been carried over to all kinds of text messaging and has "grown like Topsy," or should I say GLT. Netspeak short forms, unlike traditional acronyms, may also use a number or letter that needs to be pronounced in order to identify with a word in the underlying expression, for example, B4N stands for "bye for now," UG2BK stands for "you got to be kidding," and CUL stands for "see you later," although it may also be used for "catch you later."

Some of the acronyms of the digital age are well understood, such as OMG for "oh my gosh" or, less politely, "oh my God." However, the proper perception of some acronyms, such as LOL, standing for "laughing out loud" or "laugh out loud," may be largely confined to the younger generation. The *Parents Shouldn't Text* Website records this unfortunate message sent by an older "texter": "Your great aunt just passed away. LOL." The sender had mistaken LOL as an acronym for "lots of love," as it was in pre-digital times. British Prime Minster David Cameron made the same mistake in signing off some of his text messages to Rebekah Brooks, the former boss of Rupert Murdock's *News of the World* newspaper. Ms. Brooks testified at a public inquiry into British media ethics that she had to tell the PM that LOL meant "laughing out loud," at which point he stopped using the acronym in his messages to her. Naturally, this testimony sparked a good deal of LOLs at the expense of the Prime Minister. Like many others, I refrained from mocking the PM quite so openly, being content with LQTM or "laughing quietly to myself." Not surprisingly, there's now a growing sensitivity, in business and government, to the dangers of leaving a digital trail, especially through e-mails. The sign to revert to old fashioned oral communications is LTL for "let's talk later."

There are also many false acronyms—words that are thought to have originated as acronyms but have no such pedigree. One of these is "posh." The conventional wisdom is that it comes from the expression "port out, starboard home," used as a short-hand description of the preferred out-bound and in-bound cabin locations, for shade-loving passengers, on sailings between Britain and India. The truth is that "posh" is simply a stylish word for "stylish" that never had an earlier incarnation as an acronym. Thus, in the contemporary expression "too posh to push," it describes a pregnant woman who opts for a cesarean section simply because natural childbirth is beneath her and "too hard to stomach."

Another way of portraying an expression, short of its complete form in words, is pictorial. The American game show *Jeopardy*, in an April 2009 episode, had a category of answers that was called Animated

Word Puzzles. The contestants had to identify the expressions that were suggested by the following images:

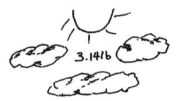

The correct responses, which had to be put in the form of a question, were "What is pi[e] in the sky?" and "What is act out of character?"

These graphic illustrations of expressions are part of a long tradition, of portraying expressions pictorially, that goes back to the sixteenth century. This kind of illustration, now usually in cartoon form, will often interpret an idiomatic expression literally, to humorous effect. Several examples are provided in later chapters of this book.

Some of the most mystifying coded expressions, at least to anyone not born within the sound of Bow Bells in London, are those that are Cockney slang. In this form of idiom, the expression takes its meaning from an unrelated rhyming word. That word, however, is not part of the expression itself. Therefore, it's not like the usual rhyming expressions, such as "drunk as a skunk" and "helter skelter." As an example, "peas in a pot" is a Cockney expression used for "hot." To confuse matters further, the rhyming word in the expression (in this case "pot") is often dropped along with any preposition or article that comes before it. A Cockney speaker would, therefore, say of an overheated room, "it's a bit peasy in 'ere," which also involves a creative evolution of the noun "peas" into an adjective. This is a fairly mild example of the idiom. Many other rhyming slang expressions are marked by their cheeky—even wicked—humor, such as "trouble and strife," which is used by Cockney males as a substitute for the word "wife."

Cockney rhyming slang has served very effectively as a secret language used by the members of a particular community that keeps rank outsiders in the dark. Some have suggested that the Cockney argot was actually developed as a thieves' code. Its jargon is certainly hard for the law abiding masses to decipher. Indeed, it's "a far cry from" being "as plain as the nose on your face," which translates to rhyming slang as "a far pipe your eye from" being "as plain as the 'I suppose' on your boat [race]."

Australian rhyming slang may have been the offspring of Cockney rhyming slang, imported to Australia by the original convict settlers from England. In any case, it largely follows the same principles as Cockney rhyming slang. Some of the slang expressions from Australia feature local notables. "Having a Captain Cook," shortened to "having a captain's", means having a look, such as the English explorer did, with amazement, when he first came upon the southern continent. In London, the notion of having a look might just as easily come out as "having a butcher's" which is built on the fact that "look" also rhymes with "hook," a hanging device used in the meat trade. "To do a Harold Holt," or simply "to do a Harold," means to bolt. This last expression may not be founded exclusively on a rhyme, but may have some other logic to it. Holt was an Australian Prime Minister who disappeared mysteriously at sea in December, 1967 when he went swimming alone in treacherous waters, suggesting to some that he wanted to be free of his duties as first minister. His tragic final act has been referred to, with "more than a touch" of black humor, as "the swim that needed no towel."

5

ALL OVER THE MAP: THE GEOGRAPHY
OF EXPRESSIONS

If the world is your oyster, there's no need to clam up.

Anon.

The narrative at this point proceeds "all over the map" in the sense that it discusses expressions that refer to a particular country, state or city. It also goes all over the place in identifying and discussing four categories of expressions; those that say the same thing in different ways in various parts of the English-speaking world, those that aren't readily exportable because they're apt to be offensive outside their original borders, those that are peculiar to a particular part of the world, such as expressions set in Strine, a native Australian manner of speaking, and those that have been imported into English from a foreign language.

Quite distinctive expressions signifying the same thing often take seed in different countries. For example, there's a trilogy of expressions to mark extreme happiness, each with a different geographic origin and usage. In the United States and Canada, one is apt to be "happy as a clam," in the U.K. to be "happy as a sandboy" and in Australia and New Zealand to be "happy as Larry." A "sandboy" was a lower class, male worker who sold sand from door to door, usually to commercial establishments. The sand was used as a crude floor covering to absorb mud and moisture. It was later replaced by sawdust, which those of us who are "long in the tooth" may remember as covering butcher shop floors. In the Australasian expression, "Larry" may refer to the undefeated Australian boxer Larry Foley (1847-1917) or it may come from "larrikin," a slang term for a young hooligan or rowdy type. As with many expressions, it's difficult to pinpoint the precise derivation.

Similarly, "not worth a brass farthing," which is used in the U.K. to indicate that something is virtually worthless has a North American counterpart in "not worth a plug nickel" and an Australasian counterpart in "not worth a brass razoo" or "not worth a zac." A farthing was a quarter of a penny. Had the farthing coin been cast in brass, it would have had an intrinsic value even less than that. A plug nickel was a five cent coin defaced with a plug of a cheap metal so that it was no longer legal tender. A razoo was a coin, supposedly of trivial value, that never actually existed, while a zac was sixpence, a coin that disappeared with the introduction of a decimal currency system in 1966-67. In every instance, the coin is "not worth diddly squat," to use an emphatic expression of U.S. origin referring, euphemistically, to something found in abundance in a barnyard.

In fact, there are many expressions that refer to currency which, of course, may have different designations and denominations in different countries. In that case, the expressions are not readily exportable. Thus, the British expressions "in for a penny, in for a pound," "penny wise, pound foolish" and "not worth a brass farthing" were never broadly espoused in the U.S. On the other hand, the American expressions "phony as a two [or three] dollar bill" and "not worth a plug nickel" and "more bang for the buck" never "gained wide currency" in the U.K.. This is not to say that expressions with local connotations never cross borders. They often do through literature, movies and television shows, news media, travelers, immigrant settlers and personal or business communications. In the colonial era, of course, many such expressions inevitably travelled from Britain to her colonies, including those in North America and Australasia.

There are some expressions that are notorious for having a perfectly respectable meaning in one country but a coarse slang meaning in another. An American woman visiting the U.K. is likely to be shocked when asked by a local hotel clerk whether, or when, she wants to be "knocked up in the morning." This expression is an innocent reference to a wake-up call, which was traditionally given with a knock on a bedroom door, usually followed by the delivery of morning tea. But to the Yankee visitor, the expression is likely to bring to mind the American slang term "knock up," meaning "to make pregnant." A downhearted American man visiting the U.K. who is told "keep your pecker up" may be equally shocked by what he's likely to take as a call to overcome an erectile dysfunction when he's simply being told "keep your chin up." In other words, remain cheerful. No wonder it's said that "England and America are two countries divided by a common language," an observation often attributed to the Irish playwright George Bernard Shaw but reflecting an earlier insight by his compatriot Oscar Wilde.

An American visitor invited to attend an Australian Rules football match in Melbourne would generate a lot of smirking on the part of his local hosts if he were to announce that he was going to "root, root, root for the home team." The reason for this reaction is that "root" is Australian slang for having sexual intercourse. It would be best, therefore, if the visitor were to adopt the local lingo and propose to "barrack for the home team." For their part, the Australian hosts should probably refrain from calling the visitor a "septic," even though that's perfectly acceptable local rhyming slang for Yank.

Geographic locations feature in many expressions. If you claim "to be from Missouri," although you don't actually come from this Show-Me State, then you're probably skeptical about something or everything and waiting, therefore, for "the proof of the pudding." "In a New York minute" suggests that the minute hand of a clock or watch in the Big Apple moves at a different rate than that of timepieces elsewhere. In fact, the expression refers to the frenetic pace of life in the city and simply means in a very short time. That timeframe has been defined as the period between the traffic light in front of you turning green and a New York cabbie behind you honking his horn. This impatient behavior by taxi drivers continues, as ever, despite a recent city ban on horn blowing. At the other extreme, someone who is "on African time" is moving at a slow pace, *polepole* (rhymes with "slowly slowly") as they say in Swahili, and will arrive for an appointment or at a destination "sooner or later," but would sooner be there later.

A few expressions are based upon the known quantities of a particular commodity in a certain location. To take, carry or bring "coals to Newcastle" is to do something that is completely superfluous because Newcastle-upon-Tyne in northeast England always had plenty of coal on hand from the mines in its vicinity. But all that has changed. The last of the coal mines have been closed and Newcastle has "changed its colors" from coal-dust grey to environmental green. It's now striving to become the first carbon-neutral city in the world. Yet, the expression persists, although its use would seem to be on the decline. The futility of "taking coals to Newcastle" is much like the futility highlighted by the lesser-known expressions "taking sand to the Sahara" and "trying to sell refrigerators to Eskimos."

If someone wouldn't do something "for all the tea in China," he wouldn't do it no matter what the reward. Put another way, he wouldn't do it "for love nor money." The geographical point of reference for this expression continues to make sense, for China remains the world's largest tea producer. The expression is one of many that are used in a negative way. "Not in a month of Sundays" signifies that something will never happen; "not playing with a full deck" suggests that someone is mentally challenged; and, as we've just seen, "not worth a brass farthing," and its counterparts outside the U.K., mean that something is virtually worthless. These expressions are almost never turned around and used with "not" omitted.

There are many Australian words and expressions that are part of a distinctive Downunder vocabulary. The expression that's perhaps best known, but least understood by foreigners, is "fair dinkum," which is "as Australian as meat pies." It's a malleable term that can mean genuine, honest, true, or fair and square and can be put to work as an adjective, an adverb, an exclamation or a question.

The expression "fair dinkum" doesn't travel well beyond its homeland. *The Sydney Morning Herald* reported, in a news item a few years ago, that an Australian woman on a U.S. domestic flight had asked the stewardess for a bag of pretzels in place of the crackers she was offered. When told that there were no pretzels left, the passenger said "fair dinkum" meaning, in this situation, "you've got to be kidding!" When the flight landed, three uniformed officers confronted the passenger, claiming that she had sworn at the stewardess which was against U.S. federal rules. In the end, however, no charges were laid which, in the circumstances, was "fair dinkum." The story is certainly apocryphal, even though it didn't appear in an April Fool's Day issue of the *Herald*.

When my wife and I sent our son, who was nurtured in Canada, off to kindergarten at a school in Melbourne, Australia, he and his class-mates seemed, at first, to be communicating well. But one day he came home terrified because some of his mates had threatened to "dob him in." He calmed down eventually when we told him that it was unlikely that they were proposing to "do him in," but were more likely to be bent on "ratting him out," apparently for some technical breach of the school's rules. My Scottish ancestors might have said that the lads were going to "clype on him" and my English cousins would probably have said that his pals were going to "grass him up." Neither alternative manner of speaking would have left him any better informed about his probable fate.

"Strine" is the name given to the language that is supposedly spo-ken by Australians. The word is a syncope since it reflects a synco-pated pronunciation of "Australian" as it would flow from the mouth of someone with a broad Aussie accent. The language itself is based on similar transformations of English words and phrases. It was first documented, in the 1960s, by Afferback Lauder, whose very name is a syncope for alphabetical order. One of his famous countrymen, Dame Edna Everage, comedian Barry Humphries in drag, also sports a Strine name, in this case a surname that's a corruption of the word "average."

In his book *Let Stalk Strine*, Professor Lauder, in real life Alistair Ardoch Morrison, compiled a number of words and phrases that were previously used only in the oral tradition and established their definitive spellings in the process. Through his assiduous research as Professor of Strine Studies at the University of Sinny, known to foreign-ers as the University of Sydney, Lauder was able to trace back the ori-gin of the Strine expression "flesh in the pen" which sounds amazingly like the English expression "flash in the pan," describing someone who shines for a brief period. The latter expression comes from the frequent misfiring of muskets when the powder in the depression or pan would flash up without igniting the main charge. According to Lauder, the Strine expression had a different derivation, coming down from the early Australian settlers who "fashioned pens from goose quills—often without first removing the goose." He claimed that the expression was originally "gooseflesh in the pen," only later shortened to "flesh in the pen." Lauder contended that the expression refers to shaky or illegible writing, such as would be caused by the struggles of the goose.

In a subsequent book, *Nose Stone Unturned*, Professor Lauder developed these bilingual signs imparting standard warnings and instructions, in English with Strine subtitles, the latter to provide clarity for the general Australian public:

NO ADMITTANCE
Key Powder Vere

BEWARE OF ONCOMING TRAFFIC
War Chaffer Ong-calming Veagles

PLEASE DO NOT SMOKE
Nouse mogen!

Strine can not only be mystifying to those who aren't "dinky-di" or "true blue" Australians, it can also be misleading. When the English writer Monica Dickens, the great granddaughter of Charles Dickens, was at a book signing session in Sydney, a city known as "steak and kidney" in rhyming slang, a bookstore customer handed her a copy of her latest book while saying two words to her. Dickens took the book and inscribed the title page with the words "Emma Chisit" over her own signature and handed it back to the customer. She thought that she had been responsive to the customer's direction as to how the book should be signed. As it turned out, the customer's words were a simple inquiry as to the price of the book.

As English speakers, we borrow liberally, without translation, from true foreign languages in the expressions we use. A wealth of expressions have been taken on loan from classical Latin, samplings of which appear in a later chapter, entitled "Things go Better with Latin" (c. 12). From the national language of France, we get such stand-bys as *bons mots* (good words), *carte blanche* (a white slate, i.e. a clean slate), *entre nous* (between us or, in other words, confidentially), *joie de vivre* (joy of living) and *savoir faire* (the ability to act appropriately, especially in a social context), which entails the avoidance of any *faux pas* (false steps). The use of these expressions adds a certain *je ne sais quoi*, which means that I can't quite "put my finger on" what they "bring to the table," although they sound impressive. That alone may be their principal *raison d'etre* (reason for being) as borrowed expressions.

The mixed language expression "*déjà vu* all over again" also sounds impressive although it involves a redundancy since its French and English parts come to the same thing. Yet it remains ever popular as a light-hearted way of saying "been there before." The expression is generally thought to have originated with Yogi Berra, the famous New York Yankees catcher and manager, who had a full roster of linguistic *faux pas*. Berra never explained or apologized for his creation, but he's reported to have made the following general confession later in life: "I really didn't say everything I said."

6

THE PLAYERS IN EXPRESSIONS: GETTING TO KNOW THEM WITHOUT A PROGRAM

What's in a name? That which we call a rose by any other name would smell as sweet.

William Shakespeare, from his play, *Romeo and Juliet*

If only there was a playbill, we'd know something definitive about the actors. As it is, there's a lot of speculation about many of the characters whose names surface in the expressions we use. We'll see, in this chapter, that some of those characters have emerged from literature, some can be identified as real folks, others are generic caricatures, while the rest remain clouded in anonymity.

Similes, in particular, are often populated with the names of historical, biblical or mythological personalities. In each case, the analogy is drawn from a legendary trait of the person. Accordingly, someone may be described as being "wise as Solomon," "patient as Job," "rich as Croesus," "old as Methuselah," "eloquent as Cicero," "handsome as Adonis," or "lovely as Venus." By comparison, "pleased as Punch" is an unlikely simile to highlight extreme delight since it refers to the grotesque puppet of Punch and Judy fame, whose pleasure was perverse and sadistic, derived as it was from glorying in his evil deeds. The Australian expression "game as Ned Kelly" paints a picture of a brave and tenacious individual. Kelly was an elusive outlaw who roamed the bush in the nineteenth century and would later become an iconic figure for his resistance to authority.

The players in all of these similes are exceptional characters in their own right. But who is "the average Joe"? Certainly not Joe the plumber, who was liberally referred to in the course of the American presidential campaign of 2008 by the Republican candidate, John McCain. He was held up as a symbol of middle-class values and concerns. But "when all was said and done," Joe the plumber didn't live up to his Everyman image. He wasn't even an accomplished plumber—he was a "Johnny come lately" to the trade who didn't actually have a license to plumb. This became apparent when an investigative reporter decided to "plumb the depths" of his background.

Some might equate the "average Joe" with "the man on the Clapham omnibus" who, we are to assume, hails from that once middle-class part of south London. This expression got its start with the civil court judges. They used it for the principal purpose of describing the ordinary reasonable man, whose conduct was taken to set the standard of care in negligence actions. If a defendant's conduct failed to measure up to what might be expected of this hypothetical man, epitomized by the Clapham transit rider, then he would be liable for the damages caused by his conduct, but not otherwise.

Although Joe is sometimes given the surname Blow, Shmoe, Doakes, Bloggs or Six-Pack, that hardly helps to place him in the pantheon of potential "average Joes." In truth, the "average Joe" may simply be "any Tom, Dick or Harry." Joe is certainly ubiquitous but nobody seems to know for sure where he came from, possibly Clapham, or what distinguishes him other than his average characteristics, which is probably "a distinction without a difference."

Joe has a mysterious Spanish namesake who keeps getting rebuffed with the putdown "no way José." José must, by now, be suffering from a serious inferiority complex. No doubt he feels better every time he's by-passed in favor of Nelly, whose name is invoked in "not on your Nelly," another way of saying "no way." That expression is a form of rhyming slang which has fallen into the mainstream. It comes, in a circuitous route, from "not on your life." First, "breath of life" is taken as a proxy for "life;" second, a "puff" is introduced into the mix because it can provide a "breath of life;" third, the name "Nelly Duff" is singled out for its rhyme with "puff;" and, fourth, "Duff" is ditched in favor of just plain "Nelly." Therefore, "not on your life" translates to "not on your Nelly." Nelly hasn't been any easier to identify than José. She's certainly not the same Nelly who's best known for being nervous. Even "blind Freddy could see that," as they say in Australia with no particular Fred in mind. The unrelated "nervous Nelly" has something in common with "a moaning Minnie," for each of them is perturbed in an alliterative manner of speaking.

Another actor in the dramatic world of expressions is Robert whose nickname is immortalized in the curious expression "and Bob's your uncle," meaning you're all set, "you've got it made" or "there you have it." "Truth be told," all we can say about Robert, other than remarking upon the good fortune that he bestows upon his nieces and nephews, is that we "don't know him from Adam," using "know" in the sense of "recognize" and not "in the biblical sense." But, we're likely to know a good deal about Adam through the Old Testament's account of creation. Therefore, it's quite silly to say that we don't know someone from Adam, especially if we've seen the person but simply failed to recognize him. If that person was clad in more than a single fig leaf, he would be easily distinguishable from Adam. Better to say: "His face didn't ring a bell."

In the north of England, the expression "you'll end up in Dickie's meadow" sounds an alert to the dangers of acting foolishly. A Yorkshireman might guess, correctly, that the most likely candidate for Dickie is Richard, the Duke of York, who was killed on the Wakefield Green in 1460 when he attacked the forces of the ruling House of Lancaster without waiting for the reinforcements he had called for. Those of us who weren't Yorkshire bred would be more likely to confess that we "know dick about" this miscalculating Richard, using "dick" in the sense of "nothing," one of the more respectable slang meanings of the word. The Richard who "met his maker" at the Battle of Wakefield is the same Richard who is up front in the mnemonic "Richard of York gave battle in vain," which helps us remember, in proper top-down order, the colors of the rainbow; red, orange, yellow, green, blue, indigo and violet. Of course, there's another name that, by itself, serves the same colorful purpose, namely Roy G. Biv.

"A good time Charlie" is an upbeat, pleasure loving person who is "out for a good time." The on-line *Urban Dictionary* describes him as "an imaginary person who makes you spend all your money at a bar." But even Charlie "has his ups and downs." The "downs" are the subject of the American country music classic "Good Time Charlie's Got the Blues."

There are two named players in the Robin Hood scenario that play out in the expression "robbing Peter to pay Paul." They may have been singled out because they bore the same names as two of the early apostles of Jesus Christ who were alike in many ways and were commonly associated with one another. The alliterative result of putting the names together may have clinched their selection. The expression is meant to emphasize the pointlessness of taking from one and giving to another who is similarly situated, or, interest factors aside, incurring a new debt just to pay off an old one.

Arthur and Margaret are another couple who are paired up in an expression. An Australian may "not know whether he's Arthur or Margaret." This doesn't mean that he's AC-DC and "swings both ways," as one might expect. Rather, he's simply confused, as he would be if "he didn't know whether he was punched or bored," to use an alternative expression of some vintage. We don't know who Arthur and Margaret were in real life, and all we can fairly assume about them is that they are of opposite sexes. Therefore, any confusion between them is, "by all appearances," hard to countenance.

A gay man is sometimes described as a "friend of Dorothy." Dorothy in this coded expression is, actually, the central character in *The Wonderful Wizard of Oz*. In the 1939 movie made from this Frank Baum fantasy novel, the young Judy Garland played the role of Dorothy. She would later become an icon amongst members of the gay community. In a circuitous fashion, a "friend of Dorothy," therefore, identifies someone who is likely to have an affinity for Judy Garland given her appeal to gays.

During and following the Second World War, the message "Kilroy was here" appeared in graffiti on building walls and other public spaces.

The message was often accompanied by a distinctive doodle that portrayed the elusive and peripatetic Kilroy like this:

Kilroy's signature piece did not go unnoticed and unchallenged by other graffiti artists. In his book *Graffiti Lives, O.K.*, Nigel Ross records two series of responses that appeared in the tradition of graffiti dialogue, the first of which began with:

Pearls of laughter
Screams of Joy
I was here before Kilroy.

This was obviously written by a killjoy (no relation) who was out to spoil Kilroy's fun, but it was followed by this further inscription by a Kilroy defender:

Shut your mouth.
Shut your face, Kilroy built the ruddy place.

A second challenge to Kilroy's primacy was contained in this graffiti message:

Sing and shout
And dance with joy
For I was here before Kilroy.

This too was followed by a further inscription by a defender of Kilroy's claim to being first on the scene:

> Alas, my friend, before you spoke,
> Kilroy was here, but his pencil broke.

While Kilroy is known to have had American roots, he's never been clearly linked to a real person although there are some usual suspects. Apparently, Hitler once thought that Kilroy was a spy for the Allied Forces since his infiltration into Axis-controlled areas was so pervasive. Consequently, "his name was mud" in the eye of the Fuehrer.

Kilroy had an Australian counterpart who wrote "Foo was here" and sketched in a Kilroy-like image on any available public space. A British version of the same character went by the name of Chad or Mr. Chad but his doodled picture was usually accompanied by a query about wartime rationing. "Wot, no bread?" was typical. The answer to that was only too obvious at the time. Although simple and monochromatic, these various verbal and pictorial trails that Kilroy, Foo and Chad left behind remain among the most famous examples of graffiti art.

A surname in an expression is more likely to be traceable to a real person than a first name. "A Hobson's choice", which means no choice at all, invokes the last name of an English stable owner of the sixteenth and seventeenth centuries who offered a selection of horses for rent. He always insisted, however, that a customer take the horse closest to the stable door. Anyone who was unhappy with "Hobson's choice" could always opt to go "on Shank's pony," sometimes referred to as "Shank's mare." But this option would mean having to walk, or "to leg it out," for Shanks was simply a made-up name derived from the term for that part of the leg below the knee.

A "Hobson's choice" should not be confused with a "Sophie's choice." A "Sophie's choice" refers to an agonizing decision that one is forced to make when there's little prospect of reducing the amount of grief by choosing one option over another. In a novel of the same name by American author William Styron, a Polish mother called Sophie finds herself "on the horns of a dilemma" upon her arrival at the Auschwitz concentration camp. The Nazis force her to choose which of her two children will be put to death. At that point, she could be described as being in a "Catch-22 situation," a state of affairs that draws upon another book title, that of Joseph Heller's satirical war novel.

If everything is "according to Hoyle," it means absolutely correct or in keeping with reputable authority as exemplified by the rules for playing various card games set out by Edmund Hoyle in his definitive treatises of the eighteenth century. Sir Edmund would probably "roll over in his grave" if he knew that his legacy was invoked by Robert Service, the Bard of the Yukon, in these opening lines from "The Quitter," as support for "taking the easy way out:"

> When you're lost in the Wild, and you're scared as a child,
> And Death looks you bang in the eye,
> And you're sore as a boil, it's according to Hoyle
> To cock your revolver and…die.

The expression "in like Flynn," meaning that you're a shoe-in to get what you want, may have been based, originally, on the example of Edward "Boss" Flynn. He was an extremely successful campaign manager for the Democratic Party in the South Bronx in New York City, who invariably managed to get his candidates elected. However, the sexual exploits of the Australian-born Hollywood actor, Errol Flynn, later led to the expression being understood, in the popular mind, to refer to the ease with which this other Flynn was able "to have his way" with women. Then, following the 1967 release of the parody spy film *In Like Flint*, starring James Coburn, many people came to believe that the expression was actually "in like Flint." However, there was nothing in the reputation of agent Derek Flint in the movie that matched the notorious track records of the two Flynns of earlier times or that otherwise suggested an assurance of success.

Someone who's labelled a "wrong way Corrigan" has a reputation for making a big blunder or for getting things backwards, much as the American aviator and aircraft mechanic Douglas Corrigan did back in 1938. After filing a plan for a solo flight out of New York for California,

Corrigan headed east across the Atlantic, in what was apparently a calculated miscalculation, landing in Ireland twenty-nine hours later. He became something of a hero for this exploit. His airplane, which he had modified himself, came to be dubbed "The Spirit of $69.90," emphasizing that it was a very "poor relation" to "The Spirit of St. Louis," built in San Diego at a cost of $10,000, which Charles Lindbergh had flown in the first solo flight across the Atlantic some eleven years earlier. The circumstances prompted the comment that Corrigan was "flying by the seat of his pants," adding credence to that idiomatic expression.

While several of these named individuals in expressions can be traced back to their origins, it has never been firmly established which of the many McCoys is "the real McCoy," meaning the genuine article. Whoever he was, he must have had many imposters, prompting the development of a singular expression to confirm his authenticity. The McCoys of Kentucky were on one side of a prolonged feud (1860-1891) with the more affluent Hatfields, their neighbors across the border in West Virginia. These families were certainly "for real" and perfectly genuine in their mutual hatred. Their sometimes violent antagonism was so notorious that "a Hatfield-McCoy feud" became a popular description of any bitter blood battle.

"Keeping up with the Joneses" involves maintaining a status equal to that of one's neighbors as exhibited by the conspicuous possession of material goods of the latest and best variety. Of course, this kind of emulation can be a costly proposition. It prompted the English writer Quentin Crisp to advise: "Never keep up with the Joneses. Drag them down to your level; it's cheaper." The expression "keeping up with the Joneses" comes from a comic strip of that name which ran for twenty-six years in the *New York Globe* in the early 1900s. The strip wasn't based on the lives of a real Jones family. It simply used the common surname "Jones" as a hypothetical description of a typical neighboring family, much like "the average Joe" was used to refer to the typical man.

Someone who is "leading the life of Riley" is unlikely to worry about "keeping up with the Joneses" for he has, by definition, a contented and carefree existence. Once again, it's the media that popularized the expression, in this case through a radio show of the 1940s starring William Bendix, followed by a feature film, a TV series and a comic book, all of which took their titles from the expression. Riley was likely of Irish heritage as the name reflects an alternative spelling of Reilly. Apparently, another Irishman horned in on his good life, as this epitaph reveals:

Here lies Kelly
We buried him today
He lived the life of Riley
When Riley was away.

The slang expression represented by the acronym SFA, where "S" stands for "sweet," "F" stands for the "f" word and "A" stands for all, is sometimes dressed up in a euphemistic way as "Sweet Fanny Adams," which avoids any crass language but preserves the saccharine quality of SFA. There really was a Fanny Adams. She was a young English girl who was murdered in 1867 at the age of eight and was remembered because sailors in the Royal Navy called an unappetizing variety of tinned meat, introduced into their messes, "Fanny Adams," in the gruesome suspicion that the meat may have come from her remains. Consequently, something that's worth "Sweet Fanny Adams" is actually worthless. In other words, it's "not worth a pinch of raccoon excrement," to coin a euphemism from another slang expression.

"What in the Sam Hill?" signifies a quizzical reaction to something "coming from out of left field," to use a baseball metaphor. But no one seems to know "who in the Sam Hill" this man was. The expression is actually a minced oath, a form of euphemism sometimes called an expletive-deletive. It calls to mind, "what in the name of hell?" but it avoids any actual expletive.

"For Pete's sake," used to express annoyance, is another example of a minced oath. It avoids the more overtly sacrilegious "for God's sake" and takes up a less offensive, oblique reference to St. Peter. Similarly, "for the love of Mike" is used to express exasperation by calling in aid a nickname for St. Michael rather than the name of God. The saints have thus preserved us from outright blasphemy by "lending their names" to these exclamatory expressions.

"Omygosh," "son of a b" and "I'll be darned" are other minced oaths with barely concealed cover-ups. "Jumpin' jehosaphat" involves a somewhat better disguise. It probably became popular because it avoided the profanity of invoking the names of Jesus or Jehovah in vain. But it owes its popularity, to a large extent, to its alliterative form.

The old-fashioned American expression "heavens to Betsy," now something of an anachronism, may also be a minced oath, serving as a respectable alternative to the seemingly unrelated "hell's bells." The latter expression sometimes appears in an elaborated form, "hell's bells and buckets of blood," which has the benefit of both rhyme and alliteration and can be used if "hell's bells" alone and "heavens to Betsy" are too mild for the occasion.

7

THE EVOLUTION OF EXPRESSIONS

Change is inevitable, except from a vending machine.

Anon.

Expressions don't stand still any more than time does. Sometimes, they go completely off-track because they've been misheard or misunderstood and then constantly repeated in an erroneous way. At other times, they've been adapted, taking on new forms or meanings in response to changes in society. Or they've suffered "from wear and tear" through overuse and have, therefore, acquired the dubious distinction of being clichés. "On the other side of the ledger," fresh expressions are often churned out, in fun or in all seriousness, using standard formats. Other expressions emerge from the specialized jargon of particular activities, such as sports, from the language of commerce or technology or from catchphrases, to take on more general meanings or usages. This chapter is all about these transitions.

Many expressions have evolved over time with changes in wording, sometimes accompanied by changes in meaning and sometimes not. The expression "to eat humble pie" means to admit wrong and face humiliation, which is also the result of "eating crow," a less palatable alternative. The original expression referred to eating "'umble pie," which also signaled a humiliating apology. "'Umbles" were the offal—the heart, kidneys, liver and entrails of a deer that were left over after the nobility, those who were "to the manor born," had their fill on the choice parts of the animal. The "'umbles" were often made into a pie for the humble servants, many of whom would have described themselves as 'umble servants, dropping the "h" in "humble" in the manner of their dialects.

If someone is being "kept on tenterhooks," he would be in anxious suspense about something. But he would be unlikely to know that tenterhooks were devices used to hold woven cloth in place while it was being tentered or stretched during a drying process. This procedure explains why being "kept on tenterhooks" means being tense. Lack of familiarity with the word "tenterhooks" has led some to mistake the expression and unwittingly convert it to the similar sounding "kept on tender hooks" but without losing sight of the original meaning.

This type of error, caused by a misunderstanding, that is evident in "to eat humble pie" and to be "kept on tender hooks" has recently been given the name "eggcorn," derived from one woman's practice of saying "eggcorn" when referring to an "acorn." A word or phrase that has come to be substituted for a similar sounding original has also been called "sparrow grass," a term that was used in the eighteenth century to refer to "asparagus."

An eggcorn is often quite plausible in the context in which it's used. Being "left on tender hooks" could refer to the practice followed by butchers of leaving meat hanging on a hook in order to age and tenderize it. If its feelings could be determined in this situation, the meat might be in a state of pained helplessness. That would be akin to the anxious suspense that is meant to be conveyed by the expression in its original form. A "bit of a stretch" but not impossible!

An eggcorn is similar to the more impressive sounding "mondegreen." A mondegreen is also the result of a misunderstanding but, in this case, typically of a song lyric so as to make it quite nonsensical. The name comes from a mishearing of "laid him on the green," a phrase in a Scottish ballad that was often mistaken for the sound-alike "Lady Mondegreen." "Doughnuts make my brown eyes blue" is a modern day example. It comes from a real or feigned misunderstanding of "Don't it make my brown eyes blue," a line from a song popularized by country-pop artist Crystal Gayle. The expression "at someone's beck and call" has become, for many, the similar sounding, "at someone's beckoned call." This still incomplete transition has received some impetus from the fact that "beck," like "umble" and "tenterhooks," is an unfamiliar fossil word. In fact, the noun "beck" is related to the better known verb "to beckon" so that the sense of the expression hasn't really changed at all.

"For all intensive purposes" is another common corruption of an expression. It involves a misunderstanding of "for all intents and purposes." But it certainly doesn't suggest anything like "for all practical purposes," the real meaning of the original expression. On the sheer nonsense scale, the corrupted version of the expression ranks up there with "the ants are my friends, they're blowing in the wind," a mondegreen that "makes a mockery of" the Bob Dylan lyric, "the answer my friend is blowing in the wind."

William Shakespeare has been widely credited as the first to use the expression "to the manner born" in a literary work. He wrote that phrase for Hamlet who used it in explaining his opinion about the heavy drinking habits of the Danes, of which he was no fan, although, as he said, "I am native here, and to the manner born." In other words, he was familiar with the local custom of overindulging because he was born into it. Over time, a homophone came to be substituted for "manner," whether in jest or in simple error, with the result that the more common rendering of the expression became "to the manor born." The result was a significant change in meaning. The expression now meant someone of high station who would be likely to occupy a manor house. The altered version was popularized by a very successful English comedy TV series which took that version as its title.

This is not the only expression born of a misquotation from Shakespeare. "At one fell swoop," which the Bard of Avon used in his play *Macbeth* became, in some quarters, "at one foul swoop" or "at one fowl swoop" when the word "fell" apparently "fell on deaf ears." The original meaning—all in a single action or event—survived through this evolution. However, it's been argued that "at one foul swoop" bears a more specialized meaning, namely a police sweep in which several miscreants who have "run afoul of the law" are rounded up.

In another of Shakespeare's plays, *King John*, the Earl of Salisbury protests the second coronation of the King with these words:

Therefore, to be possessed with double pomp,
To guard a title that was rich before,
To gild refined gold, to paint the lily...
Is wasteful and ridiculous excess.

Somehow the third line was eventually collapsed to become "to gild the lily," even though it would be unlikely that a layer of gold could be successfully applied to something as soft and brittle as a lily. But the same thing could be said about applying paint to a lily. Therefore, there's little to choose between the flowery language of the original line and the gold-plated language of the imposter. Both paint verbal pictures of over-embellishing something.

King Midas of Greek mythology is the only well known figure reputed to have succeeded in turning flowers into gold. He did this, quite simply, with his god-given golden touch, which would come to be known as "the Midas touch." But it wasn't long before he regretted this uncommon ability and asked the god Dionysus to withdraw his special power. Dionysus obliged and restored the flowers, and everything else King Midas had turned into gold, to their original form. By some accounts, the king turned against wealth and avarice, as a result of his experience, and became a nature lover, taking up the worship of Pan, the god of the fields and the woodlands, where flowers flourish in their natural unadorned state.

"To call a spade a spade" takes its present form because of an error in translation. The original Greek expression should have been translated as "to call a fig a fig, a trough a trough." But when the Dutch humanist Erasmus translated the original into Latin, he mistook the Greek word for trough for a similar Greek word that denotes a digging tool. He, therefore, used the Latin word for a spade in his translation. While he may have thought he was "calling a spade a spade," he was actually calling a trough a spade. The modern English version of the expression comes from Erasmus' inaccurate Latin translation, but with the fig bit lost somewhere along the way. In another evolutionary thread entirely, by the 1930s the word "spade" had taken on an additional role, to that of a digging tool, as a slang term for a Negro, a use that became largely derogatory. Therefore, the suspicion arose that "calling a spade a spade" implies contempt for those who are black even though it's simply used as a substitute for "saying it like it is." And so an expression that had no historical connection to race and was never commonly used as a racial slur came to be stigmatized as politically incorrect. The expression "as black as the ace of spades" is similarly suspect as racist even though the obvious allusion is to the color of a suit in a deck of cards and even though the expression is used, more often than not, to describe the jet blackness of something other than skin color.

Popular culture, current events or modern techniques may change an expression or, as is the case with the spade expressions, the association that it brings to mind. Thus, the description of uninteresting people as "dull as ditchwater" became "dull as dishwater" as ditches were filled in and replaced by pipes that carry wastewater away underground "out of sight, out of mind," as the saying goes.

Established expressions may have new applications as human experience unfolds. A novel twist on "taking justice into your own hands" came out of Zimbabwe a few years ago. According to newspaper reports, the victims of crime were asked by the prison service to drive those accused of committing a crime against them to court, for any required appearances or trials, since the prison vans were all out of petrol. According to the reports, this invitation was taken up by victims with vehicles and access to scarce fuel who wanted to avoid postponement of the proceedings against those who had wronged them. This proves, of course, that while "the wheels of justice grind slowly," they can be speeded up when "the squeaky wheels get the grease," in this case by virtue of the victims of crime lending their own "wheels" to accelerate the judicial process.

There are formulas that are now frequently used, particularly by journalists and writers, to turn out new expressions. These end products and the formulas from which they're generated have been given the new name "snowclones." One such formula is "the _____ from hell." It has spawned "the date from hell," "the neighbor from hell" and "the roommate from hell."

Someone who just doesn't get a particular message, of which "X" is the crucial part, may be asked "what part of X don't you understand?" The most common query in this form is "what part of 'no' don't you understand?" That's typically asked by a woman who's trying to rebuff a man's persistent sexual advances, having already told him that she's not interested.

The formula "X is the new Y," has been used to make the point that X has taken the place of Y in contemporary society. You simply need to insert the appropriate words for X and Y into the template. Thus, in the last recession, there were repeated comments in the press that "flat is the new up," thus "lowering the bar" on the level of economic activity to be hoped for.

The substitute for Y is often the word "normal." The changed conditions that are recognized as the "new normal" have included frugality, plunging house prices and government deficits, all spin-offs of a recessionary economy. Obesity and dementia, both aspects of a decline in health and wellness, have also been singled out as so common that they represent the "new normal" rather than isolated conditions. Indeed, the possibilities for filling the role of X are many and varied.

The formula "X is the new Y" has produced a number of not-so-serious snowclones, including the following:

Rehab is the new casting couch.
Moody is the new bipolar.
Videogames are the new pain pill.
Mumbai is the new Bombay.
Square watermelons are the new normal watermelons.
Old (or pre-owned) is the new new.

Taking their cue from "old is the new new," many senior citizens are heard to proclaim, in a serious and wishful vein, that "70 is the new 40."

An established expression, rather than a recognized formula, may also provide some of the impetus for a new expression in a similar form. This happened recently when "jump the shark" came to serve as a moving force for "jump the couch." The shark expression comes from a scene in an episode of the TV series *Happy Days*, broadcast in September 1977, in which the always cool Fonzie, played by Henry Winkler, jumps over a shark while he's waterskiing, still wearing his trade mark leather jacket. This incident came to be viewed as "a bit of a stretch," an "over the top" attempt to build up the audience for the show. But the ratings continued to decline. "Jump the shark" then evolved as an expression to describe the turning point at which something that was once great begins to suffer a decline in quality and popularity.

The expression "jump the couch" was coined later, building upon another incident on television. In May of 2005, the movie actor Tom Cruise was a guest on a segment of the *Oprah Winfrey Show*. In the course of her interview, Winfrey asked Cruise the widely anticipated question about his relationship with actress Katie Holmes, at which point he got so pumped up about his love for Holmes, who was then pregnant with his child, that he jumped up onto the studio couch and proceeded to bounce on it. This strange behavior delighted the audience and attracted considerable media attention. It bolstered the ratings for the *Oprah Winfrey Show*, proving that it didn't mark a jump-the-shark moment. But it did become labelled "jump the couch," signifying strange and frenetic behavior, which was recognized as the American slang expression of the year for 2005. Unfortunately, the bounce went out of the relationship between Cruise and Holmes as they divorced in 2012 after six years of marriage.

"Jump the shark" and "jump the couch" have been described as catchphrases because they were originally associated with a well known figure and caught on with the public, as part of the popular culture, through the media. But both matured into conventional expressions as they became more widely used. "Who'd a thunk it?" and "you ain't heard nothin' yet" are two earlier catchphrases that followed the same path.

"Who'd a thunk it?" is a funky way of posing the rhetorical question "who would have thought it?" The expression was popularized by Mortimer Snerd. He was one of the puppets of ventriloquist Edgar Bergen, which makes him the brother of the actress Candice Bergen, as she likes to say. In his appearances on radio and TV, Mortimer showed himself to be even dumber than your average dummy. When something very commonplace was explained to him by the elder Bergen, he was often taken by surprise. He would shake his wooden head and say "Who'd a thunk it." Of course, his rhetorical question was put in a perfectly logical form. If "sink" and "drink" become "sunk" and "drunk" in the conditional tense, why shouldn't "think" become "thunk" in the same way? The trouble is that logic and consistency often fail to prevail with the English language, something that Mortimer didn't appreciate given that he was a mere dummy.

"You ain't heard nothin' yet" also became famous as an expression originating in the entertainment world. Al Jolson was one of the first actors whose voice was heard, in a full length commercial film, properly synchronized with a moving picture. *The Jazz Singer* was to be a big step up from silent movies with a technological breakthrough that allowed for the reproduction of Jolson's singing voice in tandem with his movements. But while the orchestra played the first few bars of the opening vocal number, "Toot Toot Tootsie Goodbye," Jolson impetuously spoke the line "wait a minute, wait a minute, you ain't heard nothin' yet." This happened while the mike was open, but before he launched into the song, and his words were preserved on the sound track of the movie. "You ain't heard nothin' yet" became imprinted in the public mind and has been taken to mark the auspicious birth of the "talkies." There may have been a sub-text here, for Jolson had used the expression before and had released a record titled "You Ain't Seen Nothin' Yet," the sales of which could only have benefitted by Jolson's outburst in the course of the filming of *The Jazz Singer*. Another song with the same title would later become a number one hit in North America for the Canadian rock group, Bachman-Turner Overdrive. Other song titles have helped foster the wider acceptance of "ain't," including "Ain't She Sweet," "It Ain't Necessarily So" and "Ain't That a Shame."

I was always reminded by my parents and teachers that "'ain't' ain't in the dictionary" whenever I uttered the unsanctioned word as a child.

But when I joined the local pack of cub scouts, the Akela (cubmaster) taught us the campfire song "There Ain't No Flies on Me," the refrain of which repeated the title expression several times. As I had the Boy Scout credo of respecting my elders drummed into me, I didn't openly question the use of "ain't." But I was understandably confused about when the word could be used despite its absence from that sacred tome, the dictionary. Suffice it to say that nowadays "ain't" just doesn't have the same taint it once had and it's no longer true that "'ain't' ain't in the dictionary." It seems to be all right to use "ain't" at the appropriate time and place so long as you're likely to be taken to have done so with a bit of levity and not in the mistaken belief that you're using the Queen's English.

Some expressions started out as exclusive to the argot or jargon associated with a particular group, activity or way of life and then fell into more general usage. This has happened with many sports expressions. "Throwing a Hail Mary pass" describes a football play in which a quarterback lobs the ball into the air, without much precision and "on a wing and a prayer," as it were, hoping that one of his teammates, rather than an opposing player, will manage to grab it. Roger Staubach, the quarterback for the Dallas Cowboys, is credited with popularizing the expression when he used it to describe his last minute desperation pass that allowed the Cowboys to "seize victory from the jaws of defeat" in a 1975 play-off game against the Minnesota Vikings. The expression is now used to portray any kind of desperate maneuver. Several of John McCain's tactical moves during the 2008 U.S. presidential election, including his selection of Sarah Palin as a running mate, were described as "Hail Mary passes."

In cricket, someone who is "out for a duck" is a batsman who's retired without scoring a single run. One might say that he's "gone for naught," "naught" being another word for zero or zip. The word "duck" in the expression "out for a duck" refers to the entry on the score sheet for the batsman's runs, namely "0," which has the shape of a duck's egg. In North America, a "0" score would more likely be described as a "goose egg," a term that also doubles as a description of the swelling occasioned by a blow to the head. Although originally confined to the game of cricket, "out for a duck" is now used to describe someone who has "fallen flat on his face," figuratively speaking, whether on or off the cricket pitch.

The explanation for a batsman being bowled or caught out may be that he was "batting on a sticky wicket," which happens when the pitch around a wicket is tacky because of recent rain, causing the ball to bounce erratically. In this situation, it's difficult for the batsman to hit the ball or to hit it squarely. "On a sticky wicket" then came to describe being in any difficult or embarrassing situation. An Australian newspaper, *The Age*, used the expression in this 2003 headline, "WTO on a sticky wicket against Japan's rice bowlers." The underlying article was about that country's protective rice tariff that threatened to derail World Trade Organization talks on farm trade reform. The situation could also have been described, but not "in a sporting way," as a sticky rice problem.

In boxing, "it's not cricket" to "hit below the belt" or, to put it another way, "it's not according to Hoyle." Indeed, it's a direct violation of the Marquis of Queensbury Rules that have governed the sport since their first publication in 1867. If a boxer "lands a low blow," his opponent is liable to suffer severe pain if the blow lands in the area of the groin. Accordingly, to "hit below the belt" is to do something that's unfair and hurtful.

If a boxer is "out for the count," he's been floored by a punch and is unlikely to get up before the referee counts to ten. If anyone else but a boxer is "out for the count," he's totally exhausted or in a deep sleep and "dead to the world." Therefore, he's unlikely "to get up and at 'em" any time soon. But if he's simply "on the ropes," he has a slim chance of recovery although, like a boxer "hanging on for dear life" to the side of a boxing ring, he's probably going to face defeat unless he's "saved by the bell" in the form of a timely intervention at the last minute.

A boxer who takes mercy on his opponent may "pull his punches." If someone was described as having done that outside the ring, it would indicate that he was less forceful or frank than he might have been. However, the expression is more likely to be used in the negative.

Someone who is "not pulling his punches" isn't "putting a lid on" his criticisms.

Rather than pulling his punches, a boxer may be "punching above his weight," as when a middleweight manages to "hold his own" against a light heavyweight. If some other person is "punching above his weight," he would be engaging in an activity or contest above the expected level, given his skills and experience. The baseball expression "hitting out of his league" carries a similar meaning.

The game of golf has given us "par for the course," meaning as expected. This expression became an irresistible target for manipulation by journalists reporting on a widely witnessed incident on television in February of 1960. The host of *The Tonight Show* had walked off the set to protest the censoring of an off-color bathroom joke that was part of his monologue for the previous evening's show. The network executives had deemed it too *risqué* and edited it out. The host was the late Jack Paar and the censored material was described by the press, in the spirit of William Spooner, as "coarse for the Paar." He ultimately "let everyone in on" the censored joke in a chapter, entitled Plumbing Can Make You Famous, of his autobiography.

An individual or other living thing that has seriously "bitten the dust" may be described as "deader than last year's tennis balls." This is an alternative expression to "deader than a doornail." In reality, of course, there are no degrees of "deadness," any more than there are degrees of pregnancy. Moreover, inanimate objects, such as tennis balls and doornails, do not have "life and death experiences."

"Deader than last year's tennis balls" now borders on the extinct, even though it has more logic to it than the ever popular "deader than a doornail." Tennis balls are commonly viewed as being alive or dead depending on their resilience. Last year's balls that haven't been in play over the winter months are singularly lacking in that quality. New balls, by comparison, have "more bounce to the ounce," in the words of a Pepsi-Cola slogan of the 1950s or, to coin a comparable phrase for the metric world, "more slam to the gram." The demise of the tennis-balls expression has, no doubt, been hastened by the fact that tennis has become a year-round sport in the colder, northern climes with the advent of heated indoor courts. Therefore, for many players, there's no seasonal hiatus during which tennis balls can "catch their death of cold" or of simple inactivity.

While many commercial messages incorporate established expressions, at least one expression has evolved from a commercial message, rather than the other way around. "Where the rubber meets the road" had its debut in the late 1950s as part of an advertising jingle that was used for the next twenty years by the Firestone Tire and Rubber Company, now part of Bridgestone Corporation. The complete jingle went as follows:

> Wherever wheels are rolling,
> No matter what the load,
> The name that's known is Firestone
> Where the rubber meets the road

The last line has survived as a stand-alone expression used to denote "the moment of truth."

"Just do it" is one of the most widely recognized advertising slogans in the world today. It has been used since 1988 by Nike, the athletic shoe manufacturer, often alongside its tick logo, known as the "Swoosh." It's meant to say something like this: Start pursuing your dream right away by calling upon your natural determination and passion.

Before Nike's remarkable success with its slogan, the expression "just do it" was probably best known as a command to a child who had the temerity to pose the question "Why?" in response to a parental direction to do something. The expression has also been used to urge somebody to do something he really doesn't want to do and has put off for some time. It's implicitly critical of the person to whom it's directed for not "getting off his ass" sooner. Nike was able to turn an expression that's used to suppress youthful defiance and criticize procrastination into a positive message to embolden its customers. After Nike's shares had had a good run on the stock market during 2013 and were expected to mark time for a while, one newspaper ran with the catch line "just do it (but do it 'for the long run')" to introduce a business story suggesting that the shares were not a good bet for "investors interested in the dash to the top 2014 returns."

The terminology of computer and electronic communications technology has recently made its appearance in broader modes of non-technical expression. Thus "to go offline," has come to mean talk in private, "to ping [someone]" has come to mean get in touch [with someone], "to give [someone] a brain dump" has come to mean tell [someone] all you know and "to receive a pile of spam" has come to mean get a lot of unwanted junk by way of old fashioned "snail mail."

The term "spam," which appears in the last of these examples, is the name of an unappetizing canned meat product that was widely tolerated when staples were in short supply during the Second World War. However, the immediate inspiration for the use of the word to describe unsolicited e-mails, sent indiscriminately to a large number of people, is a popular comedy sketch from the British TV series *Monty Python's Flying Circus*. In this sketch, a waitress expands upon the menu options by adding spam, sometimes more than once, to each and almost every combination of the standard "eggs, bacon and sausage." She recites the seemingly large number of choices for two customers against a background chant of "spam, spam, spam, spam," from a group of Viking patrons, that builds in an increasing crescendo. One way or another, a clear and consistent spam message dominates the scene. Against this background, one of the customers insists all along that she wants no part of spam either alone or as part of a combination plate. In a later movie, *Monty Python and the Holy Grail*, spam is much better accepted, King Arthur's Knights belting out "We dine well here in Camelot, we eat ham and jam and spam a lot." Those lyrics then became the inspiration for the title of the musical comedy *Monty Python's Spamalot*, yet another parody on King Arthur and his Knights of the Round Table.

Over time, many expressions have become trite or hackneyed through overuse and have, therefore, been branded as clichés. It's been said, "tongue in cheek," that "clichés should be avoided like the plague." But if you're not "sick to death" of a cliché, you can try to get away with using it by adding a request for forgiveness in the form "excuse the cliché."

The Lake Superior State University, in Sault Ste. Marie, Michigan, publishes an annual list, based on informal public input, that "unfriends" certain words and phrases and declares them "shovel-ready" because of their overuse, misuse or general uselessness. The University's list of banished words and phrases is a helpful marker of some of the expressions that have become clichés. The lists of recent years have included the following:

> "It's a game changer."
> "Been there, done that."
> "Don't even go there."
> "Getting in touch with your feelings."
> "In your face."
> "Pushing the envelope."
> "More bang for the buck."

The 2013 list added "kick the can down the road," which has been a favorite way of describing what politicians are inclined to do when faced with a difficult problem, such as how to avoid falling over a fiscal cliff, a prospect that the U.S. has repeatedly faced. Politicians are thus portrayed as "buying time," sometimes with a partial fix, in the hope that the problem will go away or that there will be "another kick at the can," in a Canadian manner of speaking.

Some expressions have evolved as spin-offs from proverbs and can, therefore, be described as proverbial expressions. Such an expression draws strength from the recognition factor that is likely to be associated with the proverb. The expressions "bite the hand that feeds you," "throw the baby out with the bathwater" and "change horses in mid stream" are easily recognizable as proverbial. They all come from proverbs that differ only in that they begin with the word "don't."

The structure of a proverb is relatively fixed but a proverbial expression can usually be adjusted to suit the circumstances. Thus, "bite the hand that feeds you" could take the form of a metaphor as in the sentence: If you were to "spill the beans" on your boss, you'd be "biting the hand that feeds you." It could also be put in the form of a simile as in the sentence: "Spilling the beans" on your boss would be like "biting the hand that feeds you."

Some expressions simply allude, in a cursory fashion, to a proverb. "Birds of a feather," for example, brings to mind the proverb, "birds of a feather flock together." The expression therefore refers, figuratively speaking of course, to "peeps with similar likes, appearance or behavior," as the *Urban Dictionary* puts it. If some act or situation is described as a case of "the blind leading the blind," it's meant to foretell a consequence of like proportions to that described in the biblical proverb, "if a blind man leads a blind man, both will fall into a pit." When someone says "that's the last straw," we're likely to be reminded that "it's the last straw that breaks the camel's back," a notion that was conveyed, in earlier times, by the similar proverb, "it's the last feather that breaks the horse's back."

8

METAPHORICALLY SPEAKING THROUGH SAYINGS

Life is a journey. Time is a river. The door is ajar.

Jim Butcher, from his novel *Dead Beat*

We've now reached the juncture, in this journey through various manners of speaking, at which sayings take over the lead from expressions. A saying—sometimes called a proverb, an adage, or a maxim—is simply a statement, familiar through widespread use in oral or written communication, that imparts some sort of wisdom, or advice, or embodies a principle, a rule of conduct or a truth. A saying may also be described as "an old saw," but that notion didn't "cut any ice" with American humorist James Thurber, for he wrote that while "a new broom may sweep clean," referring to a well known proverb to that effect, you should "never trust an old saw."

Sayings are often built upon metaphors. I'm tempted to say that "I never metaphor I didn't like," borrowing the title of a book by language maven Dr. Mardy Grothe that feeds off Will Rogers' improbable assertion "I never met a man I didn't like." However, it would be an exaggeration to say that all metaphors are likeable and "hit the mark," although most are commendable for doing a good job by portraying a colorful image that readily leads us to appreciate an underlying concept. The metaphors in sayings that I really do like are those that can be manipulated in a witty way. This chapter explores the world of metaphorical sayings with an emphasis on those that have been used to humorous effect; with plays upon their literal sense, or as sources for clever punch lines in shaggy dog stories, or as the subject of funny takes by young children on the wisdom of the world or through the mixing of metaphors, largely for nonsense value.

Metaphorical sayings are close relatives of idiomatic expressions. The lesson that such a saying is meant to convey is not to be found in its literal terms but in its symbolic statement of a larger truth. "Don't bite the hand that feeds you" and "never look a gift horse in the mouth" counsel against ingratitude. "The early bird gets the worm" extols the virtue of preparedness and hints at the perils of sloth. "People who live in glass houses shouldn't throw stones" tells us that we should refrain from attacking others when we're vulnerable, particularly to the same form of attack as we might mount.

Some metaphorical sayings use the literary device of personification, attributing a human characteristic to an inanimate object or an abstract concept. "Walls have ears" uses the human feature "ears" in reference to inanimate objects, "walls." The saying sounds the warning that some unseen person or concealed recording device may be listening in. In a modern turnaround, it's sometimes said that "ears have walls," a commentary on a frequent human failing, the inability to listen carefully and absorb what's being said, as if walls were getting in the way as barriers to hearing. This contemporary observation carries overtones of the old saying, "there's none so deaf as will not hear." "Fields have eyes and woods have ears" is the out-of-doors, rural equivalent of "walls have ears." It alerts us to two ways in which our personal privacy can be invaded.

Although love, as an abstract concept, can't give vent to its emotion as a human can, it's said that "love laughs at locksmiths." This saying simply means that nothing at all can stand in the way of true love, for which there are no barriers. The biblical proverb "the truth will set you free" embodies a personification of the abstract concept of truth as if it too were capable overcoming restrictions. However, the freedom that it promises isn't always a good thing, which is revealed by another, painful truth, "tell the boss what you really think of him and the truth will set you free."

"The thought is father to the deed" does a good job of portraying the notion that human conduct is almost always preceded by thoughts along the same lines. The saying attributes physical existence, as a father, to a thought. "Necessity is the mother of invention" attributes physical existence, as a mother, to the notion of necessity. This kind of attribution of substance to an abstraction is "cemented in our minds" by the term "concretive metaphor."

"Time is money" embodies a concretive metaphor, using money to conceptualize time. Money is a suitable metaphor for time because it's something with which we have considerable experience. In particular, we've learned, sometimes to our chagrin, that it's not to be wasted. The saying tells us that time should be viewed in a like manner. Of course, time and money can never be fully equated, although economists and actuaries try "to pull off that trick" from time to time.

The punch lines of shaggy dog stories, a form of long-winded joke, are often derived from metaphorical sayings. They typically alter the saying, with one or more word plays, so that it's tailored, in a literal sense, to the story. In the process, any suggestion of the larger, metaphorical meaning of the saying is lost or seriously impaired, but that's never of consequence to the narrator.

One such story involves a familiar tale about a primitive warlike tribe, the members of which lived in grass huts. In a shortened version, the story goes like this:

> In keeping with custom, whenever this particular tribe prevailed in combat, the victors would take the enemy's most prized possession as a spoil of battle. After one conquest, they seized a golden throne which they then stored in the loft of their chief's house. But the grass ceiling was not strong enough to hold it and it fell through the ceiling and onto the chief, killing him instantly.

Like many allegorical stories, this one ends with a powerful moral: "People who live in grass houses shouldn't stow thrones."

An original shaggy dog story ("you read it here first") unfolds this way:

> A stone quarry was opened in a residential community. Its operation soon proved to be a real nuisance for the locals because

of the dust and noise, which interfered with the use and enjoyment of their properties. A neighbor on one side of the quarry was "quick off the mark" in complaining to the quarry operator, maintaining that the quarry should be shut down or an embankment built around it to shield the residents. Later on, the residents on the other sides of the quarry raised their voices in protest, echoing the concerns of the first complainant. In the end, the quarry operator refused to be guided by the saying "when you're in a hole, stop digging." However, he did construct an earth barrier on the side of the quarry from which the initial "hue and cry" had arisen, while ignoring the claims to protection that had come later from the residents on the other sides of the quarry.

Of course, this only goes to show that "the early word gets the berm."

The punch lines of both of these shaggy dog stories involve a transposition of sounds within a saying. They demonstrate the use of the Spoonerism as a humorous device, which we have also observed, in an earlier chapter (c. 3), in similar distortions of popular expressions.

Some other shaggy dog punch lines that sound like common sayings are set out below, followed by one line summaries of their lead-ups, an order that blatantly ignores the admonition "don't put the cart before the horse:"

"If it ain't bracken, don't fax it." A message sent by a botanist to fellow scientists. He was indicating that while he had asked for their research results on ferns, by return fax, he was only interested in what they had learned about one particular variety.

"Never lock a gift mouse in the hearse." The moral of a story about a pet rodent, received as a birthday present. The mouse disappeared at a funeral and ended up locked in the undertaker's vehicle never to be seen again.

"With fronds like these who needs anemones." A fish that would normally hide among sea anemones to be safe from predators discovers that a fern-like coral offers even better cover.

"You should never book a judge by his cover." A "lesson learned the hard way" by a police officer. He was disciplined for arresting a member of the judiciary who was on his way to a costume ball dressed as a convict. The officer had, obviously, forgotten the old adage, "appearances are deceiving."

The literal sense of a saying has sometimes inspired humorous observations about the saying itself. For example, the advice that "before you criticize someone, you should walk a mile in their shoes" has been explained in a couple of similar ways: "That way, when you criticize them, you are a mile away from them, and you have their shoes," and "That way, when they come after you, you've got a mile head start and they're running barefoot." Of course, the saying really means that you shouldn't judge a person without first putting yourself in his position. It has nothing to do with borrowing footwear except as an illustration of this point. Another saying, supposedly Native American in origin, provides a similar illustration of the general principle with its proposition, "don't judge a man till you've walked two moons in his moccasins." This alternative saying is enriched by its alliterative quality but requires a much longer period of sensitization, a couple of months, to the other man's situation.

"It's no use crying over spilt milk" usually means that it's pointless to fret over a misfortune that has already happened. But if you should think of "crying over spilt milk," there's some mitigating action that is often recommended, i.e. "try to condense it," flippant advice that is deliberately ambiguous. Is it the milk or the grieving period that should be condensed?

"Out of the mouths of babes..." means that children sometimes speak with considerable wisdom. Art Linkletter, who was a great hit with his interviews of youngsters on his TV variety show *House Party* in the 1950s and '60s, certainly found this to be true. In order to induce innocent gems or "pearls of wisdom" from his young subjects, he often used the tactic of asking them what they understood by a particular expression or saying. Not unexpectedly, the replies were usually triggered by a literal understanding. He recorded some of his favorite exchanges with his subjects in his book *Kids Say the Darndest Things*. One child was asked what he thought of the saying "the early bird gets the worm," which elicited the comment: "He's welcome to it. I ate one once and it tasted like cold spaghetti." Although he never had the same gastronomic experience, Mark Twain expressed a similar sentiment when he said:

> The early bird catches the worm...is a seductive proposition, and well calculated to trap the unsuspecting. But its attractions are wasted on me, because I have no use for the worm.

In any case, the most delectable and plumpest variety of worms, dew worms, are caught in the middle of the night, often by those who have stayed up late rather than by early risers.

Another of Linkletter's young interviewees was asked what "the grass is always greener in the other fellow's yard" meant to him. "That's easy," he replied, "he's using better fertilizer than you are." In another explanation for the greenest grass, the humorist Erma Bombeck titled one of her books *The Grass is Always Greener Over the Septic Tank*, a bestseller that was soon followed up by a sequel, reflecting her questioning of another saying, *If Life is a Bowl of Cherries, What Am I Doing in the Pits?*

A primary school teacher is reported to have fed her six year old charges the opening words of a number of sayings and asked them to complete the sayings, producing the following results:

> Strike while the... bug is close.
> It's always darkest before... Daylight Saving Time.
> Don't change horses... until they stop running.
> If you lie down with dogs... you'll stink in the morning.
> Don't put off till tomorrow... what you put on to go to bed.
> Children should be seen and not... spanked or grounded.
> Better late than... pregnant.
> A miss is as good as... a Mr.

Where there's smoke there's ... pollution.
A penny saved ... is not much.

The last four of these creative completions indicate how attuned children are to the world around them even though they may not be able to recite many common sayings with perfect accuracy.

Mixed metaphorical sayings are coined by combining two or more sayings to create a new, usually nonsensical saying, such as:

There's a watched pot at the end of every rainbow (combining "there's a pot of gold at the end of every rainbow" and "a watched pot never boils").

The squeaky wheel gets the worm (combining "the squeaky wheel gets the grease" and "the early bird gets the worm").

Don't count your chickens in one basket (combining "don't count your chickens before they're hatched" and "don't put all your eggs in one basket").

Don't burn your bridges until you come to them (combining "don't burn your bridges behind you" and "don't cross the bridge till you come to it").

A mixed metaphorical saying may make perfect sense at the literal level even though it doesn't make sense at the metaphorical level. Who could challenge the patent accuracy of the proposition that a bird in the hand isn't fouling its own nest? This newly crafted saying combines "a bird in the hand is worth two in the bush" with "it's an ill bird that fouls its own nest," both of which are addressing a fact of human life using a bird metaphor.

The traditional saying "a closed mouth catches no flies" states the general truth that you can avoid trouble if you keep your mouth shut. The expression "putting your foot in your mouth" describes a thoughtless and embarrassing act of saying the wrong thing and giving offence to another person. The saying and the expression have been neatly combined to produce the modern saying, "a closed mouth gathers no foot," which comfortably blends two ideas that are quite similar. This new saying is all the more memorable because it carries echoes of the familiar saying, "a rolling stone gathers no moss."

Not all sayings are metaphorical. We will see many examples, in subsequent chapters, of sayings that are meant to be taken literally, in which case the opportunities for manipulating those sayings, in jest, are more limited.

9

THE STYLE AND FORM OF SAYINGS

Substance without style is like truth without beauty.

Anon.

"It's just a matter of style" downplays the importance of style but in sayings style can go a long way toward "keeping up appearances," which counts toward the continuing popularity of a saying. Therefore, it makes sense to consider, as we do here, the various stylistic devices that have been used to advantage in sayings, in particular; parallelism, rhyme and alliteration. It seems logical to couple this with a consideration of the ways in which sayings are structured generally, including their common patterns, their grammatical accuracy or lack thereof, their form as laws, such as Murphy's Law, or as principles, such as the Peter Principle, and their contraction as acronyms.

First, let's look at the three stylistic devices that are most prevalent in the structure of sayings, namely parallelism, rhyme and alliteration, starting with the first of these devices. A saying exhibits a parallel structure if it is made up of similarly constructed and balanced parts as in "seldom seen, soon forgotten," "once bitten, twice shy," and "penny wise, pound foolish." Each of these examples also involves a contrast between the two parts, which enhances the saying. They are all elliptical since a word is omitted that is necessary to complete the sense of the saying. In particular, a connective "is" has gone missing, between the parallel parts, where the comma appears. The omission adds punch to the saying without sacrificing understanding since it's quite obvious what word is omitted and needs to be read in. Parallelism may also build upon the repetition of words as in "let bygones be bygones," "easy come, easy go," "out of sight, out of mind," "nothing ventured, nothing gained," and "enough is enough."

The TV and film star Groucho Marx took the saying "time flies like an arrow" and added "fruit flies like a banana" to mimic a parallel structure. Was he comparing the flying patterns of time and fruit or the preferences of two different kinds of flies? Neither of course, for he was using the word "flies" in the two parts of the sentence in different senses. Consequently, he was mixing an observation about the fleeting nature of time with an unrelated observation about the feeding habits of fruit flies. Marx used a similar, incongruous blend of contrasting ideas when he played with another saying to produce this one-liner: "Outside of a dog, a book is a man's best friend; inside of a dog it's too dark to read." In a similar unnatural combination, it's been said that "silence is golden but duct tape is silver."

"He who fails to plan, plans to fail" exhibits parallelism of a special kind called chiasmus, a verbal pattern in which the order of words in one of two parallel clauses is reversed in the other. Chiasmus is also evident in the sayings "the best of men are but men at best," "you can take the boy out of the country but you can't take the country out of the boy," "when the going gets tough, the tough get going" and "it isn't the size of the dog in the fight, it's the size of the fight in the dog." This last saying no doubt inspired Mae West's famous summation of her priorities: "It's not the men in my life that counts, it's the life in my men."

This uninhibited American actress was also responsible for coming up with "a hard man is good to find." Here, there's an implicit chiasmus because her line embodies cross-overs with the well known saying "a good man is hard to find." In a similar kind of turnaround, it's sometimes said that "good news is no news," when the original saying is "no news is good news." The reversed form makes particular sense in the newspaper world where it's used to affirm the fact that good news isn't particularly newsworthy since readers seem to prefer a story of violence or misfortune, causing editors to take the approach that "if it bleeds, it leads."

The movie actor W.C. Fields, who had a reputation for heavy drinking, is reported to have said: "I'd rather have a bottle in front of me than a frontal lobotomy." The singer and variety show host, Dean Martin stated his preference more precisely: "I'd rather have a free bottle in front of me than a pre-frontal lobotomy." This drinker's "druthers," in either form, can be best described as an example of assonant chiasmus since each of the two parallel parts simply sounds as if it's the inversion of the other. In a similar fashion, comparatively good news is sometimes passed on in the following way to someone who's having a serious coughing fit: "It's not the cough that carries you off, it's the coffin they carry you off in." The comparison in all of these various quips is almost as absurd as Groucho Marx's comparison between the fleeting nature of time and the feeding habits of fruit flies.

Single-barreled sayings have sometimes been supplemented so that they take on a parallel, chiastic structure. "Better late than never," for example, has been expanded to "better late than never, but never late is better," providing some additional wisdom in the process. In a lighter vein, the comedian George Carlin is often given credit for the line "don't sweat the petty things and don't pet the sweaty things," which builds on the saying "don't sweat the small stuff."

Some sayings follow a structural formula much like snowclones, which are expressions that conform to a set pattern. "Once a ___, always a ___," a formula for parallelism, has been completed in several ways, including "once a thief, always a thief," "once a priest, always a priest," "once a whore, always a whore." It's also been said, in the same pattern, with an added rider, that "once a king always a king, but once a knight is enough."

"X is as X does" is the form taken by several sayings, some serious and some not so serious. "Handsome is as handsome does" dates back to Geoffrey Chaucer's *Canterbury Tales*. Notwithstanding this pedigree, some consider the saying to be quite senseless because they assume that "handsome" has to do with good looks. But the saying probably means that someone is a chivalrous person if he acts in a generous manner, which is consistent with another meaning of "handsome." Therefore, it's very close to the simpler alliterative proverb "manners make the man."

Other sayings that follow the form "X is as X does" trumpet an undesirable, rather than an admirable, quality. Forrest Gump, the hero in the 1994 movie of the same name, popularized the saying "stupid is as stupid does." This was his standard rejoinder when he was called stupid. He was likely saying, if we can credit him with sufficient "smarts," that a person can only be considered stupid by the stupid acts he commits, but in the absence of such acts the moniker doesn't fit. All of these sayings are really telling us that the measure of a person is determined, for better or for worse, by his deeds or behavior.

In a take-off on this form of saying, Rowan Atkinson, playing the role of Lord Edmund, the Black Adder, in the short-lived British TV comedy series *Blackadder II*, proclaimed magnificently, on the subject of fungal wood decay, that "dry rot is as dry rot does."

Sayings that have "no rhyme nor reason" are unlikely to survive but if they take the form of a rhyme, at least they "have half a chance." Consider the current popularity of "you snooze, you lose," "no pain, no gain," "if you're going to talk the talk, you've got to walk the walk," "health is wealth," "haste makes waste," and "different strokes for different folks."

"Haste makes waste" has sometimes been characterized as an epigram, which is to say a particularly pointed saying or observation. The English poet Samuel Taylor Coleridge cleverly defined an epigram, by example, as a "dwarfish whole, its body brevity and wit its soul." Some epigrams aren't particularly poetic but are simply clever and amusing remarks, usually associated with a particular individual, such as Oscar Wilde, who was responsible for the famous line "I can resist everything except temptation." In fact, Wilde was so famous for his well-crafted examples of the style that Dorothy Parker wrote:

> If, within the literate, I am
> Impelled to try an epigram,
> I never seek to take the credit;
> We all assume that Oscar said it.

Wisecracks are often crafted out of rhyming sayings by substituting a new concluding phrase that preserves the rhyme. "Early to bed, early to rise makes a man healthy wealthy and wise" has been an easy target for this kind of manipulation. Professor Wolfgang Mieder, a prominent proverb expert, has collected a number of common variations on this proverb in his book *Twisted Wisdom: Modern Anti-Proverbs*. He notes that "early to bed and early to rise" has been supplemented, variously, with "work like hell and computerize;" "and your girl goes out with the other guys;" "and you wake up with a family of a pretty big size;" and "you'll never see red in the whites of your eyes;" and "makes sure you get out before her husband arrives" (which only works, of course, if the husband sticks to the night shift).

Recent scientific research has established that a sleep pattern marked by early nod-off and wake-up can be caused by a mutant gene. Given this significant discovery, we can now add the following to the list of suitably modified versions of the early-to-bed proverb, "early to bed and early to rise 'cause a gene's in control of your shuttering eyes."

The American humorist James Thurber altered both parts of the proverb to come up with a brand new rhyme: "Early to rise and early to bed makes a male healthy and wealthy and dead," suggesting that there's nothing to be gained, in the end, from this nocturnal sleep pattern. An early riser and early capsizer will be an early demiser, as Ogden Nash might have said.

Several sayings without the benefit of internal rhymes were cleverly reworked by Sir William S. Gilbert, to create rhyming combinations, in the libretto for *Iolanthe*, one of the comic operas on which he collaborated with the composer Sir Arthur Sullivan:

Every journey has an end –
When at the worst affairs will mend –
Dark the dawn when day is nigh –
Hustle your horse and don't say die!
...
While the sun shines make your hay –
Where a will is, there's a way –
Beard the lion in his lair –
None but the brave deserve the fair!

...

Nothing venture, nothing win –
Blood is thick, but water's thin –
In for a penny, in for a pound –
It's Love that makes the world go round!

Another stylistic device that's often incorporated into sayings is alliteration. "Live and let live," "mind over matter," "forgive and forget," "time will tell," "death before dishonor" and "it takes two to tango" are familiar examples of alliterative sayings.

If there were degrees of "alliterativeness" and a distinction for the most alliterative of sayings, the old Scottish maxim "mony a mickle maks a muckle" would, undoubtedly, contend for the top spot. One might be tempted to ask, with apologies to the originator of the Peter Piper tongue twister, if "mony a mickle maks a muckle," how many mickles must we muster to mak a muckle?" Alas, there's no clear answer, for the Scots were simply observing that many little things make a large thing or, with an eye to their thrifty approach to savings, that small amounts can become a large amount for "every little bit adds up." This kind of thrift is demonstrated, in specific monetary units, by "pinching your pennies" or, in America, by "pinching your nickel till the buffalo bellows." "Never trouble trouble till trouble troubles you" would also be a contender for top spot among alliterative sayings if those that use word repetition qualified for entry into the competition.

Alliteration and rhyme aren't mutually exclusive. "Loose lips sink ships" combines both devices in providing a compelling reason for remaining tight-lipped. This saying originally served as a warning to Allied servicemen in World War II to be prudent in what they might say in writing home to loved ones. A similar message was conveyed by the *caveat* "be like dad, keep mum." That could be taken to intimate that a dad controls his wife in the same way as he might control a dependent mistress, also known as a "kept woman." Therefore, the saying would undoubtedly be branded as politically incorrect by today's standards.

A saying may be framed in an ungrammatical way, for example, "it's not what you know, it's who you know." Whatever happened to "whom," an object with which most of us are well acquainted? The similarly cynical saying "them what has gets" is sometimes described as the Iron Law of Distribution. That formulation of the Law is undented by any attacks from strict grammarians. Indeed, "them what gets has," while no better English, has been offered up as a reality that's just as true as the Iron Law itself.

Still, if you happen to find these sayings offensive, "you ain't heard nothin' yet," at least until you stumble over "if it ain't broke, don't fix it." "Leave well enough alone" carries essentially the same advice, but it doesn't have the same common touch. The "ain't broke" saying could, of course, be re-stated, in more formal terms. But to change it to "if it isn't broken, don't fix it" might "fly in the face of" the very caution that the saying embraces. Another, lesser known saying indicates when you can tell that "it ain't broke": "If duct tape can't fix it, then it ain't broke." This serves as an effective marketing pitch for duct tape, which is promoted as a repair-all product.

There is some justification for the unconventional wording of "softly, softly catchee monkey" because this saying is couched in pseudo-pidgin English. The saying is used to advise that caution, patience and careful planning will lead to success in an endeavor. It may have come, originally, from China or from the Ashanti tribe of West Africa. Lord Robert Baden-Powell, the founder of the Boy Scout movement, popularized the saying, attributing it to the Ashanti whom he encountered during his stay in Ghana. Or it may even have come from Borneo, a territory which the Irish poet Jonathon Swift identified with this calculated method of capturing monkeys:

Sly hunters thus, in Borneo's isle,
To catch a monkey by a wile,
The mimic animal amuse:
They place before him gloves and shoes;
Which, when the brute puts awkward on,
All his agility is gone:

In vain to frisk or climb he tries:
The huntsmen seize the grinning prize.

A few sayings end in a preposition. "What the eye doesn't see, the heart doesn't grieve over," "happy is the bride that the sun shines on" and "it's a poor dog that's not worth whistling for" illustrate this grammatical form. It was once thought that a clause or sentence should never end with a preposition. Support for this so-called "rule" was drawn from Latin sentence structure. However, the authoritative *Fowler's Modern English Usage* describes that "rule" as "a persistent myth." Sir Winston Churchill "weighed in on the subject" with this sardonic comment: "Ending a sentence with a preposition is something up with which I will not put." He might, however, have expressed real, rather than feigned, displeasure at the extreme example of dangling prepositions that occurs in the strange request that's common "Down East" in Atlantic Canada: "Stay where you're at 'till I come where you're to."

A few modern sayings take the form of so-called "laws." Many of these are attributable to a particular individual and are regularly referred to by the name of the originator coupled with the designation "Law." Parkinson's Law and Murphy's Law are the best known examples of sayings that are passed off as laws. This kind of saying reflects a light hearted view of human behavior or events. The term "law," which describes such a saying, is used in the sense of a law of nature or a law of physics. It suggests that the saying is invariably true.

Parkinson's Law proclaims that "work expands to fill the time available for its completion." In his book *Parkinson's Law or the Pursuit of Progress,* first published in 1958, Professor C. Northcote Parkinson supported this conclusion with pseudo-scientific evidence from the British civil service experience. "Data expands to fill the space available for storage" is a more modern Law, on the pattern of its predecessor, formulated to take account of one of the significant phenomena of the computer age.

Murphy's Law is to the effect that "if anything can go wrong, it will." This Law is generally credited to American aerospace engineer Captain Edward Murphy. Jon Henley, writing in the *Guardian* newspaper on the occasion of the Law's sixtieth anniversary in 2009, established that Murphy's Law is self-proving and beyond dispute. His deft, if dubious, line of reasoning is as follows: The Law states that if anything can go wrong, it will; therefore, the Law itself can go wrong, in which case things can sometimes go right. Consequently, the Law is right in stating that "if anything can go wrong, it will," the Law itself serving as a prime example of this. So the Law proves itself, *quod erat demonstrandum* (that which was to be demonstrated) or *QED*. In a departure from Murphy's Law and its inherent logic, the legendary radio broadcaster Paul Harvey once calculated that "if there is a fifty-fifty chance that something can go wrong, then nine times out of ten, it will."

In what is clearly a specific application of Murphy's Law, another Law proclaims that "toast always falls buttered side down." In this case, however, there are a couple of techniques that have been suggested for avoiding that fall-out. You can butter the toast on the flip side, rather than the top side, or you can attach the toast to the back of a cat before dropping it.

Parkinson's Law and Murphy's Law have spawned many other, unrelated Laws, such as:

Weiler's Law:	Nothing is impossible for the man who doesn't have to do it himself.
Scott's Second Law:	When an error has been detected and corrected, it will be found to have been correct in the first place.
Gumperson's Law:	The probability of anything happening is in inverse ratio to its desirability.

The last of these laws has been said to explain why you can throw a burnt match out of your car window and start a forest fire but have trouble getting a burning match to start a fire in your fireplace.

Other successor Laws are confined to particular activities but offer equally trenchant observations about "the way things shake out." Firestone's Law of Forecasting is that "Chicken Little only has to be right once." Jones Law of TV Programming is that "if there are only two shows worth watching, they will be on at the same time." This Law obviously pre-dated the widespread use of personal or digital video recorders, which eliminate many of the dilemmas that used to come with the simultaneous broadcast of two or more great shows. The Airplane Law is also about bad timing in its recognition that "when the plane you are on is late, the plane you want to transfer to is on time." On a slightly more serious note, Godwin's Law states that "as an online discussion grows longer, the probability of a comparison involving Nazis or Hitler approaches one."

Principles are somewhat lower than laws in the hierarchy of sayings. While also purporting to convey a fundamental truth, a principle is more general than a law and admits of the possibility of exceptions. The best known principled saying was formulated by Dr. Laurence J. Peter, a professor of education at the University of Southern California. His contribution came through his popular 1968 book *The Peter Principle, Why Things Always Go Wrong*, which he wrote in collaboration with fellow Canadian Raymond Hull. The Peter Principle is to the effect that "in a hierarchy every employee tends to rise to his level of incompetence." The result is that over time every position comes to be filled by an employee who is incapable of effectively carrying out the duties of the position he occupies. There's "a clot for every slot," as the authors put it. Many human resource management practices thereafter became attuned to avoiding this potentially disastrous state of affairs, taking seriously the new science of "heirarchiology" pioneered by Professor Peter.

The Dilbert Principle is a follow-up to the Peter Principle. It was formulated by American cartoonist Scott Adams, the creator of the syndicated Dilbert comic strip. The Principle is elaborated in Adams 1996 book *The Dilbert Principle: A Cubicle's-Eye View of Bosses, Meetings, Management, Fads and Other Workplace Afflictions*. The Dilbert

Principle holds that "the most ineffective workers are systematically moved to the place where they can do the least damage: management." Adams explains the subtleties of the evolution from the Peter Principle as follows: Whereas the old concept was that "capable workers were promoted until they reached their level of incompetence," his observations led him to conclude that "now, apparently, the incompetent workers are promoted directly to management without ever passing through the competence stage." Despite its light touch, Adams' book attracted the attention of many business managers just as Professor Peter's book had done earlier.

The Queue Principle stands in line behind the Peter Principle but doesn't have the same scholarly cachet. Most of us can personally attest to the validity of its proposition that "the longer you wait in line, the greater the likelihood that you are in the wrong line." The similar Driver's Principle, that "the other lane is always faster," rings true for all those who have ever gotten behind the steering wheel of a car. The technique evident in all of the Principles is to take the most annoying or frustrating of situations, apply a pessimistic perspective, à la Murphy's Law, and state them as if they were the norm, dignifying them by calling them Principles.

A lot of sayings are commonly put in the form of acronyms. There are obvious gains in efficiency and speed when acronyms are sprinkled liberally throughout text messages exchanged between those who know the codes. The ancient sounding BCBC has been used to sum up "beggars can't be choosers." GMTA, which has nothing to do with Greenwich Mean Time, has been substituted for "great minds think alike." These are but two modern examples of acronyms that are in play for established sayings.

No doubt inspired by the cost accounting acronyms FIFO (first in, first out) and LIFO (last in, first out), used to describe different methods for valuing inventory as it's sold, GIGO has recently been added to our stock-in-trade of acronyms. It usually stands for "garbage in, garbage out," emphasizing one of the hazards of the computer age; if you input rubbish, you'll generate rubbish by way of output. One would have thought this would be a self-evident truth for we were warned long before computers that "you can't make a silk purse out of a sow's ear." Yet some people continue to put their faith in the message of another form of GIGO, "garbage in, gospel out," which is a sardonic comment on the unwarranted trust that we sometimes place on computerized data.

"Keep it simple, stupid" came out of a concept of design engineering which recognized that it was best to design a product so it could be readily repaired, in the field, by someone with limited resources and sophistication. It is sometimes stated as the "KISS principle." The complaints to which the principle responds include that of the military arising from its experience that "the more advanced your equipment, the further you will be from civilization when it fails." This, of course, is simply an application of Murphy's Law, an illustration of the rule that "if anything can go wrong, it will." In fact, aerospace engineer Captain Edward Murphy was motivated in enunciating the very prescription that bears his name by the need to design repair parts so they could only be fitted in one way. He concluded that if they could be fitted in more than one way, a "wrong way Corrigan" would eventually come on the scene and do it the wrong way.

The word "stupid" was probably added to the conventional advice to "keep it simple" in order to produce a saying that would lend itself to representation by way of an acronym that mimicked a memorable word. Some reverse engineering may have been involved, working backwards from the desired acronym to arrive at the saying from which the acronym or backronym, as it might then be called, could be drawn.

After its general acceptance as an acronym for "keep it simple, stupid," KISS inspired other widely circulated explanations of what it represents, including "keep it simple sweetheart," "keep it short and simple," "keep it simple sista" and "keep it simple Sherlock," drawing on the reputation of the sleuth of Baker Street. All of these alternatives avoid the irreverent and insulting tone struck by "keep it simple stupid." So does the more balanced advice that "everything should be made as simple as possible but not simpler," which warns against both over complication and over simplification. However, this aphorism, which is generally attributed to Albert Einstein, doesn't lend itself easily to representation by acronym.

TANSTAAFL must be one of the longer acronyms to be used for a saying; it's certainly not short and simple like KISS. It stands for "there ain't no such thing as a free lunch," the colloquial version of the saying "there's no such thing as a free lunch." That saying was closely associated with the American economist Milton Friedman although he wasn't the originator.

LSMFT was popularized in the 1950s and 1960s as an acronym for "Lucky Strike Means Fine Tobacco." This marketing slogan for the American Tobacco Company's popular brand of cigarettes was so persistently drummed into the public perception that its simple repetition called up the full message in the minds of smokers. The acronym served as something of a mnemonic memory aid. But it wasn't long before it spawned a mock proverb to fit the letters; "loose suspenders mean falling trousers."

There's one saying that has come to be represented by a distinct visual image, much as the expression "Kilroy was here" came to be identified with a characteristic doodle portraying the elusive Kilroy. "See no evil, hear no evil, speak no evil" is commonly represented by three wise monkeys, one covering his eyes, one covering his ears and one covering his mouth. Statuettes of the threesome gather dust on mantelpieces, knick knack corners and whatnots in homes around the world.

Notwithstanding the visual clue, it's not entirely clear what the saying means. Some maintain that it's telling us not to be nosy or gossipy. Others suggest that it warns us to steer clear of bad situations so that we won't get into trouble ourselves. However, the most common contemporary use of "see no evil, hear no evil, speak no evil" is to describe, in a critical way, someone who ignores an impropriety by "turning a blind eye," by "turning a deaf ear," and by refusing to condemn it "by word of mouth."

Occasionally, a fourth monkey has been observed with the threesome. He's usually shown crossing his arms, apparently to signal "do no evil." But one cartoonist has given us a different story about the fourth monkey, as shown in this illustration:

The most likely suspect as the political incarnation of the fourth monkey is former U.S. Senator Gary Hart. He was the clear frontrunner for the Democratic nomination in the 1988 American presidential campaign when rumors surfaced in the press that he was having an extra-marital affair. He strongly denied any such relationship. But then the supermarket tabloid the *National Enquirer* ran a picture of him with a model, by the name of Donna Rice, seated on his lap. They were pictured aboard the luxury yacht *Monkey Business* and he was wearing a T-shirt with "Monkey Business Crew" emblazoned across the front. The publication of the picture brought effective closure to his presidential ambitions. If he had only been content to remain a Senator, recognizing that "the higher the monkey climbs, the more he shows his tail…"

10

MAKING SENSE OF SAYINGS

If you wish to live wisely, ignore sayings including this one.

Anon.

While sayings are usually meant to provide guidance or wise comment on everyday life, they aren't always clear, straightforward or up-to-date in their message. They can be ambiguous, paradoxical or enigmatic. They can be "out of sync" with current scientific reality or social norms. They can be based on beliefs that have been largely debunked or on long forgotten folklore or terminology. They can have the appearance of simply stating the obvious, in which case they have no readily apparent rationale. This chapter attempts to "get to the bottom" of these and other challenging sayings.

Some sayings are ambiguous and liable to mislead for that reason. "It's an ill wind that blows no one any good" can be taken as a simple statement of a pessimistic message that a bad event can bring no benefit to anyone. However, the conventional view is that the saying is telling us that an event would have to be really bad for it to bring no benefit to anyone. Someone is usually in a position to profit from an unfortunate occurrence or, to put it even more positively, "every cloud has a silver lining," which is an optimistic message. If this point is easily missed, it's because of the archaic and cryptic structure of the ill-wind saying, which was recorded as far back as 1546 by the English writer John Heywood in his *Dialogue of Proverbs*.

Nonetheless, the saying and its variations have often been viewed as a lament. That is true of Harold Arlen's lyrics for "Ill Wind (You're Blowing Me No Good)" from the 1933 Cotton Club Revue, *Paradise in*

Harlem. Arlen treats an ill wind as the purveyor of nothing but troubles that "creep up from out of nowhere when love's to blame." Some musicians have applied the saying, with a minor modification, to certain wind instruments that are particularly difficult to master. But it was the fictional character Walter Mitty, a ne'er-do-well with dreams of stardom in many pursuits, who was instrumental in popularizing that musical challenge. In the 1947 film, *The Secret Life of Walter Mitty*, Danny Kaye, playing the central role, described the oboe in song as "an ill wind that nobody plays good."

The saying "a friend in need is a friend indeed" seems to embody an unlikely proposition. It's more likely that "a friend in need is a friend to be avoided," as British politician Herbert Louis Samuel, 1st Viscount Samuel, is reported to have said. While the obvious interpretation of the saying may not make a lot of sense, there's another, less obvious, interpretation that does, namely; someone who is a friend when you are in need is a true friend. But that formulation doesn't scan nearly as well as the traditional poetic rendition of the saying.

The harsh reality, however, is that a friend will often "turn his back on" you when you're in need. That reality was neatly captured by Ambrose Bierce, the American newspaper columnist, in his definition of "back" as "that part of your friend which it is your privilege to contemplate in your adversity." Bierce's observation has been described as an aphorism, a statement that is distinguished by its originality and depth of thought, in a short compass of words, and its good literary style. It's akin to a saying but may not be particularly long standing or as widely repeated. Bierce had the distinctive habit of putting his aphorisms in the form of definitions, which he collected in his *Devil's Dictionary*.

Some sayings are puzzling because they are based on folklore that has not "held up to the test of time." The saying, "don't eat oysters unless there's an 'r' in the month" seems to impart advice that's arbitrarily restrictive and, in any event, seems a poor candidate to serve as a general "pearl of wisdom." The first thing to note about the saying is that it was once thought that oysters were unsafe to eat during the warmer months of the year in the northern hemisphere, from May through August. None of those months has an "r" in it while all the other months do. According to Mark Kurlansky, author of *The Big Oyster: History on the Half Shell,* some New York oystermen in the 1850s started referring to the month of August as "Orgust," with a view to accelerating the start of the oyster season. This happened after the injunction embodied in the saying had become a prohibition in the law. Ogden Nash declared in verse that he fancied the life of an oyster but he took the saying to heart in carefully limiting his metamorphosis with this concluding couplet:

I'd like to be an oyster, say
In August, June, July or May

That way he wouldn't be "consumed in the process."

The second thing to note about the saying is that, unlike many others, it is situation specific. It isn't meant to be anything more than a dietary direction relating to the consumption of oysters. In its limited reach, it's much like some other adages about consumables or treatments, such as "an apple a day keeps the doctor away" and "feed a cold and starve a fever." These sayings lack a larger, metaphorical meaning. The same is true of many sayings about the weather, for instance "April showers bring May flowers," "when the wind is in the east, 'tis neither good for man nor beast" and "red sky at night, sailor's delight; red sky in the morning, sailor's warning," All of these sayings are simply predictive in and of nature, unlike the ill wind saying, which is metaphorical.

While these predictive sayings are usually sustained by some experience, others can be put down to superstition "pure and simple." Who doesn't remember as a youngster warning playmates, "step on a crack, break your mother's back" and then demonstrating fine hopping skills so as to avoid the seams in the sidewalk. The saying was used as an excuse for this childish game. If you landed on a crack, it was understood that this wasn't "the mother of all disasters." Indeed, it was quite harmless beyond potential defeat in the hopping contest.

Many other sayings perpetuate superstitions by promising good or bad fortune from certain actions or circumstances. There's the dated invocation of good luck that comes from a nursery rhyme; "see a pin and pick it up, all the day you'll have good luck," which is coupled with the warning, "see a pin and let it lay, bad luck you'll have for all the day." We're told to let the pin "lay," rather than "lie," no doubt in the interests of achieving a rhyme. There haven't been any serious suggestions that this error should be corrected, perhaps on the theory that we should "let sleeping dogs lie," or should I say "let sleeping dogs lay?"

Many superstitions around numbers are preserved in sayings. Since "there's luck in odd numbers," it's not surprising that "all good things come in threes" and that it's "third time lucky." But the number three might cause someone a good deal of concern who happened upon another saying "all bad things come in threes" or the proverbial warning that it's "three strikes and you're out," which comes from the game of baseball but is now used as a description of laws under which you can be put away for a long time on a third offense.

"All good things come in threes" and "all bad things come in threes" aren't, strictly speaking, opposites. It would be surprising, however, if either proved to be statistically correct, let alone both. The fixation on "three" in these two sayings may simply be the result of a general affinity, in our communications, for catchy three-fold descriptions of actions, happenings or things. Triads are quite commonplace in our lives, from the marriage vow "to love, honor and obey," to the Holy Trinity, representing the Father, the Son and the Holy Ghost in the Christian faith, to the popular three cheers "hip, hip, hooray." They are also evident in many sayings, such as "eat, drink and be merry," "see no evil, hear no evil, speak no evil," and, on the subject of children, "one is one, two is fun, three is a houseful."

The supposed luck in odd numbers is likely to be a hard sell to cats. For them, it's nine times and out. But for humans, "a stitch in time saves nine," which seems to place some special significance on the number nine as the measure of the protection secured by acting in a timely manner. It's more than likely that "nine" in this saying was the result of an attempt to come as close as possible to creating a rhyme with time, rather than any notion of good fortune in this odd number.

For many, the number thirteen is likely to strike a note of foreboding. That reaction is sufficiently common that novelty "megawords" have been dreamed up, from Greek components, to describe a fear of the number thirteen. "Triskaidekaphobia" describes a general fear of that number and "paraskevidekatriaphobia" describes a fear of Friday the thirteenth. It's said that if you suffer from either of these phobias but learn to pronounce the name of your condition, you'll be cured as a reward for your accomplishment.

Some sayings that seem to reflect nothing more than silly superstition have been reinforced as a result of scientific research. Recent studies support the proposition that "you have to eat a peck of dirt before you die." The study results show that the ingestion of dirt allows you to get friendly with lots of germs, build up the immune system and prolong life by protecting against serious ailments, such as heart disease and autoimmune disorders, which could do you in. The same results also lend some credence to the old adage that "what doesn't kill you makes you strong."

The notion that "you are what you eat" receives some backhanded support from a growing body of evidence that what you don't eat may contribute to your disposition. For instance, a lack of zinc in your diet may make you irritable and aggressive. This prompted Dr. Edward de Bono, the father of lateral thinking, to conclude that the seemingly intractable conflicts in the Middle East might be attributed, in large part, to the widespread consumption in the region of unleavened bread, which is made without yeast, a great source of zinc. His solution: Ship jars of Marmite, a yeast-based spread that is marketed in the U.K. under the slogan "love it or hate it," to the Middle East. His idea was that, when consumed, it would have a leavening effect on peace negotiations. But for many, especially those who tag Marmite as "tar-in-a-jar," it's a solution that would be "hard to swallow."

The latest survey techniques have sometimes been used to determine the extent to which public opinion continues to reflect the values of traditional sayings. The current acceptance of the saying "a woman's place is in the home" was measured in a 2010 survey, of 24,000 adults in twenty-three countries, carried out on behalf of Reuters, the international news and information services organization. The resulting conclusion was that the saying continues to reflect the accepted wisdom for one in four adults. In India and Turkey, at the high end, support for a purely domestic role for women reached over fifty percent. It ranged between twenty and twenty-five percent in Australia, Canada and the United States. The reality, however, is that over forty-five percent of the Australian workforce is made up of women and over fifty percent of the Canadian and of the American workforce is made up of women. It may be too soon to consign the saying to "the dustbin of history" given the levels of support that it continues to have, even though the saying can be taken to suggest an inferior societal role for women.

The modern saying "men are from Mars, women are from Venus" doesn't raise the same male chauvinist suspicions as "a woman's place is in the home." It simply emphasizes the fact that there are serious differences between the sexes, Mars being the god of war and Venus being the goddess of love, which makes the two planets "as different as chalk and cheese." It doesn't imply the importance of one sex over the other, because we simply don't know the relative merits of the specific attributes of Martians and Venusians. Therefore, the saying tells us little about how earthlings may differ depending on their sex, apart from the fact that men may be more bellicose and women more affectionate. The 1992 self-help book by John Gray, the title of which adopted and popularized the saying, provides one person's understanding of the differences that may affect relationships between the sexes, differences that have long been celebrated by the French in the expression *vive la difference*.

When "put on the spot" by a insistent women's rights advocate who asked "what is the difference between man and woman," Professor John Pentland Mahaffy, who served as provost of Trinity College, Dublin in the early part of the twentieth century, is reported to have responded "off the cuff" with this fine example of clever repartee: "Madam, I cannot conceive."

Many old sayings that demean women, or are otherwise offensive to women by today's standards, have largely "fallen by the wayside."

This has been the fate, thankfully, of "women are necessary evils," "a woman's tongue wags like a lamb's tail," "he that has a wife has strife," "a woman and a ship ever want mending," "a whistling woman and a crowing hen are neither fit for God nor men" and "a woman, a dog and a walnut tree, the more you beat them the better they be." Another old saying "the cock may crow, but it's the hen that lays the egg," which lauds the greater productivity of the female of the species, experienced a revival of sorts when it was called upon, on several occasions, by that consummate "ruler of the roost," British Prime Minister Margaret Thatcher.

As if there weren't enough seasoned sayings that are demeaning to women, a number of perverted proverbs with a humorous bent keep the tradition of those "old chestnuts" alive. A common form involves taking a proverb that uses "man" in the sense of a human being and treating it as if it refers to a male person by adding a contrasting observation about a female to the original. Here are a few gems of twisted wisdom in this form:

"Time and tide wait for no man" but a woman expects all three to wait for her.
"A man is known by the company he keeps" but a woman is known by the company she keeps waiting.
"Every man has his price" but brides are given away.
"Clothes make the man" and lack of them the woman.
"Man does not live by bread alone": woman is not bred to live alone.

Most of these perverted proverbs are, of course, prime targets for attack in the movement to political correctness.

The role of women as mothers has generally been treated as sacred and has been idealized, rather than denigrated, in sayings from around the world. "God could not be everywhere and therefore he made mothers" is a Jewish proverb; "An ounce of mother is worth a pound of clergy" a Spanish proverb; "The greater love is a mother's; then comes a dog's; then a sweetheart's" a Polish proverb; and "The hand that rocks the cradle rules the world," an English proverb.

The accuracy or continuing value of some sayings has been challenged in the comments of astute observers of the human condition. One perceptive person raised this logical question: "If ignorance is bliss, why aren't more people happy?" An eminent American politician and diplomat, Adlai Stevenson, is reported to have said that "there was a time when a fool and his money were soon parted but now it happens to everyone." Subsequent investment frauds and financial institution failures have confirmed the accuracy of Stevenson's comment. Finally, a driver who was obviously experienced in the pitfalls of thruway driving was moved to observe that "he who hesitates is not lost but miles away from the next exit." Drivers operating in the high tech world would "take in stride" this turn of events as their GPS (Global Positioning System) would automatically reconfigure their route and, as a result, they would avoid the need to double back from the next exit.

Other sayings have been modified by humorists, so that they reflect a more accurate or fuller representation of the truth, through the addition of an ironic aside. Ever a seminal thinker, Mark Twain coined a variant of the saying "familiarity breeds contempt" by adding "and children." Of course, his version is only true for someone who hasn't heeded the flippant send-off, "be good and, if you can't be good, be careful," which implies that contraception should be "the order of the day" on every conceivable occasion. A second fall-back has, sometimes, been added to this advice: "And if you can't be careful, name the first child after me."

The comedienne Phyllis Diller drew from her maturing experience when she said "Maybe it's true that life begins at fifty; but everything else starts to wear out, fall out or spread out," which was ultimately addressed in her case through plastic surgery. That remedy may never "get to the heart of the matter" for, as Dorothy Parker famously observed, "beauty is only skin deep," but "ugly goes clean to the bone."

Other revised sayings that temper the tone of the original with a reminder of unpleasant realities include:

"All good things come to those who wait"...arthritis, heart disease, rheumatism, diabetes, clogged arteries, etc.

"April showers bring May flowers"...also weeds and crabgrass.

"A bird in the hand is worth two in the bush"...but it can also be very messy.

"Money isn't everything"...usually it isn't even enough.

These spliced sayings provide a bit of value-added information by drawing our attention to some taxing consequences when the sayings play out.

The sardonic treatment of a saying, an expression or a simple statement may take the form of a Wellerism, a kind of humor that was introduced in an earlier chapter (c. 2). The following samples of the form are built on popular sayings or, in the last instance, a spoof on a saying:

"Out of sight, out of mind" as the warden said as the escaped lunatic disappeared over the hill.

"You can't keep a good man down" as the lion said when he coughed up the Christian martyr.

"No noose is good noose" as the convicted murderer said when finally reprieved after waiting some time to learn his fate.

It's often hard to reconcile the lessons of different sayings. That conundrum has been put down to the fact that "for every saying there is an equal and opposite saying." This is consistent with the liberal notion that "there are two sides to every coin." Both of these statements are suspect for their unqualified generality, a frequent criticism of sayings. Although every saying doesn't have a flip side, it's easy to come up with many pairs of sayings that seem to offer opposing principles, such as:

"The early bird gets the worm."
BUT "The second mouse gets the cheese."

"He who hesitates is lost."
BUT "Look before you leap."

"Great minds think alike."
BUT "Fools seldom differ."

"All good things come to those who wait."
BUT "Time and tide wait for no man."

"Many hands make for light work."
BUT "Too many cooks spoil the broth" (or, as the Chinese would say: "Too many bricklayers make a lopsided house").

"You're never too old to learn."
BUT "You can't teach an old dog new tricks."

"The bigger the better."
BUT "Good things come in small packages."

"Absence makes the heart grow fonder."
BUT "Out of sight, out of mind."

"Clothes make the man."
BUT "Clothes don't make the man."

These pairs are sometimes called dueling sayings or proverbs to emphasize their competition for our attention as guiding life lessons. We are left to make our choice of which of two competing sayings to recite, or to pay attention to, on the basis of which best fits a particular situation.

"Clothes don't make the man" and "clothes make the man" are, obviously, precise opposites with no room for possible reconciliation such as there may be with some of the other pairs. Mark Twain would seem to have preferred the second of these two sayings for he was quick to note the bare fact that "naked people have little or no influence in society."

The American actress and temptress Mae West deliberately turned around an established saying when she proclaimed that "flattery will get you everywhere." Her saying soon became equally as popular as the original, which promises that "flattery will get you nowhere." West's restatement is often spoken, "tongue in cheek," to indicate that the speaker is alert to the fact that she's the target of flattery. It's not usually meant to indicate that flattery is likely to achieve its apparent objective. After all, most people realize that "flattery is soft soap, and soft soap is ninety percent lye (lie)," in the words of a nineteenth century American saying.

Anxious to postpone "the day of reckoning," procrastinators are guided by the self-serving advice "never do today what you can put off to tomorrow," a clear reversal of the saying "never put off to tomorrow what you can do today." "No good deed goes unpunished" is a saying that sounds as if it's the result of upending conventional wisdom to the effect that no bad deed goes unpunished. It's actually a cynical observation on the unfair results that can come from considerate conduct. It carries echoes of another cynical observation, "only the good die young," which leaves us wondering whether the bad are left to live long lives. That might be implied by this epitaph on a tombstone in the province of Nova Scotia:

Here lies
Ezekial Aikle
Aged 102

The Good Die Young

The inscription was either an attempt at *post mortem* humor or a deliberate snub at the admonition "never speak ill of the dead." Mr. Aikle would have enjoyed some redeeming grace, in the eyes of his surviving family and friends, if only the epitaph had added another, competing saying, "he lives longest who lives best."

A paradoxical saying is one that seems contradictory, senseless or absurd but purports to express a truth. The saying "there's an exception to every rule" turns out, on careful consideration, to be self-contradictory. If this saying itself states a rule, which seems to be the case, then there must be an exception to it. If that exception is that there are no exceptions to this particular rule, then how can it be said that "there's an exception to every rule"?

There are many other sayings that seem to be contradictory but are really making a valid, if subtle, point. "Less is more" originated with the poet Robert Browning and was later espoused by the German architect Ludwig Mies van der Rohe as his credo. Its sense is that simplicity can lead to a better result. "The more things change, the more they are the same" (*plus ça change, plus c'est la même chose*), attributed to the French novelist Alphonse Karr, is frequently recited as a description of the end result of many of the changes taking place in the modern world, namely those that "take things full circle." "Make haste slowly" (*festina lente*), was a favorite saying of the Roman Emperor Augustus and was adopted by him and later by Cosimo de Medici, the Grand Duke of Tuscany, as a motto extolling the merit of proceeding with deliberation in order to accomplish something quickly. "Sometimes you have to be cruel to be kind," from a line in Shakespeare's *Hamlet* has a contemporary application through ToughLove, a self-help organization for parents dealing with children who have "gone off the rails." The organization's philosophy for dealing with such children, toughness prompted by love, is expressed through its name. Taken literally, all of these sayings are contradictory, prompting their designation as oxymorons or oxymora. However, the sayings have a claim to the truth if the mind is stretched beyond the most obvious literal meanings of the words that make up the sayings.

"Don't go near the water until you learn to swim" seems absurd in its literal sense for dry land training alone can hardly make a swimmer out of you. But the saying rings true in the metaphorical sense; that you shouldn't dive into a new and difficult situation or environment until you're capable of handling it. Therefore, without going "too deep into it," the paradox can be resolved.

The Bible records these words of Jesus, spoken to his disciples; "it is easier for a camel to go through the eye of a needle than for a rich man to enter the kingdom of God." This saying embodies the literary device of hyperbole. In this and other situations, Jesus resorted to exaggeration to motivate his followers. Had they been unfamiliar with his technique and "taken his word as gospel," they would have been totally discouraged by his virtually unattainable standards.

Sometimes we "can't make head nor tail" of a saying because it uses a word in a different sense than is common today. The verb "to prove" and the related noun "proof" were, at one time, understood to refer simply to the act or result of testing something. These days, we would be more likely to take them to involve establishing the truth of something. Only if we were aware of the other meaning could we get an accurate read on what is meant by "the exception proves the rule." As Bill Bryson points out in *The Mother Tongue: English And How It Got That Way*, the latter proposition is patently illogical if it's understood as advancing the notion that the existence of an exception to a rule establishes that the rule is true. Actually, the exception waters down the rule and, if joined by a lot of other exceptions, may undermine the rule completely. Of course, neither of these consequences would be of concern to anyone who has subscribed to the counterintuitive maxim that "rules are made to be broken," which echoes the sentiment of the homespun saying, "promises are like pie crust, made to be broken."

Some sayings appear to have no value because they do no more than state the obvious. These include "nothing succeeds like success," "enough is enough," "a promise is a promise" and "it is what it is." "It's not over till it's over" is similarly uninformative as is its fulsome equivalent "it ain't over till the fat lady sings," which alludes to the fact that buxom sopranos frequently have the concluding arias in operatic performances (think *Brunhilde*). Clearly, all sayings aren't packed with deep insights into important facts of life. However, occasions do arise, from time to time, when we need to be reminded of what should be patently obvious. The sayings that state self-evident propositions serve that purpose.

"Boys will be boys" also seems to state an obvious fact, but it's actually more subtle than that. It can not only be used to explain the expected juvenile conduct on the part of boys; it can also be used to explain childish behavior on the part of grown men, for instance their play with "boy toys," typically mechanical equipment such as riding lawn mowers. "Boy toys" are not to be confused with "toy boys," who are attractive young men pursued as boyfriends or lovers by much older and more prosperous women or men. The popular singer Madonna is reported to have had many "boy toys" at her "beck and call" or, if you prefer, her "beckoned call."

A surrealist proverb—the classic example is "elephants are contagious"—usually makes no sense at all to the "average Joe," which is to say most of us. This unusual form of proverb came out of the movement in art and writing of the 1920s that attempted to stimulate the subconscious with a free flow of representation or thought. Surrealist proverbs exploit the unexpected, often containing a surprising twist to a well-known proverb. Hence, the perplexing proverbs, "one albino doesn't a summer make," and "when reason is away, smiles will play." We can surely be forgiven if we simply put these proverbs down to an irrational experimentation with *non sequiturs*.

Other proverbs or sayings that don't owe anything to the surrealist movement can be equally enigmatic. "The child is father of [to] the man," for example, appears to state a reproductive impossibility, yet it appears in the poem "My Heart Leaps Up" by the Romantic poet William Wordsworth. The later English poet-priest Gerard Manley Hopkins feigned mystification in this triolet, an eight line poem with a distinct pattern of rhymes and recurring lines:

"The child is father to the man."
How can that be? The words are wild.
Suck any sense from that who can:
"The child is father to the man."
No; what the poet did write ran,
"The man is father to the child."
"The child is father to the man!"
How can that be? The words are wild.

In fact, the wild words simply recognize the logic of the proposition that the traits of character evident in early childhood tend to carry through to maturity. "As the twig is bent, so is the tree inclined" bears the same message while staying true to biological reality. "The apple never falls far from the tree" is to similar effect, although it's not as neutral as the other comparable sayings since it's used, most often, to explain the failings of the offspring, recognizing that "a wild goose never lays a tame egg."

A mock proverb is seemingly profound but is actually a meaningless, senseless or platitudinous statement. While it's proverbial in form, it has no application or practical use except to entertain. Many mock proverbs were collected through popular competitions run by the English magazine *The New Statesman*, beginning in the late 1960s, and by *The New York Magazine*, in 1997. Others were collected by Tom Weller and suitably illustrated in his 1982 book *Minims or Man is the Only Animal that Wears Bow Ties*. Here's a sampling from these three sources:

In the City of the Bald, barbers are beggars.
A big pot makes shallow soup.
He digs deepest who deepest digs.
Nosh by day, mosh by night.
Always buy sheep and sell deer.
A horse without a nose will not win close races.
No one achieves immortality in his own lifetime.
Fortune favors the lucky.
Scissors always travel in pairs.
A piece of string has two ends but no beginning.
Happy is the man whose pig has no avatar.
No leg's too short to reach the ground.

Most of these mock proverbs have a degree of logic to them, but they do little to advance our understanding of anything important that we didn't already know or couldn't have guessed. At least, they may prompt a gentle smirk, while surrealist proverbs typically provoke nothing more than a quizzical gaze.

11

THE ORIGINS AND THE COMMERCIAL
APPLICATIONS OF SAYINGS

I'm tired of hearing the claim that Vince Lombardi was the first to say "fatigue make cowards of us all" but I really don't have the courage to say so.

It pays to advertise and if you don't it's like winking at a pretty girl in the dark; you know what you're doing but nobody else does.

Sayings from the world of advertising

We now turn to answering two distinct questions about sayings: Where do they come from and how have they been exploited for commercial purposes? The originators of several sayings turn out to be the usual suspects, Chaucer, Shakespeare and Confucius, while the original language of many sayings, such as those of Confucius, turns out to have been foreign. Indeed, some alien sayings, such as those in Latin and French, have crept into the English idiom without translation.

There's no shortage of business mottos and advertising slogans that pick up on popular sayings while, in a reversal of direction, some generic slogans have become catchphrases or sayings. Not to be left out, the perverted proverb and the mock proverb have also been featured in product messages, including those embedded in fortune cookies and those featured on the front of T-shirts.

Although sayings generally reflect traditional wisdom, some have been attributed to a single person as the one who initiated or first popularized them. However, the original wording of such sayings, if they go back some centuries, has often been refined over the years. In his *Canterbury Tales*, from the fourteenth century, Geoffrey Chaucer, the Father of English Literature, has given us the sayings that we now know as "strike while the iron is hot" and "there is a time for everything." Two centuries later, William Shakespeare was the first notable writer in English to popularize, if not to initiate, the sayings that remain familiar in the form, "desperate diseases must have desperate remedies," "every dog has his day," "discretion is the better part of valor," "neither a borrower nor a lender be" and "all that glitters is not gold."

"All that glitters is not gold" has a Roman antecedent in *non omne quod nitet aurum est* (not all that shines is gold). When Shakespeare picked up the thought, he wrote "all that glisters is not gold." That wording changed over time with little or no change in meaning. "Glitters" and "glisters" both mean "sparkles," although "glitters" is now preferred because it's more commonly understood as conveying that meaning. The original saying concludes the final verse of Thomas Gray's "Ode on the Death of a Favorite Cat Drowned in a Tub of Gold Fish," first published in 1748:

> From hence, ye beauties, undeceived,
> Know, one false step is ne'er retrieved,
> And be with caution bold.
> Not all that tempts your wandering eyes
> And heedless hearts, is lawful prize;
> Nor all that glisters, gold.

The Favorite Cat, which actually belonged to Gray's writer friend Horace Walpole, lost all of its nine lives when it stretched to reach a goldfish in a tub, slid on the edge of the tub, falling in head first, and drowned after emerging eight times from the water, all as lyrically described in the earlier verses.

The philosopher Confucius (551-479 B.C.) is thought to have been responsible for many Chinese proverbs the sense of which is often reflected in later English proverbs. Perhaps the best known of the similar Confucian and English proverbs are "what you don't want to be done to yourself, do not do to others" and "do unto others as you would have them do unto you." This last proverb is drawn from the Bible and its message is commonly described as the Golden Rule, although that name has been high-jacked to describe the mock proverb "he who has the gold rules." Confucius' early proverb is essentially the mirror image of the Golden Rule of biblical origin, stated as a negative restraint rather than a positive direction.

Several other Chinese proverbs, said to come from Confucius (although no one can be sure), have English counterparts, including:

"It does not matter how slowly you go as long as you don't stop." COMPARE "Slow and steady wins the race."
"To be wronged is nothing unless you continue to remember." COMPARE "Forgive and forget."
"The nobler man first practices what he preaches and afterwards preaches according to his practice." COMPARE "Practice what you preach."
"The superior man is modest in his speech but exceeds in his actions." COMPARE "Speak softly and carry a big stick."
"When anger rises, think of the consequences." COMPARE "Never let your anger get the better of you."

Confucius-say jokes owe little or nothing to the proverbs of the great Chinese philosopher. They follow a standard format and involve a word play in English, which usually has a sexual element that is blatantly obscene. Such a joke typically begins with "Confucius say" followed by a supposed saying that is in a grammatically incorrect form intended, no doubt, to make fun of the way a speaker whose primary language is a Chinese dialect might construct an English sentence. Some cleaner examples of these juvenile jokes go like this:

Man who runs in front of car get tired.
Man who runs behind car get exhausted.
Man who crosses the ocean twice without washing is a dirty double crosser.

Man who leap off cliff jump to conclusion.
Man who tell too many light bulb jokes soon burn out.
Man who eats photo of father soon spitting image of father.
People who live in glass houses should use bathroom in basement.
Man who stand on toilet is high on pot.
House without toilet is uncanny.

These are, essentially, mock proverbs purporting to be oriental in origin.

If we compare sayings from many different national and linguistic communities, we're likely to find a lot of inconsistencies amidst a remarkable number of similarities. The inconsistencies can often be explained by different geographic, social, cultural or economic circumstances.

"All roads lead to Rome" was, not surprisingly, expressed in Latin originally, only to become an English proverb in the late fourteenth century. It tells us, in a metaphorical way, that there are many routes to the same goal or many different ways of reaching the same objective. One of the several forms in which this principle can be stated is to observe, rather grotesquely, that "there's more than one way to skin a cat."

An ancient Chinese proverb insists that "all roads lead to Peking" and, as such, is inconsistent, in its literal sense, with the Rome-centered view of the world. China was outside the Roman Empire, but one of its major trading routes, which later became known as the Silk Road, connected with the Empire. In the new, flattened world, the Chinese proverb may be the more appropriate one since many more roads that carry commercial traffic now lead to Beijing, the new name for Peking, than to Rome, Eternal City though it may be. However, traffic bound for the Chinese capital regularly comes to a complete standstill for days on end as the road approaches that destination, which is reputed to have the world's worst traffic congestion. Therefore, the Chinese proverb should, perhaps, be modernized as "all roads lead, in time and for those with the necessary patience, to

Beijing." But that may be a bit too long-winded and qualified to serve as a memorable proverb.

Some foreign language sayings have been effectively incorporated, holus-bolus and without translation or other alteration, into the English idiom. For instance, *plus ça change, plus c'est la même chose*, often shortened to *plus ça change*, is a saying that is used in that form by both French and English speakers alike. It means that the more things change, the more they remain the same. It's commonly used to remark upon a situation where change has not resulted in any noticeable improvement.

Noblesse oblige, signifying that noble rank entails responsibility, is also used in both French and English communications. It became particularly well known in the English-speaking world as the title of a 1956 book, edited by the British writer Nancy Mitford, collecting a number of essays on the characteristics of the English aristocracy.

Carpe diem, entreating us to seize the day, is one of many Latin sayings that are frequently used in their original language in communications which are otherwise carried out in English. The utility of this and other Latin expressions and sayings is explored in a subsequent chapter (c. 12).

"Que sera sera" is often mistakenly taken to be a Spanish saying that has made a similar transition to that experienced by *plus ça change, noblesse oblige* and *carpe diem*. It has become mainstream in many English speaking countries largely as a result of a popular song of the same name recorded by the singer and actress Doris Day in the 1950s. The lyrics of the song tell us that the saying means, in English, "whatever will be, will be." However, "que sera sera" is not the Spanish equivalent of that English saying. The English saying would actually translate into Spanish as *lo que será, será*. The use of these and other sayings in their foreign language form, actual or assumed, may be viewed as elegant or refined but, in some circumstances, may be considered as "putting on airs."

Several sayings in foreign languages have been adopted as mottos. The motto of the state of Maryland, for example, is *fatti maschii, parole femine*, which is in archaic Italian. It was originally the motto of the Calvert family, headed by the Lords Baltimore, who founded the colony of Maryland in 1632. The motto is now in trouble with a segment of the Maryland electorate because, in translation, it means "deeds are men, words are women." There's an implicit hierarchy here for "actions speak louder than words," as we're often reminded, and "fine words butter no parsnips," as they used to say. Therefore, the motto could well be proclaiming that men have more meaningful roles than women in society, a proposition that's also thought to be advanced by the saying "a woman's place is in the home." Those who would avoid this possible interpretation of the motto, because of its political incorrectness, haven't proposed to change the motto itself, which is accepted as sacrosanct. But they have offered up modern, replacement translations such as "manly deeds, womanly words" and, in the longest leap from the literal translation, "strong deeds, gentle words." So far, there's no agreement on a new official interpretation.

Some corporations promote themselves with visionary mottos as part of their "branding," to use a contemporary marketing term. The movie studio Metro-Goldwyn-Mayer adopted the motto *ars gratis artis* (art for art's sake). It appears on the studio's trade mark logo featuring Leo the Lion. The motto is actually a Latin translation of a French bohemian creed, *l'art pour l'art*, of the nineteenth century. When the multi-talented Stan Freberg came to establish his very successful advertising agency, incorporated with the name "Freberg, Ltd. (but not very)," he adopted the conflicting motto *ars gratis pecuniae* (art for money's sake), which appears on the company's seal along with the image of a seagoing seal, wearing sunglasses. This is the same free-wheeling Stan Freberg who became the bane of most of the American advertising world with his recording, in 1959, of "Green Chritma," a satire on Madison Avenue's commercial exploitation of Christmas. At that time, "green" meant money, particularly of the green paper variety, and not environmental consciousness.

The American saying "it pays to advertise" became popular in the first half of the twentieth century. It states a well known business proposition. The proof of that proposition was provided, strangely enough, by laying hens, as this verse of unknown origin explains:

The codfish lays ten thousand eggs,
The lonely hen lays one.
The codfish never cackles
To tell you that she's done.
And so we scorn the codfish,
While the humble hen we prize,
Which only goes to show you
That it pays to advertise.

One of the pioneers of modern advertising, Andrew Barratt, head of the English soap company A. & F. Pears, must be given some of the credit, along with the hen, for laying the groundwork for the saying "it pays to advertise." One of his many masterful marketing coups was obtaining an endorsement for Pears soap, in the late nineteenth century, from the famous American clergyman Henry Ward Beecher. Drawing on an old proverb, first recorded in a sermon by John Wesley, the founder of Methodism, Beecher wrote that "if cleanliness is next to godliness, soap must be considered as a means of grace." He went on to endorse Pears soap as a preferred means to that state. Given this significant product testimonial, "cleanliness is next to godliness" became a prominent tagline in advertisements for Pears soap, leading to the remarkable commercial success of that product.

In the second half of the twentieth century, a note of skepticism about the value of advertising was struck by the business guru Norman R. Augustine. His Law No. IV, promulgated in 1983, states that "if you can afford to advertise, you don't need to." Like Augustine's other Laws, this one was crafted as much for its humor as its wisdom.

Since 1911, the Morton Salt Company has marketed its product under the slogan "when it rains, it pours," drawing strength from the public's recognition of the proverb, "it never rains but it pours." The free flowing slogan is usually accompanied by a picture of the Morton

Umbrella Girl happily treading along, fully sheltered by her umbrella, in the midst of a rain shower.

Other advertising slogans trade on perverted proverbs as a means of grabbing the attention of consumers. The American brewer Anheuser-Busch has marketed its popular Budweiser brand of lager with the line "where there's life, there's Bud," which has echoes of the proverb, "where there's life, there's hope." The Bud ad might also bring to mind the English proverb "life isn't all beer and skittles," which hardly encourages beer drinking. But this proverb isn't likely "to ring a bell" with most American consumers, for whom skittles are candies rather than a pub game.

"An apple a day keeps the doctor away" has, understandably, inspired a lot of advertising slogans for consumables, usually emphasizing or implying health benefits. Naturally, it's been used, with little modification, to promote the sale of apples, as in Horticulture Australia's "eat an Aussie apple a day" campaign. But it's also been converted into perverted proverbs as in the Mars candy bar ad of the 1960s: "A Mars a day helps you work, rest, and play." We've recently been advised that "a toke a day keeps memory loss at bay," although that hasn't yet been adopted as an advertising slogan. It appeared as the headline over a newspaper article about a scientific finding, offered up as the "the acid test," that small doses of marijuana improve the functions of aging brains. Obviously, if you put together an apple, a Mars bar, and a bit of weed every day, you have an infallible recipe for a healthy body and mind, ready to excel in all aspects of life into "the golden years."

Spoonerisms have even worked their way into promotional messages. A sign on a podiatrist's office reads, "Time wounds all heels," emphasizing the need for the professional's services amongst all but the youngest. This modern saying, an inversion of "time heals all wounds," is more commonly used for another distinct purpose, that of foretelling the eventual fate of someone who has acted like a "heel," the slang term for a jerk, usually of the male variety. The notion is that he'll ultimately "get his just deserts" for his dastardly behavior.

Some generic marketing slogans that owe nothing to traditional sayings have become so well known that they have become sayings in their own right. This is true of "say it with flowers," which has been used by members of the FTD (Florists Transworld Delivery) organization since 1917. The florist industry would even have us believe that different kinds of flowers "say" different things. This is fraught with all sorts of dangers for the unwitting. For instance, a young man who sends yellow water lilies to his girlfriend, to demonstrate his love, is courting disaster. These flowers, we are told, signal growing indifference. What he should do is "say it" with asters, lavender, honeysuckle or even dandelions and that way he'd be expressing his undying love.

Since 1947, DeBeers Consolidated Mines has also been using a generic marketing slogan, "a diamond is forever." This slogan was further popularized by *Diamonds are Forever*, one of Ian Fleming's books featuring James Bond, Secret Agent 007, and by the successful 1971 movie, of the same name, that was made from the book. The result of all of this is that "a diamond is forever" has become a popular saying.

These generic marketing slogans may also be called catchphrases by virtue of the fact that they have caught on with the public through repeated exposure in advertising and other media. "If you want to get ahead, get a hat" and "drinka pinta milka day" are two other classic catchphrases of the same kind. Although they are now dated, they were clever enough to capture the public mind in their time. The first catchphrase was used by the former British Hat Council in the 1930s and 1940s, an era when formal men's hats were *de rigueur*. The second catchphrase was used by the former British Milk Marketing Board, in the pre-metric days of the late 1950s, to get people to drink more milk, both the flavored variety that was popular at the time and the plain and simple variety that never "fell from grace." The word "pinta" became so well known as a result of the slogan that it eventually made it into the *Collins English Dictionary*, where it's defined as an informal British rendering of "pint of" in phonetic form.

Sayings have other uses in commerce besides marketing and advertising. They may also be used to enhance or embellish a product. The planted messages in fortune cookies are, certainly, a fundamental feature in the attraction of those consumables. The cookie itself is not particularly appealing. It's been described as "a cross between desiccated cookie dough and a stale communion wafer."

The messages in fortune cookies are, typically, in one of four different forms; predictions of good fortune, advice addressed directly to the consumer on how to enhance his prospects, favorable comments on the qualities of the consumer, and sayings or proverbs. A few unconventional messages may be thrown in, such as the plaintive alarm; "Help! I'm a prisoner in a Chinese bakery."

Although fortune cookies are often served, in many parts of the world, at the end of a meal in a Chinese restaurant, they are actually an American invention with an oriental influence that is principally Japanese. The sayings that are contained in fortune cookies may be traditional, modified traditional or freshly minted. But, generally speaking, they are not Chinese in origin. Here are some of the cookie sayings that are particularly clever, wise, amusing or perplexing:

The world may be your oyster, but it doesn't mean you'll get its pearl.
Love thy neighbor, just don't get caught.
A different world cannot be built on indifferent people.
Better be the head of a chicken than the tail of an ox.
When you get something for nothing you just haven't been billed for it yet.
Birds are entangled by their feet and men by their tongues.

Many of these sayings, all of which are either perverted or mock proverbs, will be familiar to those who don't have a taste for the fortune cookie, for they often have other lives outside the confines of a fortune cookie.

Naturally, the astute restaurateur will be anxious to make sure that the sayings in the fortune cookies he serves are responsive to the "signs of the times" as the following cartoon aptly illustrates:

The amusing lines that are stenciled on T-shirts, to enhance their appeal, often take the form of perverted proverbs. "If at first you don't succeed, skydiving is not for you" is one such line. The dire warning that it proclaims has got to be related, in some way, to the marketing pitch: "FOR SALE: Parachute, only used once, never opened, small stain," which has also been incorporated into T-shirt designs.

The perverted proverbs applied to T-shirts may involve a Spoonerism, as in the Oscar Wilde quotation, "work is the curse of the drinking class," derived from the proverb "drink is the curse of the working class." Or they may involve a pun as in "two rights don't make a wrong; they make an airplane." They may also address contemporary issues such as computer capacity. That's the subject of comment in the message, "a picture is worth a thousand words but it uses up a thousand times the memory," a line that's only likely to fit onto extra-large shirts.

Some of the messages on T-shirts purport to be much more personal, reflecting on the attributes or desires of the wearer. "If we are what we eat, I'm fast, cheap and easy" and "where there's a will, I want to be in it" are two perverted proverbs that carry this kind of message. The second of these parodies is one of several humorous variations on "where there's a will, there's a way." Others include "where there's a will, there's relatives" and "where there's a will, there's lawyers." All three variations exhibit the distinctive characteristic of a paraprosdokian, the term for a figure of speech involving a surprising change of direction in a sentence because of a word taking on a change of meaning. In each of the examples above, the word "will" in the initial clause suggests determination since that's what it means in the identical initial clause of the familiar proverb "where there's a will, there's a way." But the final clause assumes an alternate meaning of "will," namely a testamentary instrument.

12

THINGS GO BETTER WITH LATIN

Quidquid latine dictum sit, altum sonatur
(That which is said in Latin sounds profound)

Anon.

"And now for something completely different." That Monty Python catchphrase serves as a versatile segue that can lead almost anywhere. The "completely different" in this case is a dead language that plays an important *post mortem* role by contributing to our inventory of words and expressions and our inventory of sayings or, as they're usually called when rendered in Latin, maxims.

Imagine the opportunities that would open up for us if we English speakers weren't just occasional dabblers in these Latinisms but were fluent in the classical language of Rome. Dan Quayle, a former U.S. Vice President, was sensitive to the missed opportunities when he said: "I was recently on a tour of Latin America and the only regret I have was that I didn't study Latin harder in school so that I could converse with these people." Another American politician, who will go unnamed, had no such regrets, confidently stating that "if English was good enough for Jesus Christ, it's good enough for me."

More than half of the words in our language have Latin roots. But our Latin linguistic heritage is not just reflected in word derivations. We also use many words, alone or in combination, in the original Latin in the course of communicating with one another. Some have been effectively assimilated into English, such as *alma mater, alumni, caveat, habeas corpus, subpoena, quid pro quo* and *verbatim*. Others are simply borrowed to suit particular occasions, such as *sui generis* (of its own kind or one-off), *mens sana in corpore sano* (a sound mind in a healthy body) and *sic* (thus or so). I use italics in this chapter to call attention to Latin words, whether those words are truly foreign to the English language, have been naturalized as English words or are simply imposters with false Latin credentials.

There is a danger of being misunderstood if you slip the occasional Latin word or words into your speech or writing. Take the word "*sic*," which is sometimes inserted in the midst of a quotation for the purpose of indicating that, although apparently wrong, the preceding part of the quotation is faithful to the words of the person who uttered or penned them. A journalist is reported to have sent a letter to the Duchess of York pointing out an error in something she had said and quoting her *verbatim* but inserting "*sic*" in brackets, at one point, in the quotation. This prompted the Duchess, who was reputed to have a compulsive eating disorder, to write back in anger: "It's one thing to accuse me of getting something wrong; it's quite another to refer to my eating problems." She obviously thought she was the target of an *argumentum ad hominem* (argument to the person or a personal attack) and not just a criticism of how she had expressed herself.

There are many reasons why we might choose to use an unassimilated Latin word or expression in the course of what is otherwise a discourse in English. Sometimes it's for lack of a suitable English word or expression that conveys our message equally well. Imagine Ogden Nash, after composing the first line of his poem "Sedative Reflection," straining to find an appropriate rhyme and ultimately resorting to the Latin for "love conquers all," thus emerging with this couplet:

How doth the hippie cure insomnia
By murmuring *amor vincit omnia.*

A Latin word or expression can be used for emphasis, as when Queen Elizabeth described her past year as an *annus horribilis* in her 1992 Christmas address. This contemporary turnaround of a classic Latin expression, *annus mirabilis* (a wonderful year) is usually translated as "a horrible year." But the British tabloid, *The Sun*, couldn't resist the temptation to go for a double entendre and irreverently took the Queen's choice of expression as meaning "a bum year." The year of which Her Majesty spoke, 1992, was the year in which the marriages of her children Prince Charles, Princess Anne and Prince Andrew all broke up and Windsor Castle had a serious fire. With the benefit of this royal *imprimatur* (let it be printed or official approval), the popularity of the modern Latin expression to describe any kind of bad year has been enhanced.

Latin may be a convenient vehicle for dealing with a delicate subject, such as sex, in a gentler fashion than would be the case if English were to be used. *In flagrante delicto* (while the misdeed is blazing), which "covers a multitude of sins," is often used to convey the notion of being caught red-handed in the act of having sex, particularly of the illicit variety. The saying "after sex every animal is sad" is sometimes rendered in the seemingly more clinical Latin form, *post coitum omne animal triste est.*

A Latin word or expression is often used simply to import some *gravitas* (seriousness) to a statement or to add an air of "verisimilitude to an otherwise bald and unconvincing narrative," to borrow a phrase used, for other purposes, by Poo-Bah, a central character in Gilbert and Sullivan's comic opera *The Mikado*. How many of us would have to say *mea culpa* (my fault or, loosely, whoops; I'm guilty), or even *mea maxima culpa* (I'm super guilty), to this practice? Finally, a Latin word or expression may simply be used "to put on airs" or to confound a listener or a reader.

The Latin maxim *carpe diem*, in its popular translation, tells us to "seize the day." Its origin is a poem by Horace, the great Roman lyric poet, in which he adds, in Latin of course, that we should place no trust in tomorrow. The *carpe diem* message frequently appears on sundials where its purpose isn't entirely clear. Henry II of England popularized the Latin phrase on early timepieces when he gave Eleanor of Aquitaine a diamond laden sundial ring, inscribed with the words *carpe diem*, before their marriage in 1152. Of course, a sundial can only provide the time during daylight hours and, even then, only when the sun co-operates. Therefore, a sundial's reminder to "seize the day" could be taken to suggest that we should embrace the daylight hours and "make hay while the sun shines." That would leave us with perfect license to fritter away the nighttime hours. This isn't likely what Horace had in mind, although it may have been what King Henry was thinking when he presented Eleanor with her ring. Looking at it "in the larger picture," a timepiece such as a sundial may simply be an appropriate place for an inscribed reminder that *tempus fugit* (time flies) and that it's best to make the most of it before it's too late, which is the thrust of the *carpe diem* injunction.

Carpe diem has proven to be a very flexible maxim, however, serving as a rallying cry to action, a call to transcend the mundane, a warning against procrastination, a reminder of our mortality and an appeal to basic hedonism. A couple of sharply contrasting interpretations are brought out in this Doug Pike cartoon:

You carpe diem your way, and I'll carpe diem mine.

The unorthodox English teacher John Keating, played by Robin Williams in the movie *The Dead Poets Society*, used the rallying cry of *carpe diem* to inspire his prep school students to embrace a love of literature and to "live life to the fullest."

Carpe diem poems make up a distinct genre of poetry. The most famous is Robert Herrick's "To the Virgins, to Make Much of Time," which includes this familiar verse:

Gather ye rosebuds while ye may,
Old time is still a-flying:
And this same flower that smiles today,
Tomorrow will be dying.

While Herrick's "bottom line" is to urge marriage upon unmarried women, many other *carpe diem* poets use the notion of *tempus fugit* as a reason to make the case for the seduction of young women "without benefit of clergy," to use an old expression that pre-dates the advent of civil wedding ceremonies.

René Descartes, known for his dual paternity as Father of Modern Philosophy and Father of Analytical Geometry, was responsible for the well known philosophical statement *cogito ergo sum* (I think therefore I am). The maxim means that if I think about my existence, this is proof in itself of that existence for otherwise I wouldn't be able to do the necessary thinking. The logic of this may be undermined by IBM which is currently working on the development of cognitive computing, which would allow us to rely on electronic circuits to do our thinking for us.

There is some debate as to whether there's a flip side to the *cogito ergo sum* proposition, as suggested by this barroom tale:

Descartes walks into a bar and asks for some scotch. The bartender asks him if he wants it on the rocks. Descartes says "I think not," and then immediately disappears into thin air.

There's also some question about what Descartes may have been thinking upon his demise, as posed by this clerihew, a form of whimsical poem invented by the English journalist and mystery writer, Edmund Clerihew Bentley:

Did Descartes
Depart
With the thought
Therefore I'm not?

Cogito ergo sum has spawned several maxims in mock Latin, often called Dog Latin (*Canis Latinicus*), including:

Cogito ergo zoom, which has been translated as "I think, therefore I drive fast;"

Regate ergo sum, which has been translated as "I row, therefore I am" and has been adopted as the motto of several university rowing clubs;

Tesco ergo sum, which has been suggested as a suitable ad for British based Tesco, the world's third largest retailer and, with that in mind, has been translated as "I shop, therefore, I am."

Several other sayings, besides the maxims *carpe diem* and *cogito ergo sum*, are frequently used in their Latin form even though they have a readily recognizable English form as well, including *tempus fugit* ("time flies"), *caveat emptor* ("let the buyer beware"), *in vino veritas* ("there's truth in wine") and *festina lente* ("make haste slowly").

Perhaps the best known expression going back to the days of the Roman Empire is *veni, vidi, vici* (I came, I saw, I conquered). The words were originally those of Julius Caesar. The occasion was Caesar's report to the Senate on his victory over Pharnaces at the Battle of Zela in 47 B.C. That's the same year in which he developed a liaison with Cleopatra, the recently deposed Queen of Egypt.

Veni, vidi, vici and its English translation have worked their way into the modern world in many ways; as the title song for the musical

Mame, as the name of several restaurants featuring Italian fare, as the motto of the Philip Morris tobacco company, which is fighting its own contemporary battles—over responsibilities for lung cancer deaths. The Latin expression has undergone a modern adaptation as *veni, vidi, velcro* (I came, I saw, I stuck around), which has become popular as a message displayed on T-shirts.

Caesar's bold pronouncement about his military prowess has also been re-ordered to produce a sassy pronouncement about his sexual prowess. As such, it serves as the punch line of this limerick:

> I, Caesar, when I learned of the fame
> of Cleopatra, I straightforward laid claim,
> ahead of my legions
> I invaded her regions
> I saw, I conquered, I came

This was the period of her life of which Cleopatra spoke, in Shakespeare's play *Antony and Cleopatra,* as "My salad days, when I was green in judgment." She would have been twenty-two to Caesar's fifty plus.

The mystery surrounding the stone structures at Stonehenge is fairly well known. Not so well known is the mystery that, at one time, surrounded the stone post with a hole through the top, also uncovered in Britain, which is pictured below.

The locals first thought that the inscription on the post, TOTI EMUL ESTO, was a Latin proverb of some sort, dating from the Roman occupation of Britain, with a meaning along the lines of "all things are but copies." The initial excitement dimmed when it became clear, after some scholarly research, that the message was a mundane description, in plain English, of the function of the post, *i.e.* (short for *id est*) TO TIE MULES TO, written in an odd fashion to fit, in a balanced way, within the limited space available. The suspected Roman provenance of the post immediately went *ex fenestra* or "out the window."

This fictional mystery provides a suitable re-entry point to the subject of Dog Latin. Expressions, sayings or narratives that have the look of Latin but aren't the genuine article are called Dog Latin. One of the best illustrations is provided by this poem of unknown authorship:

> *O civile si ergo*
> *Fortibus es in ero*
> *O Nobile Deus trux!*
> *Vatis Enim?*
> *Causan dux.*

While the words may be authentic Latin, they make no sense strung together as they are. In fact, the poem is simply disguised English for:

> O see Willy, see her go
> Forty buses in a row
> Oh, no, Billy
> They is trucks!
> What is in 'em?
> Cows and ducks

Illegitimi non carborundum, which has been translated as "don't let the bastards grind you down," is also a good example of Dog Latin. Carborundum is a very hard mineral that's used for grinding purposes but it's not Latin, although it appears, by virtue of its ending, to be a neuter noun like *bellum* (war). The word "*illigetimi*," which suggests that it might mean bastard in English, likewise has no legitimacy as a Latin word. A bastard would be a *filius nullius* (a son of nobody) in Latin. Nonetheless, *illegitimi non carborundum* was given credibility when it was adopted by "Vinegar Joe" Stillwell, a U.S. army general, as his motto in the Second World War. Years later, Senator Barry Goldwater, when he was the Republican nominee for president of the United States, displayed the expression, on a sign in his office, which gave it a new, civilian life.

Semper ubi sub ubi represents a form of Dog Latin. It's a favorite saying among young students of pure Latin. The translation comes out best through the spoken word. In written form, it would be "always where under where" but when that "falls trippingly from the tongue," it sounds like a proverbial caution to "always wear underwear," advice not always heeded by American pop star idol and notorious bad girl Britney Spears.

As children, my contemporaries and I would often use the expression *dorkus malorkus*, to which we might add, "as they say in Latin." This was a way of deriding someone, for the word "dorkus" sounds like "dorky," a slang term for "stupid," and "malorkus" suggests "malarky", a word for nonsense, which was apparently tortured so that it would rhyme with "dorkus." The expression was recently resuscitated when it was used by Bart Simpson in an episode of the popular television series *The Simpsons*. In fact, it means nothing in Latin; it's simply a nonsense pairing like "hocus pocus" but set in Dog Latin. On the other hand, "hocus pocus," a magician's term for trickery, is thought by many word experts to have originated in a blasphemous corruption of *hoc est corpus [filii]*, church Latin for "this is the body [of the Lord]."

Dorkus malorkus is representative of a special variety of Dog Latin known as macaronic Latin, which involves affixing Latin endings to vernacular words. Perhaps the best known example of the style is this two line poem for which no one has admitted authorship:

Boyibus kissibus priti girlorum
Girlibus likibus wanti somorum.

Dog Latin is not to be confused with Pig Latin. Pig Latin (Igpay Atinlay) is a language that used to be spoken by school children in an attempt, usually futile, to keep things from their parents and teachers. The most obvious remnant of this language is the word "eBay." The few surviving speakers of the language will recognize this word as meaning "be," which translates to "eBay" by following the standard Pig Latin rule of moving the initial consonant to the end and adding an "ay" after that. However, it's hard to fathom why a disguised form of the word "be" would be used as the label for an on-line auction system.

Some people get enjoyment from coming up with the possible meanings of Latin terms, expressions and sayings that are suggested by the pronunciation of their words as if they were English. Here are some examples of these homophonic translations, most original but some from other sources, set against the proper translations:

Latin Expression	Apparent Meaning	True Meaning
Ad nauseam	A commercial message on an airline barf bag	Endlessly
Ars longa, vita brevis	Long in the bum, short on the vital signs (a warning about the dangers of obesity)	Skill takes time to acquire but life is short
Carpe diem	The day of the fish (which is the seventh day of feasting following a Moroccan wedding)	Seize the day
Casus belli	A civil case worthy of the King of Torts, the late California attorney Melvin Belli	A situation justifying or precipitating war
Cave canem	An underground facility for preserving food	Beware the dog

Latin Expression	Apparent Meaning	True Meaning
Corpus delicti	The corpse was delectable (a cannibal's compliment to the chef)	The body of the crime
Deus ex machina	A low platform mechanically produced; a god who was formerly a machinist	A god out of the machine, referring to the sudden contrived resolution of the plot in a storyline, something the ancient Greek dramatists would pull off by hoisting a god onto the stage, by crane, who would then "tie up all the loose ends"
Fiat lux	A high end vehicle model produced by a European car manufacturer	Let there be light (from the Book of Genesis)
Hic et ubique	Everywhere I go I get the hiccups	Here and everywhere
In loco parentis	Parents gone wild	In the place of a parent
In medias res	In the heat of network competition during TV ratings week	In the midst of a sequence of events as in a literary narrative where the story begins in the middle of the action and the first part of the story is filled in later

Latin Expression	Apparent Meaning	True Meaning
Mens sana in corpore sano	Rational men have the sense to incorporate (*i.e.* limited liability is the way to go), or Men's saunas lead to a healthy body (a translation offered up by the Scottish writer Alexander McCall Smith.)	A sound mind in a healthy body
Noli me tangere	Don't you want to dance with me?	Don't touch me
Non omnis moriar	"Moriarity isn't omniscient" (although he may be a master criminal) (a quotation from Sherlock Holmes)	I shall not die entirely
Persona non grata	An ingrate; an ungrateful cad	Someone who's not welcome or accepted in a particular place or circle because of something he's said or because he's otherwise "blotted his copy book"
Primus inter pares	Stove burning oil buried in the French capital	First among equals
Pro bono (short for *pro bono publico*)	A U2 Fan	For the public good

Latin Expression	Apparent Meaning	True Meaning
Quid pro quo	A pound for what? (the lament of an Englishman whose change has been swallowed up by a vending machine with no merchandise in return)	Something for something or, colloquially, tit for tat
Sic gloria transit mundi	Gloria took ill while riding the bus on Monday	Thus passes the glory of the world
Sine die	"The wages of sin is [*sic*] death," a biblical warning	Without a day, meaning until an unspecified day, usually referring to the adjournment of a meeting
Suggestio falsi	Bringing to mind the expression "making mountains out of molehills"	A statement of a falsehood
Sui generis	Commencing legal proceedings against a popular talk show hostess	Of its own kind

Headline writers have had a field day with some of these Latin phrases. A particular gem was the caption on a *New York Daily News* report of the plans of the artist and socialite Gloria Vanderbilt, the mother of CNN news commentator Anderson Cooper, to fly across the country the following week, despite an illness, for an engagement (not, this time, of the pre-marital kind). The headline read: "Sick Gloria in Transit Monday."

In their book *Liberated Latin*, Richard Arndt and Otto Soglow collected, freely translated, and illustrated over forty Latin terms, expressions and sayings. A couple of their illustrations, and the associated captions that take liberties with the Latin, are reproduced below:

Bona fide
(Give the dog a bone)

De gustibus non est disputandum
(This bus is drafty and you can't deny it)

If accurately translated, the first of the Latin captions would be rendered in English as "in good faith." The second would come out as "there's no arguing about tastes." This has, roughly, the same sense as *chacun à son goût*, a saying that French and English speakers alike use to remark upon the fact that it's "everyone to his own taste."

Some modern English expressions have been translated into rough Latin equivalents. Here are some samples for use by those who think they can impress by "putting new wine into old bottles:"

Honk if you speak Latin	*Sona si Latine loqueris*
Make mine bacon wrapped	*Da mihi porco amictum*
Not in my backyard	*Ne ponatur in mea vicinitate*
(sometimes put simply	
as NIMBY)	
Holy cow!	*Sacra bos*
See you later alligator	*Vale, lacerte*
Let it all hang out	*Totum dependiat*

You can bet that these expressions were not in common use in ancient Rome.

There are three kinds of institutions in which Latin terms, expressions and sayings are particularly prevalent, *viz.* (short for *vidilicet*, meaning "that is to say") churches, universities and courts. In church, congregants sing hymns with Latin names, sometimes rendering the verses in Latin, as in the case of *Adeste Fidelis* (O Come all ye Faithful), and priests of the Roman Catholic rite commence mass with the words *In nomine Patris et Filii et Spiritu Sancti* (In the name of the Father, the Son and the Holy Ghost) while making the sign of the cross.

In university, students are inspired by a motto that is often in Latin; if they're indisposed at exam time, they get an *aegrotat* (he is sick); and the better students aspire to graduate *cum laude* (with praise), *magna cum laude* (with great praise) or *summa cum laude* (with highest praise). At the end of their educational journey, the members of the graduating class assemble to listen to an address delivered by a distinguished person who has just received a degree *honoris causa* (for the sake of honor); then stand to sing the drinking-song-turned-graduation anthem *Gaudeamus igitur* (Therefore let us rejoice); and, finally, receive their degrees with the chancellor's invocation, *admitto vos ad gradum* (I admit you to the rank of graduate), at which point they pick up their diplomas, which may be entirely in Latin. And so they become *alumni* (foster children), except that those who miss the graduation ceremony receive their degrees *in absentia* (in absence).

The first task after receiving a university diploma is usually to prepare a *curriculum vitae* (course of life), sometimes blandly called a résumé, to help open the doors to "the working world."

Latin was the language of the courts in early Britain. Moreover, the common law that was administered in those courts was influenced by Roman law. Many Latin words and expressions persist in the law today in those parts of the world that follow the English common law system just as they do in those parts that have inherited Roman law. This may have deterred some from pursuing a career in the law. Peter Cook did a very funny monologue, as part of the *Beyond the Fringe* revue of the 1960s, in which he spoke as a coal miner. He compared judging and coal mining, saying that he could have been a judge but he "never had the Latin for the judging." He did, however, express a preference for judging over mining because of the absence of falling coal.

Legal Latin is sometimes referred to as the Latin that judges and lawyers used to know. Indeed, many familiar Latin terms, such as *subpoena, in camera* and *ex parte*, have been banished from the rules of civil procedure in the courts of England and Wales *pro bono publico* (for the public good). The writ of *habeas corpus* (you must have the body), a well known process that requires that a person be brought before the court to determine the lawfulness of his detention, has so far survived the purging of Latin terms. Writing in *The Guardian* newspaper, lawyer-turned-journalist Marcel Berlins commented on the prospect of this writ ultimately becoming a "you-must-have-the-body claim form:"

> Where is the romance, where is the atmosphere of ancient rights, the rattle of history? It is almost better to remain in unlawful

custody than to be freed under such a dull-sounding procedure. If we get rid of *habeas corpus*, we might as well start talking about the great charter, and forget *Magna Carta*.

This last statement is, of course, a *non sequitur* (it doesn't follow).

The move against legal Latin has its fervent critics, including barrister John Gray, who passes this judgment in his book, *Lawyers' Latin: A Vade-Mecum*; "to attempt suppression of Latin in a civilized country is, in the scale of cultural atrocities, on a par with burning books." It's much too soon, however, to say *RIP* to legal Latin, even in the U.K. It would be inappropriate to apply that epitaph, in any event, as it's originally an acronym for the Latin expression *requiescat in pace* (may he rest in peace). The fact is that it's pretty hard to get completely away from Latin, even in death.

Lawyers remain fond of using Latin maxims to state legal principles. You would expect that these maxims would introduce an element of precision, at least for those who are alive to the nuances of a dead language. But, in fact, the legal propositions advanced by Latin maxims are very general. Consequently, they are true most of the time, but not all of the time, for "circumstances alter cases." The hit-or-miss nature of these maxims is camouflaged by the Latin garb in which they are dressed. It adds an aura of *veritas et utilitas*, a phrase that my *alma mater* (bounteous mother) has adopted, as its motto, to encourage us to aspire to truth and usefulness.

I suspect that those who accuse lawyers of interminable nitpicking will be surprised by the maxim *de minimis non curat lex*, which proclaims that the law does not waste time with tiny unimportant things. This emboldened the accused who was the subject of this bawdy verse:

There was a young lawyer named Rex
who had very small organs of sex.
When charged with exposure,
he said with composure
de minimis non curat lex.

Rex was thus exposed as having "more flash than substance."

We don't know if the *de minimis* argument that Rex advanced was successful since limericks don't take us beyond a five line stanza. Alas, the poor devil "had a fool for a client" since he represented himself. Therefore, he was probably no better endowed with legal sense than with certain physical attributes. The trial judge may well have countered, in his judgment, with another Latin maxim, *minima maxima sunt*, emphasizing that the smallest things are the most important. As is the case with English sayings, Latin maxims often lead us in opposite directions.

The *de minimis* maxim has sometimes been translated as "the law does not concern itself with trifles". This prompted one wag to ask what desserts might be of concern to the law if not trifles. Could it be just deserts and making sure that everyone gets theirs? Probably not, for law and justice are not the same thing, which is implicit in this famous aphorism of Oliver Wendell Holmes, Jr., speaking about the U.S. Supreme Court, of which he was an Associate Justice: "This is a court of law, young man, not a court of justice."

The assumption of risk is something about which the law is concerned, with more than trifling consequences. The maxim *volenti non fit injuria* expresses the principle that an individual who voluntarily puts himself in a position where harm may result can't complain if that harm ensues. This is so because the individual will be taken to have consented to the harm or to have waived his right to complain about it.

The *volenti* defense is often invoked in response to a damages claim for injuries suffered by someone who has taken part in a sporting activity. If you choose to get into the ring with Mike Tyson, the former world heavyweight boxing champion, you can't complain if you're injured when he decks you, although you can complain if he bites you, causing "earsplitting pain." The possibility of a bite is not a risk that you would reasonably assume by getting into the ring, particularly if you weren't aware of the ex-champ's reputation for taking a bite out of opponents.

Sometimes, however, there can be consent to rough play beyond the rules of the contest and, therefore, to the assumption of the related risks. That's what professional ice hockey players are seeking when they ask an opposing player "wanna go?" before starting a fight. In other situations, that question is an invitation to step into the parking lot, or some place else outside, and settle things like real men. Hockey players don't usually have the parking lot in mind, as the appropriate arena, since that would mean waiting until after the game "to settle the score" and disappointing the fans they are paid to entertain.

Some Latin maxims appear, on first impression, to state the obvious. One such maxim is *nemo dat quod non habet*, which means, literally, that no one can give what he doesn't have. In its legal application, the *nemo dat* principle means that no one can confer a better title to property than he actually possesses. The principle is well illustrated by an episode of the *Simpsons* TV series, entitled "The Devil and Homer Simpson." Homer enters into an agreement with the devil to sell his soul for a doughnut. A trial ensues to determine whether the devil is entitled to enforce the agreement. Marge Simpson assumes the role of representative of her husband Homer at the trial in a desperate bid to save her soulmate from his bargained fate. Marge then produces, for the court, a marriage photograph on which Homer had written that he pledged his soul to Marge. In the result, the devil lost his claim to enforce the agreement on the basis that Homer had no remaining property in his soul to sell at the time he made his bargain with the devil, having long since pledged his soul to Marge. This was the devil's second big loss of this kind, the first having occurred in an earlier case in which eminent counsel Daniel Webster appeared against him. That earlier proceeding is recounted in "The Devil and Daniel Webster," a short story by Stephen Vincent Benét.

Sometimes, Latin offers more than one maxim to capture a single legal concept. For example, *qui facit per alium facit per se* carries the same sense as *respondeat superior*. The former can be translated as "he who does an act through another does it for himself." Thus, an employer is liable for the actions of his employees. *Respondeat superior* tells us that we should let the master or employer answer, which also carries the notion that an employer is responsible for the actions of his employees.

The expression *qui facit per alium facit per se* hasn't been confined to the legal sphere. It's also been adopted as a motto by the Perse School in Cambridge, England where it's used to extol the selfish benefits of altruism; he who does things for others does them for himself. The last two words of the motto are a play on the name of the school's founder, Dr. Stephen Perse. As such, they're a form of *rebus*, a riddle or puzzle made up of letters, pictures or symbols.

Mottos usually state a motivating ideal, a high sounding principle or a guiding objective. Often that's thought to be better reflected in Latin, although this is obviously at the risk of some people missing the point of the motto. Some Latin mottos consist of a single word while others encapsulate all or part of a saying or an expression.

The motto *e pluribus unum* (out of many, one) appears on the Great Seal of the United States of America, signifying the unification of the original thirteen colonies into one confederated state. The motto also accompanies the official motto, "In God We Trust," on U.S. coins. The Latin motto is said to have evolved from a recipe for a salad set out in a poem entitled "Moretum," which has been attributed to the Roman poet Virgil (70–19 B.C.). The poem describes the crushing of cheese, garlic and green herbs together, in the process of preparation of the salad, so that the colors blend into one, a result described in Latin as *color est e pluribus unum.*

However, there's a much more prosaic explanation for the origin of the motto, *i.e.* that it came from *The Gentleman's Magazine.* That English publication was popular in 1776 when the Continental Congress struck a blue ribbon committee, consisting of Benjamin Franklin, John Adams, and Thomas Jefferson, charged with the task of coming up with a Great Seal for the new American nation. *The Gentleman's Magazine* regularly published an anthology of articles to which it applied the tagline *e pluribus unum*, which may or may not have been inspired by the recipe for *moretum*. While the committee's design for the Great Seal wasn't ultimately adopted, the motto that it proposed, *e pluribus unum*, was carried through to the final design.

One of the most popular Latin mottos is *semper fidelis* (always faithful or always loyal). For the United States Marine Corps, it's more than just a motto as it epitomizes the *esprit de corps* of the Marines. It describes a way of life during and after military service and it's the title of the official march of the Corps composed by the American March King, John Philip Sousa. The motto is often shortened by the Marines to *semper fi*, with "*fi*" pronounced as if it rhymes with "pie." In a play on the abbreviated form of the motto, the members of the Corps have adopted the phrase "Semper I" to describe a selfish "comrade in arms" who always puts his own interests ahead of those of the Corps. This is, of course, inconsistent with the Corps' motto, which commands primary loyalty to the Corps and fellow Marines.

In J.K. Rowling's Harry Potter book series, the Hogwarts School of Witchcraft and Wizardry enjoys the motto *draco dormiens numquam tillandos*, which is translated as "never tickle a sleeping dragon." In the 1991 black comedy movie, *The Addams Family*, Morticia Addams, played by Angelica Houston, reveals the family motto, *sic gorgiamus allos subjectatos nunc*. Morticia undertakes to translate this and renders it in English as "we gladly feast on those who would subdue us," which is consistent with the family's macabre instincts. There's a strong hint that the motto is Dog Latin because Gorgias is the Latin name for a Greek philosopher who had a reputation as a sophist, a person who reasons with clever but fallacious arguments.

13

ANIMAL IMAGES

I have been studying the traits and dispositions of the "lower animals" (so called) and contrasting them with the traits and dispositions of man. I find the result humiliating to me.

Mark Twain from *Letters to the Earth*

The animals that surround us commonly serve as points of reference in our expressions and sayings. Domestic pets and farm animals are, of course, particularly familiar to us, both in their physical and behavioral characteristics. This explains why they figure prominently in expressions and sayings. But wild creatures, from elephants to fleas, also make their appearance. This chapter explores all of this animal imagery for its origins, its underlying significance, its appropriateness, its variety, its fairness to the animals involved and its political correctness.

Several of the earliest examples of animal sayings and expressions come from *Aesop's Fables*, first published in English in 1484. Many of Aesop's fables illustrate sayings or expressions that are in use today. Animals usually feature in these fables, often as major players in the story, sometimes with speaking parts. Aesop himself had a fabled existence as it's never been firmly established that there was an Aesop. The stories attributed to him were most likely passed along in the oral tradition for some time before they were collected and recorded. In the manner of fables generally, Aesop's stories are short allegories the narrative of which is an extended metaphor symbolic of a larger truth.

One of the most familiar of these fables tells of a race between a tortoise and a hare. The hare stops for a rest and a doze in the midst of the contest fully confident that he'll be able to overtake the tortoise before the finish line. But when he awakens, it's too late to close the gap on the plodding tortoise, who prevails, proving that "slow and steady wins the race." Because the tortoise's victory was "against all odds," there has been some speculation, on the Internet and elsewhere, that he cheated; by taking a short cut, by slipping a sleeping pill into the hare's water bottle, by taking a bus for most of the way or by doping up like Lance so that he'd have more than "half a chance." None of these allegations has been proven.

In another story attributed to Aesop, a milkmaid has her high hopes of wealth abruptly dashed. She carries a pail of rich milk on her head and, in the daze of a day dream, calculates that she will skim the cream off the milk, churn it into butter which she'll exchange for a dozen eggs which will, in turn, produce a dozen chickens that she'll be able to sell for lots of money. Unfortunately, in her inattentive state, she drops the pail, spilling the milk (we don't know if she cried over it). Therefore, she loses out on the prospects of cream, butter, eggs and, the most valuable asset of all, a dozen chickens. This, of course, illustrates the proposition "don't count your chickens before they're hatched," which warns against acting on an optimistic assumption that may turn out to be wrong.

The American humorist James Thurber would later coin the perverted proverb "don't count your boobies before they are hatched," which serves as the moral to one of his modern fables. He wasn't building his twisted wisdom upon the image of a young girl anxiously anticipating the end of puberty or the image of a brooding blue-footed boobie anxiously anticipating the arrival of her chicks. Rather, he was making a play upon "booby hatch," a slang term for an "insane asylum." Both terms are now regarded as politically incorrect and have, generally, been replaced by "psychiatric hospital." In Thurber's fable, titled "The Unicorn in the Garden," a husband notices a unicorn with a golden horn eating flowers in his garden one morning. He wakes his wife to tell her what he's seen, but she dismisses him and his story, declaring that "the unicorn is a mythical beast" and threatening to put him in the booby hatch. When she gets out of bed later that morning, she secretly phones the police and a psychiatrist, telling them to come to her house with a strait-jacket. When they arrive, she tells them that her husband saw a golden-horned, flower-eating unicorn that very morning. They wisely question the husband about whether he had reported to his wife that he had seen such an animal. He denies having done so, observing that "the unicorn is a mythical beast." At this point, they take the wife away in a strait-jacket, having concluded that she was "crazy as a jaybird," and the husband lives happily, on his own, ever after.

In another, early fable, a huntsman is frustrated in the realization of his expectations like the unfortunate milkmaid. In this story, a currier, a tanner of leather, buys a bear skin from the huntsman on the understanding that the huntsman will kill the bear the next day. The huntsman goes out faithfully the following morning in pursuit of the bear. One would think he'd be "loaded for bear," both literally and in the sense of being fully prepared for an impending confrontation. But when he finds the bear and shoots at the beast, he misses his target, "falling short of the mark," and the bear attacks him, knocking him to the ground. The huntsman wisely plays dead, saving himself from certain destruction. As the bear leaves the scene, he whispers a message into the huntsman's ear: In future, make sure of the bear before you sell the skin. And so the saying "don't sell the bear skin before you have caught the bear" was born. Ultimately, it gave rise to a spin-off saying, designed for the American frontier, namely "sell the buffalo hide after you have killed the buffalo." The celebrated American poet Carl Sandburg used this, in his book length poem *The People, Yes* as one of several illustrations, in proverb form, of the common wisdom of his countrymen.

Most tales of the hunt, whether for bears or other prey, don't end as ignominiously for the hunter as the fable of the huntsman and the bear. The hunter is usually shown in a very favorable light for "until the lion tells his own story, the story of the hunt will always glorify the hunter," as an African proverb explains. The father of modern African writing, Chinua Achebe, credited this proverb with inspiring him to spin the tales of fellow Nigerians, beginning with his acclaimed 1958 novel, *Things Fall Apart*. He became convinced that he could bring to bear a truer perspective on life in Africa than his literary predecessors of European descent, including Joseph Conrad, Joyce Cary, and John Buchan. On Achebe's recent death, at the age of 82, it was reported, fittingly, that "the lion of Africa is gone."

"Dog in the manger" and "bell the cat" are both expressions that come from Aesop's fables. A dog makes himself comfortable lying on a bed of hay in the oxen's manger. Returning from a hard day's work in the fields, the oxen are hungry and want to get at the hay. But the dog growls at them, baring his teeth and keeping them at bay. The oxen react by telling the dog that he's being very unfair in denying them the hay that he won't eat himself. "Dog in the manger" behavior on the part of an individual therefore reflects a spiteful and mean-spirited attitude that would prevent others from having something that the individual can't or won't use himself.

The fable from which the expression "bell the cat" is derived is about the plan of action of a group of mice to defend themselves against a troublesome cat. Life was good for the mice whenever the cat was off on holiday for "when the cat's away, the mice will play." But when at home, the cat had the habit of creeping up on the mice and "eating into their numbers." At a strategy session, one wise mouse proposes that a bell be tied around the neck of the cat so that the mice would be alerted to his approach. Since "forewarned is forearmed," they could "make themselves scarce." The other mice concur unanimously in this proposal. However, before the meeting adjourns, one bright mouse asks "who will tie the bell around the cat's neck?" No one volunteers. One is reminded of a famous line, written much later by the Scottish national poet, Robbie Burns: "The best-laid schemes o' mice an' men gang aft agley."

The larger metaphorical meaning of "to bell the cat" is, as might be expected, to assume a big personal risk for the benefit of the broader community. As to the unanswered question "who will bell the cat?" a suitable candidate emerges from this Irish ditty:

Some Guinness spilled on the barroom floor
When the pub was shut for the night.

Out of the hole crept a wee brown mouse
And stood in the pale moonlight.

He lapped up the frothy brew from the floor,
Then back on his haunches he sat,
And all night long you could hear him roar,
"Bring on the goddamn'd cat!"

A famous poem is the source of the expression, "an albatross around the neck." Samuel Taylor Coleridge's *The Rime of the Ancient Mariner* is the narrative of a sailor whose ship is driven off course into the Antarctic. The ship is visited by an albatross, also known as a gooney bird, the largest of all sea birds. His appearance forecasts a south wind that will carry the ship out of the dangerous southern waters. But the ungrateful mariner shoots the ship's apparent savior, an act that brings on the doldrums, becalming the ship and leaving the crew with "water, water every where, ne any drop to drink." The crew is angered by this change of fortune and forces the mariner to wear the dead albatross around his neck, as a punishment, prompting him to lament:

Ah! wel-a-day! what evil looks
Had I from old and young;
Instead of the Cross, the Albatross
About my neck was hung.

"An albatross around the neck" has since come to mean any heavy burden of guilt that has become an obstacle to success and is particularly difficult to shake off. No such guilt was felt by the cinema snack vendor in the popular albatross sketch from the British TV series *Monty Python's Flying Circus*. She's seen trying to sell a dead albatross from a snack tray strapped on her neck. When asked by a potential customer "what flavor is it?" the girl, played by comedian John Cleese, shouts back that it has no flavor since "it's a bloody sea bird." However, she proceeds to make a sale, whereupon she stops shouting "albatross!" and proceeds to call out "gannet on a stick!" One is left to wonder whether she's managed "to kill two birds with one stone" and hopes to dispose of them both "in one fell swoop" around the movie theatre.

The origin of some animal expressions can be traced to sentences that have been remembered and recorded but, like fables, are of unknown authorship. The expression "up to your ass in alligators," for example, comes from the line "when you're up to your ass in alligators, there's no time to remember that you're there to drain the swamp." Rush Limbaugh, the conservative political commentator, rose above this kind of memory lapse for, as he once said, coining his own mixed idiom, "I knew enough to realize that alligators were in the swamp and that it was time to circle the wagons."

Someone would, typically, say that he was "up to his ass in alligators" to emphasize that he was "swamped with work" to such an extent that it was "threatening to devour him." If the intimidating presence of menacing alligators were to be offered up as an excuse for not getting on with a task, such as draining the swamp, it might draw the response, "that's a croc." Understood literally, this would pinpoint a misidentification of the species of threatening reptiles. But it's more likely to be intended, in a figurative sense, to signal disbelief in the excuse. Another skeptical reaction to the excuse that alligators were preventing the work from getting done might consist of "shedding crocodile tears." This expression, describing an artificial display of grief, draws upon an old legend that crocodiles moan and cry in order to attract sympathetic victims and then shed hypocritical tears when ripping apart and devouring those victims.

Given the reputation of the crocodile for false moaning and crying, it's no wonder "that's a croc" is sometimes used to suggest that something shouldn't be believed. In all probability, the expression simply evolved from "that's a crock," which continues as the more common expression. While it has no difference in sound or meaning, this last formulation is actually a shortened version of a longer, slang expression "that's a crock of shit." The last word is used in the sense of nonsense. In Cockney slang, utter nonsense would be dismissed as "pony and trap," conceived for its rhyme with "crap." But this too is often put into a condensed form, typical of that peculiar variety of slang, as just plain "pony."

"As the crow flies" is meant to describe a distance between two points should a straight-line route be followed. In reality, however, crows are easily diverted from their flight paths, whether they're flying singly or in a group, ominously called a "murder of crows." A "gaggle of geese," which is known as a "skein of geese" when airborne, is much more likely to pursue a straight course, especially in migratory flight. Crows, on the other hand, are frequently distracted in flight by the sight or smell of carrion, by the urge to assist injured crows or by raptors to which they often give chase. However, there's a plausible historical explanation for the expression. It would seem to draw upon the behavior of seafaring crows with special navigational duties. One of these crows was released from the top of the mast of a ship, where the "crow's nest" is located, when it wasn't certain where the nearest land was to be found. It was thought that the crow would "make a beeline" for the closest shoreline, in which case the helmsman would alter the ship's course to follow the crow. The function that these crows performed was eventually taken over by radar, which was murder on the crows, ousting them from their marine role and leaving the ships' "crow's nests" empty of the birds that gave them their name.

While crows may fly in a straight line from the "crow's nest" to shore, there are remote Outback spots, such as Woop Woop, where they're bound to deviate from a straight course. Woop Woop is a backward location in Australia that's "beyond the black stump," or "back o' Bourke," and uncharted on any map. It's the fictional archetype of "the place where the crows fly backwards to keep the dust out of their eyes." Consequently, these landlocked crows know where they've been but don't have a good bead on where they're going.

"To make a beeline" is another idiomatic expression that appears to be based on the premise that one of nature's creatures moves in a straight line. Although bees don't appear to follow direct flight paths in their very short hops, scientific observation confirms that the premise of the expression is, indeed, accurate "in the long run."

The current scientific consensus is that on extended flights, bees, like many other insects, go into a compass mode, orienting themselves to the sun while making allowance, through an innate sense of time, for the daily movement of the sun across the sky. On repeat forays, they have been observed cutting corners and straightening their routes, apparently learning from experience how they can conserve time and energy. Other research supports the fascinating conclusion that bees actually engage in information sharing in order to map out their paths when they are heading out from the hive in search of nectar. The bees "take their cue from" fellow bees. Flight plans are formulated with the assistance of experienced informants, who pass along key distance and direction details through what is known as a "waggle dance." This enables the informed bees to go directly to known sources of sustenance. German zoology professor Karl von Frisch was honored with a Nobel Prize in 1973 for unraveling the meaning and significance of the "waggle dance."

Many similes are also based on the distinctive attributes, actual or reputed, of particular kinds of animals. For example, "sly as a fox," "slow as a snail," "strong as an ox" and "quiet as a mouse" are derived from a stereotypical characteristic of the named animal. "As prolific as a rabbit" and "breed like rabbits" are also particularly apt since the fertility of rabbits is undeniable. This reproductive fact has even influenced the expressions that rabbits themselves use, as indicated in this cartoon:

"Really? — my people always say multiply and conquer."

Not surprisingly, rabbits are in a hurry to get on with the business of multiplying, especially in Australia where they have a proven proclivity for procreation. The degree of haste involved is captured in another rabbit cartoon, illustrating the Australian expression "to be off like a bride's nightie," which plays off a couple of meanings of "be off."

One particular characteristic may be displayed by several animals, in which case there may be several possible similes to choose from in order to illustrate that characteristic in human traits. For example, someone may be said to be "as busy as" any of the following animals; a beaver, a bee, an ant and a cat on a hot tin roof. Of these animals, the cat is only likely to be busy for a relatively short period of time. It will probably be so uncomfortable on the roof that it will be quick to "hot foot it out of there." Amongst the various options, the expressions "as busy as a beaver" and "as busy as a bee" are often favored because they have the added attraction of an alliterative allure.

The champion boxer, Muhammad Ali, put together two contrasting animal similes to characterize his boxing style when he coined the phrase, "float like a butterfly, sting like a bee." This became a slogan that was widely associated with the boxer. In fact, he also registered it as a trade mark and recently settled an infringement lawsuit against the digital bookseller Kobo. Another sports tactic "creep like a tiger, fight like a snake" is, so far, unprotected by registration. This tactic is one that managers urge their contesting charges to follow in the Chinese betting sport of cricket fighting.

Someone may be described as being mad, either in the sense of angry or crazy, as a collection of animals in a confined space. The choice of expressions playing upon a supposed collective madness include; "mad as a bag of ferrets," "mad as a box of frogs," "mad as a bag of badgers" and "mad as a sack of weasels." These various animals could "have their dander up" because they naturally don't like being close to each other or they could have "gone off the deep end" because of their confinement.

"Mad as a March hare" signifies a third form of madness, namely foolishness. That's what the European hare, a close relative of the rabbit, demonstrates during its six month breeding season, which peaks in March. Throughout this season, hares act in a frenzied, even hare-brained, way. In the circumstances, their behavior is to be expected "in the heat of the moment," although it's odd by human standards. No doubt, they're just "following their animal instincts."

Americans are likely to say "mad as a wet hen" or "mad as a hornet" to indicate anger while Australians are apt to say "mad as a cut snake" to signify craziness or anger and "mad as a gumtree full of galahs" to signify craziness or foolishness. A galah is a rose-breasted parrot that is thought to be pretty dimwitted. It also doubles as a term for a stupid person.

In order to emphasize that someone is mad in the sense of crazy, there are further options available in the form of the expressions, "crazy as a loon," "crazy as a coot," "crazy as an outhouse rat [or mouse]" and "crazy as a bed bug." "Crazy like a fox" is not as straightforward, for it inverts the expected meaning. Its sense is that although someone may appear to be crazy, that person is actually very shrewd and crafty. That reality is consistent with the reputation of foxes reflected in the expressions "sly as a fox" and "cunning as a fox."

A lot of similes "give a bum rap" to the animals whose suggested traits are the basis for the analogy. "Drunk as a skunk," "cruel as a wolf," "violent as a gorilla," "drink like a fish," "miserable as a bandicoot" and "stubborn as a goat" would likely be found defamatory if the maligned creatures had the standing to resort to the courts to remove the stain from their reputations. But in the absence of a judicial remedy, "give a dog a bad name and hang him," for any reputation destroyed is hard to rehabilitate.

Many other similes refer accurately to familiar animal behavior patterns. For example, a strong draw or attraction, particularly to some thing, may be described as being "like bees to honey," "like moths to a flame" or "like flies to sugar." These similes all trade upon the recognized susceptibilities or instincts of the named creatures.

There are many expressions that interpret human behavior in terms of animal behavior. The "cock of the walk" is someone who's acting like a dominant rooster "strutting his stuff." He needs to be "brought down a notch," which is nicely accomplished by the Russian proverb, "a rooster today, a feather duster tomorrow." If someone is proceeding "at a canter," then becomes "hot to trot" and, finally, starts talking "at a full gallop" (the opposite of "a snail's gallop"), he's been "put through his paces" in the manner of a horse. But, in a figurative sense, he's been cruising along without much effort, getting sexually excited and then speaking very quickly. Someone who's "over the moon" is particularly delighted about something. In this case, the image is not one of normal animal behavior but of the out-of-this-world antics of the cow who jumped over the moon, to the accompaniment of the cat's fiddling and to the amusement of the little dog, in a nonsense nursery rhyme from which the expression is derived.

Someone who "bays at the moon," who's "barking up the wrong tree" or who has a "bark worse than his bite" is portrayed as doing what a dog does. But, in reality, he's being accused of clamoring to no effect, being mistaken in his course of action or being less ferocious than he makes out to be. On the other hand, "my dogs are barking" owes very little to the behavior of dogs, despite appearances. This is simply an old fashioned way of saying that my feet are aching, drawing upon Cockney slang, according to which "dogs" is a substitute for "feet" because "feet" happens to rhyme with "dog meat." "Go figure!"

"To work like a dog" may have carried a more potent message of intense activity in earlier times when dogs were more likely to carry out important tasks for their owners, then known as their masters. For example, they were once widely used to tree raccoons for hunters in the American south, although sometimes these coon dogs would "bark up the wrong tree." Nowadays, our canine sidekicks tend to concentrate on eating, sleeping, playing go-fetch and, generally, on earning our affection by being "man's best friends." Yet, some still earn their keep by working; as hunting dogs, fire dogs, guard dogs, sled dogs, guide dogs, search dogs and detection dogs. There are different sub-specialties among several of these varieties of working dogs. For example, detection dogs may be trained to sniff out dead bodies, contraband drugs, bed bugs or, to pinpoint them for release, pregnant lobsters. The concept of "working like a dog" got a big boost when it was popularized by the Beatles through the lyrics of the lead song from their 1964 film "A Hard Day's Night."

Certain canine breeds are preferred for particular working roles. Dalmatians serve as fire dogs, although it's far from clear what their responsibilities are when they "ride shotgun" in the front seat of a fire truck and eventually arrive at the scene of a fire. Some have speculated that they're used to find the location of fire hydrants. That would mean, of course, that only males of the breed would have the proper tools for the job. The truth is that the Dalmatians riding the fire engines are just for show. The original assignment of the breed was to run ahead of the horses, clearing the way for the horse-drawn fire carriages en route to a fire. Once that job disappeared with the advent of motorized fire trucks, they were kept on, apparently in order to avoid redundancy payments. Retraining for new tasks would have been "out of the question" for "you can't teach an old dog new tricks."

Alsatians, also known as German shepherds, gained a reputation as very effective guard dogs. Consequently, they often served as junkyard dogs, charged with deterring would-be thieves from entering a scrap yard and making off with valuable auto parts. But, like fire dogs, junkyard dogs became redundant in the wake of new technologies, in this case electronic surveillance and sophisticated alarm systems. The junkyard dog survives, however, in the expression "meaner than a junkyard dog." That description was applied, most famously, to Bad Bad Leroy Brown in the lyrics of a song of that name by singer-songwriter Jim Croce. If the expression doesn't go far enough, there's always the elaborated version, "madder than a junkyard dog with fourteen sucking pups."

The British newspaper, *The Daily Telegraph*, carried the story of a candidate for political office, canvassing door to door, who came to a house where an Alsatian was barking furiously. His agent said, "Just go in. Don't you know the proverb 'a barking dog never bites.'" "Yes," said the candidate "I know the proverb, you know the proverb, but does the dog know the proverb?" This apocryphal story may sound familiar as it has appeared in other forms. The Yiddish proverb "a meowing cat can't catch mice" and the folksy American proverb "a howlin' coyote ain't stealin' no chickens" also address the distraction that occurs when an animal is engaged in vocalizing in his own way, with the result that he isn't able to act "true to form."

Ominously, the Alsatian in the story of the campaigning political candidate may have been mindful of another proverb, "every dog is allowed one bite." This reflects an old common law principle that would permit him to take a single chunk out of the candidate with impunity. There are no stated exceptions preventing a barking dog from benefiting from the principle. Of course, the candidate could always hold out the hope that the dog's "bark was worse than his bite." But if he was proved wrong in that, he would be "twice shy," having been "once bitten," which would be bound to inhibit his future door-to-door campaigning.

"Work like a dog" is one of those expressions that lends itself to an add-on of one kind or another. Consequently, we have the derivative sayings: "work like a dog, play like a puppy," "work like a dog so you can party like a rock star," and "work like a dog and you'll be dog tired at the end of the day." "Work like a Trojan" carries the same meaning as "work like a dog". It too can be expanded as in this description of a zealous hog caller; "he worked like a Trojan and was horse (hoarse) at the end of the day." Of course, this calls for a further add-on, namely "pardon the pun."

In "a more serious vein," Caroline Simon, an American jurist and sometime politician, provided this guide to success for career women; "look like a girl, act like a lady, think like a man and work like a dog." The famous football coach, George Allen, had nothing but animals "on his radar screen" when he formulated his prescription for a good life; "work like a dog, eat like a horse, think like a fox and play like a rabbit." A good life is not necessarily a long life; Allen died of a heart attack in 1990 at the age of 72.

Other helpful hints for worldly success, by "taking a leaf from the book" of particular animals, include:

Be like a dog. Chase your tail in order to "make ends meet" and be sure to "leave your mark," which just "goes with the territory," but whatever you do, don't "bark up the wrong tree."

Be like a lion. Live life with pride, "grab the lion's share" "with might and mane" and, by all means, have a "rip-roaring good time," but beware of being "bearded in your den."

Be like an elephant. "Have a thick skin" and learn to "tickle the ivories" so you can stay "in tune with yourself."

In every case, the zoological advice enlists several expressions to illustrate why the animal bears copying, albeit with an important caveat in the first two examples.

While the dog has now largely lost its earlier reputation as man's working partner, the truism persists that "a dog is a man's best friend." The dog's number one position has not gone unchallenged. It was questioned by Ogden Nash in his narcissistic poem "Compliments of a Friend:"

How many gifted pens have penned
That Mother is a boy's best friend!
How many more with like afflatus
Award the dog that honored status!
I hope my tongue in prune juice smothers
If I belittle dogs or mothers
But gracious, how can I agree?
I know my own best friend is Me.

A couple of perverted proverbs, with sexist overtones, attempt to explain why "a dog is a man's best friend," in particular, "a dog is a man's best friend because it wags its tail and not its tongue" and "a dog is a man's best friend because he's not always calling for explanations."

It's also been said that, unlike the sociable dog, "a cat is its own best friend." Sir Winston Churchill compared the two companions most favored by humans in this way: "Dogs look up to us. Cats look down on us." In a sop to the undervalued pig, he added: "Pigs treat us as equals." Churchill's dog-versus-cat comparison may have been inspired by the saying "dogs have owners, cats have staff," which is often announced by message bearing T-shirts and wall plaques. In a very modern version of the comparison, Mary Bly, the American romance novelist who writes under the name Eloisa James, has astutely observed that "dogs come when they're called; cats take a message and get back to you later."

Generally speaking, dogs come off worse than cats in the expressions we use. Witness the rough experiences a person has gone through if he's been "in the doghouse," suffered through the "dog days of summer," "gone to the dogs," "led a dog's life" in a "dog-eat-dog world," been "thrown to the dogs," been "sick as a dog" and, after having been dogged by all this misfortune, "died like a dog." In fact, a dog's life is so miserable, that it takes something extremely funny to be "enough to make a dog laugh." Humans have had to be warned that the mere association with dogs may have a contaminating effect, even though they be best friends, for "if you lie down with dogs, you'll get up with fleas," according to proverb

The hapless dog is also a convenient scapegoat. "The dog did it" is used to lay blame upon a dog for any one of a variety of sins from flatulence to eating a child's homework. A similar, responsibility-shifting expression, "the dingo did it," is derived from the theory of the defense in a famous murder case, *The Queen v. Chamberlain*. Lindy Chamberlain was convicted, amidst a media frenzy, of murdering her nine week old daughter while on a family camping trip to Ayers Rock, now called Uluru, in the Red Centre of Australia in August of 1980. She maintained that a dingo, an indigenous variety of wild dog, must have taken her child. The body was never found. After several unsuccessful appeals, she was finally exonerated upon the discovery of new evidence that strongly suggested that dingoes were, indeed, the likely culprits. The whole incredible story was told in the 1988 film *A Cry in the Dark*, starring the versatile, Oscar winning actress Meryl Streep as Lindy Chamberlain.

One of the most puzzling of well known animal expressions is "raining cats and dogs." There are several fanciful explanations for this description of a heavy rainfall, including a Latin origin in *cata doxus*, meaning beyond normal experience. The most likely explanation, that cats and dogs got caught up in the run-off from storms in earlier times, is "dull as ditchwater" by comparison. However, it's reinforced by these lines from Jonathon Swift's poem "A Description of a City Shower," written in 1710:

Now in contiguous drops the flood comes down,
Threatening with deluge this devoted town.
...

Now from all parts the swelling kennels flow,
And bear their trophies with them as they go

...

Drown'd puppies, stinking sprats, all drench'd in mud,
Dead cats, and turnip-tops come tumbling down the flood.

It's easy to see why witnesses to the flood might have gotten the impression that the cats and dogs, unlike the other debris, had come down from the sky with the deluge. Had the cats, in particular, been terrestrial in origin, they would have steered clear of the flood for "a cat would eat fish but would not wet her feet."

While they're alive and earthbound, the two kinds of favored pets aren't likely to associate, even for comfort in the face of a storm, for they would inevitably end up "fighting like cats and dogs." More likely that animals of the same species, but of the opposite sex, would get together, at least if a heavy rain threatened to bring on a flood "of biblical proportions" such as Noah experienced. It's not surprising, therefore, that a very heavy downpour should also be described as "raining so hard the animals were starting to pair up."

"A hail of dead cats" sounds even more awesome than a rain of cats. It's used in American political terminology to describe a storm of criticism that accompanies an unpopular incumbent's exit from public office. In this case, the cats are probably related to catcalls, which are harsh or shrill cries, like those of an angry cat, by which an audience expresses its disapproval at a sporting engagement, a performance or a meeting.

Another dead cat expression is used to describe a frequent stock market behavior pattern. "A dead cat bounce," also known as "a sucker's rally," signals a temporary recovery in the trading price of a stock or the over-all market that is followed by a continuation of the previous decline or bear market. The idea behind the metaphor is that even a cat will bounce if dropped from a sufficient height, but that its rebound doesn't mean that it's thriving. However, a dead cat may ultimately rise again, more than once, for "a cat has nine lives." This "fact" prompted the British comedian, Jimmy Carr, to say that this "makes them ideal for experimentation."

A couple of other well known expressions that refer to cats may not be about the four-legged variety at all but the cat-o'-nine-tails, a whip with nine knotted cords that was often called a cat. The cat was used to inflict corporal punishment, especially upon seamen. "No room to swing a cat" may simply indicate a measure of space that is less than you would need to crack this variety of whip. The interrogatory expression "cat got your tongue" may have been prompted by the fact that the fear of getting the cat-o'-nine tails could explain why a seaman might be deterred from breaking silence and revealing a confidence, for which he could be punished with a lash of the cat.

Pigs pop up everywhere in expressions and sayings, where they are usually "held in low esteem" even though, as Churchill said, they treat us humans as equals. We're not inclined to reciprocate as evidenced by the fact that we portray pigs implicitly as:

heavy on the perspiration in "to sweat like a pig" (although all the scientific evidence is that pigs don't sweat);

turned on by kitchen waste in "happy as a pig in slop;"

taking more than their fair share in "to hog [something];"

over-eaters in "to pig out" and "to make a pig of [oneself]," leading to obesity, which is recognized in "as fat as a pig" and in "pigs get fat, but hogs get slaughtered;"

unappreciative in "do not throw pearls to swine;"

uncontrollable in "you can no more steer a pig than a hurricane" and **uncontrolled** in "go hog wild;"

ugly in "like putting lipstick on a pig;"

inferior, in part if not in whole, in "you can't make a silk purse out of a sow's ear;"

boorish in "what can you expect from a pig but a grunt;"

noisy snorters in "driving pigs to market," which describes someone who is, "snoring like a pig" to the annoyance of those within hearing range;

stinky in "those who run with pigs smell like pigs;"

wallowing in the prospect of getting filthy in "never wrestle a pig; you both get dirty and the pig likes it;"

bad company in "when you lay down with pigs, expect to get dirty."

A pig needs to be aware of the person with whom he chooses to "lay" down since he may also be "known by the company he keeps" as this story of "The Drunkard and the Pig" demonstrates:

It was early last December,
As near as I remember,
I was walking down the street in tipsy pride;
No one was I disturbing
As I lay down by the curbing,
And a pig came up and lay down by my side.

As I lay there in the gutter
Thinking thoughts I shall not utter,
A lady passing by was heard to say:
"You can tell a man who boozes by the company he chooses;"
And the pig got up and slowly walked away.

Fortunately for his abstemious reputation, the pig acted upon the wisdom of the boozing proverb, as if it was directed to "every man and beast," and dissociated himself from the drunkard.

"Putting lipstick on a pig" is a gesture that seems totally out of place and quite futile in terms of improving the attractiveness of the pig. It's an expression that's used, particularly in political circles, to characterize a change as purely cosmetic while what lies beneath remains the same; the pig is still a pig. The expression embraces the wisdom of a much earlier saying, "you can put nail polish on a hangnail, but it's still a hangnail."

Barack Obama applied the lipstick-on-a-pig analogy, in the course of the 2008 U.S. presidential campaign, in challenging the claim made by John McCain, the Republican candidate, that McCain's policies represented a change from those of the incumbent president, George W. Bush. In an "over the top" assertion of political incorrectness, Obama was pounced upon as being sexist and as having, inferentially, mounted an out-of-bounds attack on McCain's vice presidential running mate, Sarah Palin, even though her physical attractiveness was unquestionable. A runner-up in the Miss Alaska beauty pageant "back in the day," she didn't really need lipstick or any other kind of make-up for it would simply have "gilded the lily."

Another barnyard animal, the horse, is treated in a more neutral fashion than the pig. The many varieties of horses that have become notorious as a result of expressions and sayings include:

dark horses—which are odds-on to lose a race but sometimes come through as winners;

wrong horses—which never come through for their betting backers;

horses for courses—which are suited for different racetracks;

over-specialized, immature horses—which are known as "one trick ponies;"

blind horses—to which "a nod's as good as a wink" in order to convey one's meaning;

blind mares—as to which there's "nothing so bold" since they're in the dark about a challenging situation and, therefore, are the least likely to be deterred by it;

dead horses—which it's futile to flog because they are unresponsive;

gray mares—which are "the better horses," being the females of the species (although the old ones "ain't what they used to be," as an old song tells us);

high horses—upon which someone mounts only to show his arrogance (George W. Bush once observed, by way of a perplexing mixed metaphor, that "you can't take the high horse and claim the low road");

short horses—which are "soon curried" because there's a smaller expanse of hair to groom;

stalking horses—which disguise the presence of hunters and allow them to get within shooting range of their quarry and zero in for the kill;

gift horses—which you should never "look in the mouth" (even though it's always prudent to look in the mouth of a horse you might buy to determine the length of his teeth, a good gauge of age which, in turn, affects the value of the horse);

Trojan horses—which look deceptively like gift horses but actually harbor the enemy within;

escaped horses—after which it makes no sense to "close the barn door" because it's too late to bolt in those that have managed to bolt out;

wild horses—which couldn't drag you to a place where you don't want to be.

All of the expressions and sayings that identify these equine varieties make "a lot of horse sense" as well as a lot of human sense, although none comes "straight from the horse's mouth," that is from an authoritative source.

"When you hear hoof beats, look for horses not zebras" is one of those unusual sayings that offer advice to a very specific community rather than the world at large. In this case, the intended audience is members of the medical profession in their diagnostic roles. The saying reminds physicians that a patient's symptoms are more likely to be caused by a common illness than an uncommon one.

Several sayings and expressions that feature horses have provided fodder for humorous take-offs. For instance, "you can lead a horse to water but you can't make him drink" and "never look a gift horse in the mouth" are the bases for the mixed metaphorical saying "you can lead a gift horse to water but you can't look him in the mouth." The first of these sayings has also spawned several perverted proverbs, including "you can lead a horse to water but you can't make him brush his teeth," "you can lead a horse to water but you can't make him walk on it" and "you can lead a donkey to water but he's still an ass." Dorothy Parker was obviously mindful of the saying when she took up a challenge to use the word "horticulture" in a sentence. She's reported to have come up, in an instant, with this line: "You can lead a horticulture but you can't make her think." Another saying, "never change horses in midstream," has prompted this reminder of an equally important fact of life, that you should "never change diapers in mid-stream."

"A horse of a different color" is one way of describing something that's completely different. The expression lends itself to a Nordic pun. The Norseman Leif Ericson was the son of Erik the Red. True to his nickname "Leif the Lucky," the younger Ericson "discovered" North America, landing in Newfoundland in the early part of the eleventh century. Both father and son were inveterate explorers. One might be tempted to say of Leif the Lucky "like father, like son" except that the father, Erik the Red, was "a Norse of a different color." "By the same token," a supposed descendant, Erik the Doughnut, has been described, in an even more dubious, double pun, as "a Norse of a different cruller."

A farm animal frame of reference turns to a reptile frame of reference in a lighthearted exchange of greetings. Friends have traditionally used the salutation "how now brown cow," yet on parting they bid farewell with "see you later alligator," which often elicits the response "in a while crocodile," as if one good rhyming reptilian expression deserves another.

"Flat out like a lizard drinking" is an Australian expression that might be expected to conjure up an image of a "lounge lizard" compensating for the lack of high-end bars in the Outback where many "lounges of lizards," to use the collective expression for these reptiles, can be found. This kind of image is comfortably captured by *Canberra Times* cartoonist David Pope in this illustration:

The expression "flat out like a lizard drinking" became familiar to many beyond the land of Oz because of the Crocodile Hunter, the late Steve Irwin. He used it often, on his TV show, to highlight the great speed at which various creatures of the Outback move, usually emphasizing his amazement at that speed with a "crikey!" or two thrown in. The expression seems to be contradictory, for when a lizard drinks it's indeed flat out in the sense that its body is prone against the ground but it's hardly going flat out in the sense that it's moving at top speed, "hell bent for leather." In fact, it's in a relatively static state and, presumably, isn't at all bent on a fate that would turn it into lizard skin footwear or any other variety of leather goods. The expression is meant to be humorous in its mixture of two quite inconsistent meanings of "flat out." Someone who wasn't familiar with the expression would most likely guess that it was intended to describe the condition of lying perfectly flat on the ground or to be a sarcastic comment on a lack of speed or activity. Neither would be correct; rather it means that some person or animal is going "hell bent for leather," but only in the figurative sense.

When it's especially stressed, the American possum, also known as the opossum, goes automatically into a form of suspended animation, as a defense mechanism against its enemies. When in this state, the possum appears to be dead. This reactive behavior is the foundation for the expression "playing possum," which means that a person is pretending to be dead, or possibly dormant or disabled, in order to deceive others. It's not surprising, therefore, that Possum Lodge adopted the motto *Quando Omni Flunkus Moritati*, which is Dog Latin for "when all else fails, play dead." This fictional Canadian lodge was presided over by the character Red Green of *The Red Green Show*, a long running comedy series on television from 1991-2006.

The American possum is described in the southern states, its original home ground, as "a flat animal that sleeps in the middle of the road." Of course, this habit doesn't come from feigning death. Here we have the real thing, which means that the prostrate possum isn't in the same kind of flat out state as that of a lizard drinking. A possum that's "flat as a pancake" and "deep in the big sleep" is often put to good use in roadkill cuisine. Various cookbooks provide recipes, which are sometimes legitimate and sometimes a put-on, for possum stew, possum pot pie and other delectable "flat meat dishes."

The Australian possum, which is unrelated to its American namesake, is known for getting upset and nasty when aroused, especially from its daytime slumber. Not surprisingly, therefore, "to stir the possum" means to create a disturbance, cause controversy or simply liven things up; quite the opposite of playing dead. It's what happens when you set the cat amongst the possums, as illustrated by this David Pope cartoon:

The balding condition that plagues maturing humans isn't, generally, replicated elsewhere in the animal kingdom. Yet someone who has lost a head of hair is often portrayed as "bald as a coot," "bald as a bandicoot," or "bald as a badger." Of course, a coot doesn't have any hair to shed since it's a bird. But the white marking on its head, as distinct from its otherwise dark body, gives it the appearance of baldness, much like the American eagle, which is known, familiarly, as the bald eagle. Both the coot and the eagle are simply bald by way of a contraction of piebald, which means that they exhibit patches of contrasting colors.

The coot also features in the description of someone as "an ornery old coot." This cantankerous coot also appears in the double barreled derogatory expression "bald as a coot and twice as ornery." That description is used "to put someone down," for whatever reason or for no particular reason. The structural style of this insult is also evident in the American expression, "crooked as a hound dog's hind leg and twice as dirty" and the Australian expression, "strong as a Mallee bull and twice as dangerous," referring to a bull that has been toughened up by living off the eucalyptus scrublands. The form of these modern expressions was, no doubt, influenced by the old expression "large as life and twice as natural," which was popularized by Lewis Carroll when he used it to describe the way in which Alice was introduced to the Unicorn, one of the many fantasy characters in *Through the Looking Glass*, the sequel to *Alice in Wonderland*.

A bandicoot is an antipodean marsupial that looks like a cross between a rat and a rabbit. It's not short of hair over any part of its body and it doesn't look as if it's bare headed. The expression "bald as a bandicoot" may, therefore, simply have evolved from the much earlier "bald as a coot," preserving the familiar "coot" sound and introducing an attractive alliterative quality. The unfortunate bandicoot apparently suffers from all kinds of other handicaps since someone can be "as miserable as," "as poor as," "as blind as," "as barmy as" (meaning as mad or foolish as) or "as lousy as" (meaning as stingy as) "a bandicoot." No wonder the bandicoot is prone to suffering from deprived isolation and exclusion, as brought out in the expression "like a bandicoot on a burnt ridge," suggesting that he's much "like a shag on a rock," another

Australian simile. That expression calls up an image of a lone cormorant completely abandoned by other "birds of a feather."

The expression "bald as a badger" is actually a shortened version of "bald as a badger's bum." Badger hair was used to make bristles for high quality shaving brushes. It's believed that hair for this purpose was plucked from the rear ends of badgers, leaving them "butt naked." Therefore, the badger expression might have been perfectly intelligible at one time before the shaving brush "went the way of the dodo" or, with apologies to the Old Order Mennonites, "the way of the horse and buggy."

"Bald as a baboon's bum" would make more sense, without sacrificing any alliteration. The butt of a baboon is quite naturally bereft of hair, which is "brought to the fore" by an exposure of red skin. However, a well-worn riddle highlights an important distinction between a bald man and an ape such as a baboon. The question: What are the apparent differences among a bald man, an ape and the Prince of Wales? The answer: A bald man has no hair apparent, an ape has a hairy parent and the Prince is the heir apparent. "Ask a silly question, get a silly answer!"

In these days of brushless shaving, the expression "bald as a baby's bum" is preferable to "bald as a badger's bum" since a baby's bottom is now much more familiar territory than a badger's depilated *derrière*. Even better than any of the living creature images, "bald as a bowling ball" and "having a chrome dome" put us clearly in mind of a bare, polished and round surface that is suggestive of a perfectly bald human pate. But whatever comparative indicator of baldness is used, the individual to whom the expression is applied, in a disparaging way, can always use this comeback: "Anyone can grow hair but it takes a real man to suck it back in."

While baldness is quite rare amongst members of the animal kingdom, a state of undress is the norm, although wolves apparently go about from time to time "in sheep's clothing," as a form of disguise, thinking they're "the cat's pajamas." However, for most creatures, with the exception of wolves, sheep and cats, clothes are out of fashion and nakedness is accepted "without blinking an eye." So why is a North

American bird, the jay, singled out in the expression "naked as a jay-bird" as illustrative of stark nakedness? Two theories persist to explain the reference to a jay in this expression. It may advert to the fact that young jays are born with no feathers and very little down. But in this respect, these chicks are not much different from those of any other species of nesting birds. The alternative explanation is that the "jay" in the expression is not a bird at all; rather it's slang for a rustic simpleton who's likely to be very exposed, metaphysically speaking, because of his vulnerability. This is the same "jay" that's found in the word "jay-walk," which indicates being "out of step with" the law that requires pedestrians to cross the street at a corner.

"Buck naked," used to describe being "in the bollocky," or stark nakedness, sounds as if it may be drawing an analogy to the uncovered body of a male deer. However, it's more likely that it simply represents an attempt to dress up the expression "butt naked" in some respectability. Alternatively, it may refer to a "young buck," a high-spirited young man who might be inclined to doff his clothes and go "in the buff." "Buff" is a term used to describe the tan color of buffalo hides, which were used to make items of clothing. That color mimics the skin tone of a white person who has been exposed to the sun. The fewer the clothes, the more the exposure to the sun's rays and the more the tan.

"Cold enough to freeze the balls off a brass monkey" suggests a degree of extreme cold sufficient to do similar damage to a man as to a monkey, especially, one might expect, to a man who is "buck naked." Like "buck naked," this expression appears to offer up an animal image. However, no such image is borne out by the investigations of the word buffs who have looked into it. They offer several theories as to what the expression is all about. By most accounts, it relates to inanimate objects. The expression may refer to a pyramidal stack of cannon balls collared, at the base, by what was known as a "brass monkey," which bears no relation to the alcoholic drink of the same name. In very cold weather, the brass material of the monkey would likely contract more than the iron of the cannon balls, forcing them to pop out. Alternatively, the expression may be based on the conductive qualities of certain statuettes made of brass, in particular those cast in the image of the three wise monkeys who "see no evil, hear no evil, speak no evil." These theories lead to the conclusion that the expression doesn't reflect the impact of cold temperatures on live monkeys and demonstrate that the expression isn't as brassy as it might, at first, appear.

Some sayings, unlike the brass-monkey expression, can't be explained away as simply superficially crass. "A fox smells his own hole first" is used, in a humorous way, to identify the source of flatulence as the one who responds to it first by drawing it to everyone's attention. The expression certainly "leaves a bad odor" "no matter how you cut it." "The first chicken that cackles laid the egg" is used in the same circumstances and to the same end but without being quite as crude.

A tall tale in the shaggy dog style tells of a herring who befriends a whale. The two are always seen together. But one day the herring appears without the ever present whale. When asked by the other fish where the whale is, the herring replies: "How should I know, am I my blubber's kipper?" This response carries an ominous suggestion for it comes close to a saying, in the Old Testament, used by Cain in denying any responsibility for his brother Abel, whom he had, in fact, murdered. However, the little fish would probably dismiss this as "a red herring" with no bearing on what he might have done to lose the whale.

Sometimes, a whale can be caught by using a herring-like fish called a sprat, as is evident from the expression "a sprat to catch a whale," which indicates that a little expenditure or risk may result in much gain. A similar truth is captured by the expression "a sprat to catch a mackerel" and by a saying of French origin, "one must lose a minnow to catch a salmon."

Other seagoing creatures that are referred to in popular expressions include eels, mullet, prawns and squid. "As slippery as an eel" can mean two things: when speaking of an object; that it's so slippery it's impossible to grasp in one's hands, and, when speaking of a person, particularly one's who's evading the law; that he's "as cunning as a fox" with the result that he's unlikely to be caught. "As charming as an eel," by comparison, is an ironic simile that plays against our expectations about the characteristics of the elusive eel.

The Australian expression "like a stunned mullet," referring to the fish and not the haircut, means completely dazed, much "like a deer in the headlights" or "like a rabbit caught in the headlights." The theory is that a mullet is stunned into submission when it's landed by a fisherman. But why a mullet and not some other fish that would be equally dazed when hit over the head, or slammed against the boat, by a fisherman? This explanation for the expression, therefore, sounds like a "load of codswallop," to use a nonsense expression for nonsense. More likely, the mullet is singled out because it's slow and easily caught, which could be explained on the basis that it's stunned in the sense of simple minded.

In the province of Newfoundland, someone who's "like a stunned mullet" is, in the local manner of speaking, "stunned as me arse." That's how Chainsaw Earle is described in a song written and sung by Buddy Wasisname and the Other Fellers. The lyrics tell of Earle's return, after fifteen years, to his hometown where he was a stunned wimp in his youth. The prodigal son, now a muscular giant of a man, single-handedly clears a wide firebreak with his 10 foot chainsaw, saving the town from an advancing forest fire and certain destruction. While savoring the praise of the townsfolk, the mighty Earle lights up a cigarette and throws the match away just as he knocks over a drum of gasoline. An explosion occurs and the town burns flat, prompting his father to say that after fifteen years he's still "as stunned as me arse," while Earle runs off "like a scalded cat."

But Newfoundlanders also have their own equivalent of the stunned mullet in the form of the capelin. The capelin, a favorite fish dish enjoyed by whales, has the habit of running ashore, figuratively speaking, to spawn and then die unceremoniously. Therefore, it's not surprising that someone in Chainsaw Earle's position could also have been described, in more respectable Newfie lingo, as "foolish as a capelin."

For an Australian, "to come the raw prawn" means to attempt to deceive someone or "to pull a fast one" or "pull a swifty" on someone. The expression generally takes the form "don't come the raw prawn with me," which is sometimes put, in jest, as "don't come the uncooked crustacean with me." Either way, it's typically used by someone trying to warn off another person who is trying to "put something over" on him. To the same end, an American would be likely to resort to one of these rhetorical questions: "You think I just fell off the turnip truck?" "You think I just got off the noon balloon from Rangoon?" (with no offence to the Burmese intended) and "You think I was born yesterday?" (and am just "a babe in the woods"). An Australian might also carry off a similar rebuff with the question: "What do you think this is, bush week?" and an Irishman with the question: "You think I came down in the last shower?" In every case, the question is a light hearted substitute for the more traditional: "Do you take me for a fool?" or the exclamatory "Yeah right!" said in a pronounced sarcastic tone.

There has been plenty of speculation about the basis for the connection between uncooked crustaceans and deceitfulness, which seems to be made by the expression "to come the raw prawn." Most of this speculation is "hard to swallow," including the suggestion that preying on a person's gullibility by deceiving him amounts to forcing something that might "stick in the craw," such as a raw prawn, down that person's throat.

A "damp squid" is a British term for something that fails to meet expectations. However, the original term was a "damp squib." A "squib" is a small explosive device that will fail to ignite when water has seeped into it. The transition to a "damp squid" is a prime example of folk etymology, in this case still in progress since the original term hasn't "fallen off the table" completely. In a 2009 survey in the U.K., a "damp squib" ranked number one among the most misquoted of everyday expressions.

The land animals "on the wild side" that are found indoors, frequenting our habitations or places of work, range from large beasts, such as elephants and 800 pound gorillas, to small, less intimidating critters, such as flies. "The elephant in the room," sometimes described as pink, perhaps to distinguish it from a "white elephant," has been invoked so often that the expression has become a cliché. When asked what the expression means, one wit said "it means that you're going to need a bigger garbage bag and a shovel." In fact, it's used, in a metaphorical way, to describe an issue or problem, such as a debilitating addiction, that no one wants to talk about but that, like an elephant in the room, is hard to ignore. The expression often carries an implicit value judgment that the issue or problem ought to be addressed.

The meaning of the expression can be neatly conveyed in the question and answer style of an elephant joke, a type of silly humor that was particularly popular in the 1960s:

Q. Why do we try to ignore elephants that are in the room?
A. I know, but I'd rather not say.

"An 800 pound gorilla" unconfined by the walls of a room, symbolizes a person who will "throw his weight around" in order to get his way. But if that same gorilla is described as being in the room, this simply signifies that nobody wants to talk about him just as they would try to avoid mention of an elephant similarly situated. In other words, the gorilla-in-the-room expression is used as a direct substitute for the elephant-in-the-room expression. Both the pachyderm and the big ape have what can be best described as a looming presence, attributable largely to their size. Neither is "like a bull in a china shop" who announces his presence by his awkward, destructive movements.

The "fly on the wall" is a much envied creature since we often hear it said, "I wish I were a fly on the wall." This apparently static fly has the advantage of being inconspicuous yet well positioned to hear and see what's going on in the room. While the elephant and the gorilla try to claim our attention, if they could, the fly wants no such attention; it simply wants to observe without being observed.

"A fly in the ointment" is also unmoving like the "fly on the wall," in this case because it's more than likely drowned. It's not, therefore, in a position to carry out a spying mission as it could if it were live on the wall. But this small insect poisons the atmosphere, much like the huge elephant or gorilla in the room, for it's known to spoil a whole vat of ointment from which an apothecary, the predecessor of the modern day pharmacist, would dispense his medicinal salves.

The question "are you catching flies?" is meant to shame a person into "closing his trap" when it's been left open, usually unconsciously. Kermit the Frog, of Muppets fame, however, would be just as happy to catch flies, for as he has said "time's fun when you're having flies," his adaptation of the saying, "time flies when you're having fun."

"There are no flies on" someone means that the individual is aware, astute and mentally active so that no one can take advantage of him much as an animal that is always in motion manages to be fly-free. Those who have been involved in the scouting movement may remember the silly song that was sung around the campfire (usually artificial) that reiterated a colloquial version of this expression more than enough times and with increasing volume. The refrain goes as follows:

Oh, there ain't no flies on me
There ain't no flies on me
There may be flies on some of you guys
But there ain't no flies on me.

There's no denying that Australians are all too familiar with flies, at least as they surround mere mortals, even adopting a characteristic hand wave in front of the face "to clear the air" of the pesky "Nellie Blighs," a gesture known as the "Australian salute." That gesture is also called a "Barcoo salute," named for a shire in western Queensland that's thinly populated, except for the flies. The usual futility of the gesture is recognized in this limerick:

The blowies are buzzing that coot—
You can tell from his Barcoo salute.
He's been waving all day,
But they won't go away.
They must reckon his noggin's a fruit.

The focus of the mock proverb, "never leave undone those things that ought to be done up" is flies of a different kind. This proverb has a religious derivation; it's the result of "adding a bit of zip" to these words of an Episcopalian prayer of confession: "We have left undone those things that we ought to have done…" Apparently, Sir Winston Churchill wasn't particularly moved, "in thought or deed," by the proverb. When told, on one occasion in his later years, that his fly was open, he was quick to observe that "a dead bird does not leave its nest," creating his own, self-deflating animal image. The mock proverb could prove offensive to some Christians on the basis that it involves disrespectful treatment of a religious text. They would likely characterize it, therefore, as politically incorrect.

For some people, particularly animal lovers, political correctness also involves steering clear of so-called speciest language. This kind of language suggests that humans are the dominant species or that particular characteristics or behavior patterns of animals make them inferior to most humans. But speciest language hardly has the same potential for damage as other kinds of politically incorrect language, such as that which is racist, sexist or sacrilegious, since those "in the crossfire," namely animals, are unlikely to take offence. Expressions that are apt to be condemned by opponents of speciest language include; "no better than an animal" and "appealing to our animal instincts." Sayings that are candidates for similar condemnation include; "a dog returns to his vomit" and "what can you expect from a pig but a grunt."

Some politically correct extremists have criticized expressions and sayings that convey a violent image because they promote, or desensitize us to, violence or cruelty, especially when defenseless animals are the target. They'd be likely to place the expressions "killing two birds with one stone" and "like shooting fish in a barrel" in this category. They would also be likely to condemn the Australian exclamatory expressions "stone the crows," which is Cockney in origin, and "starve the lizards." These two expressions are often joined together for a double whammy.

The sayings that are apt to be classified as having the same vice as these expressions include; "there are more ways of killing a dog than hanging it" and "it's easy to find a stick to beat a dog." The perverted proverb "you can't teach an old dog new tricks, but you can use him as a door stop" is likely to be considered offensive as well. Cats can also be the butt of abusive sayings, as in "there are more ways of killing a cat than choking it with cream" and "there's more than one way to skin a cat." While this last saying is generally taken to refer to domestic cats, it's used in the southern U.S., with less risk of offence, to refer to the many options for preparing catfish for cooking.

There are other, humorous expressions that aren't likely to be offensive, although it's hard to be sure these days. It's probably not in bad taste to say; "I'm so hungry I could eat the leg off a low flying duck." However, it's unlikely that the expression would go over well in polite company when "ass" or "arse" is substituted for "leg," as in the racy version. The comparable Australian slang expression "I'm so hungry I could eat a galah and bark sandwich" draws some of its strength from the unappetizing nature of another member of the avian community, the much maligned galah, a species of parakeet.

"Black sheep," as in "the black sheep of the family," has been a prime target of criticism on the grounds of political incorrectness. A "black sheep" is "the odd man out," to humanize its unfortunate position, in a flock of otherwise white sheep. Its wool is, generally, worth less than that of the other members of the flock. As an idiomatic term, "black sheep" means someone of bad character who has brought discredit upon his family. In 2009, the Global Language Monitor, a Texas-based organization that analyzes cultural trends in language, listed "black sheep" as one of the top ten politically incorrect terms and phrases, because of its apparent ethnic insensitivity. "White elephant," which describes something of little or no value, has been spared the kind of criticism that "black sheep" has attracted.

In an effort to correct the incorrect, some schools in Oxfordshire, England have changed the venerable nursery rhyme "Baa Baa Black Sheep" to "Baa Baa Rainbow Sheep." But since a rainbow flag is a symbol of the lesbian, gay, bisexual and transgender pride movement, this change threatens to substitute one form of insensitivity for another. So, it may be "out of the frying pan and into the fire" for the revisionists.

If "black sheep" "doesn't wash," what of *bête noire*, which has been assimilated, in its original French form, into the English language? It translates as "black beast" and is used to describe a person or thing that is strongly detested. Yet, it seems to have avoided the same taint as has been suffered by "black sheep," perhaps because its association with the color black is somewhat obscured by its foreign language dress.

14

BODY LANGUAGE

The way to a man's heart is through his stomach but not by jumping down his throat.

Anon.

The body shapes up as a rich source of images for expressions and sayings. Sometimes, it's the anatomy of particular varieties of animals that figures in, sometimes it's the human anatomy but, in either case, body language is in play. The more conventional form of body language uses physical expressions and gestures to convey meaning. The meaning of many gestures, however, can be conveyed just as well by verbal expressions that describe the gesture, such as "giving a thumbs up."

This chapter considers the ways in which the various parts of the body, and the five senses by which the body responds to the world around it, have been used in expressions and sayings. It looks at the images that are portrayed, explains some that may not be well focused, comments on the suitability of others and identifies misconceptions about others.

Body language is often combined with animal images. Someone may get "butterflies in his stomach," "a frog in his throat" and "a flea in his ear" denoting, variously, nervousness, hoarseness and receiving an annoying hint or rebuke. That same individual could also be "up to his ass in alligators" and be plagued by "an albatross around his neck" and "a monkey on this back." If he remains silent, when asked about all these scourges, believing that "a closed mouth gathers no flies," he might well be asked "cat got your tongue?"

All of these expressions and sayings refer to human body parts and their invasion by animals. Others focus their imagery on the body parts of animals. The individual who was plagued by a variety of intrusive animals, in the situation described in the previous paragraph, might be consumed with so much anger that it "made his hackles rise," a more extreme reaction than if it simply "ruffled his feathers." The idea that he might have to accept, and therefore endure, so many annoyances might also "stick in his craw." The word "hackles" calls to mind the neck feathers of birds or the neck hairs of dogs that tend to fluff up in moments of excitement, which is particularly noticeable in fighting cocks or hunting hounds. The word "craw" calls to mind the crop or preliminary stomach of a fowl, in which stones sometimes get stuck. If someone is urged, in typical Australian and New Zealand fashion, to "rattle his dags," hopefully he knows enough to hurry up even though, fortunately, he has no "dags" to set a-jangling. These are telltale clumps of wool matted with dung that often adorn the rear end of a sheep.

Someone who is incompetent or ill-equipped to deal with a situation might be described as being "like a rubber-nosed woodpecker in a petrified forest." Of course, a woodpecker isn't endowed with a nose; a strong bill is what allows him to "live up to his name." But never mind the technicality; the rubber-nosed-woodpecker analogy in the expression does a good job of highlighting someone's complete inability to deal with a hard or difficult situation. On the other hand, if somebody is described as "bird brained," so as to signify an utter lack of intelligence, the analogy "misses the mark," for many species of birds have been shown, through modern experiments and observations, to be quite intelligent. Consider the crow who can learn the technique of dropping pebbles into a narrow container of water in order to raise the water level far enough for him to reach and devour a floating piece of meat, an ability that was foretold in "The Crow and the Pitcher," one of Aesop's fables.

The anatomy of the pig has received particular attention in the expressions we use. "To make a pig's ear" of something is "to make a hash of it," although "a pig's ear" in Cockney rhyming slang, is something you imbibe, namely beer. "On a pig's back" means living a life of luxury, "high off the hog," where the best meat is to be found, while "in a pig's eye" is used to express disbelief.

The eyes of certain other animals are also singled out as indicative of a human state, action or perspective, as in "bright eyed and bushy tailed," referring to an alertness akin to that of a squirrel, "making sheep's eyes," which involves casting amorous glances at someone, and "having a bird's eye view," suggesting a panoramic view of things from above, or, at the other extreme, "having a worm's eye view," as if a worm could see.

An adorable child is often described as "cute as a bug's ear." This is an odd expression because bugs don't have ears, any more than worms have eyes, although they do have an acute sense of sound. The ears of a hippopotamus, by comparison, are unmistakable. In southern Africa, "the ears of the hippo" is a favorite way of describing something that is only a small part of a much larger situation or problem, most of which remains concealed. That same perception is also conveyed by "the tip of the iceberg." For an African, a submerged hippopotamus, with only its ears and eyes visible above the water, is of course a much more familiar reference point than an iceberg, which is likely "to leave him cold."

If you "couldn't care less" about something, you might make that point, in disdainful slang, by saying "I couldn't give a rat's ass." The rat is held in somewhat higher esteem in the Australian colloquial expression "flash as a rat with a gold tooth," used to describe someone who is particularly dashing or ostentatious or, as the British would say, "dressed up like a dog's dinner." The image of the rat in this expression is especially appealing because it's so incongruous given the usual reputation of the rat as unattractive vermin.

Almost as absurd as the gold-toothed rat is getting something "straight from the horse's mouth," which is to say from an authoritative source. Mr. Ed, The Talking Horse, is the only horse I'm aware of who was able to speak. Never just plain "Ed," he was the star of a TV show from the 1960s. However, he was silenced by the 1970s with the show's cancellation and his steadfast refusal to accept any further speaking roles. Of course, the idea of a horse with Mr. Ed's communication skills is preposterous enough to amount to "a lot of horse feathers." Except in the case of Pegasus, the winged horse deity, feathers on a horse are about "as useful as lips on a chicken" or "as useful as tits on a bull." The last two expressions are popular ironic similes. The initial adjective "useful" sets up an expectation that an example will follow of something that has considerable utility. Then, in an ironic twist, the example actually offered up is a body part for which the animal, to which it's ascribed, would have no use whatsoever.

Of the expressions that appear to refer to human rather than animal body parts, "green around the gills" sounds fishy in its description of someone who looks ill or nauseated. But, in fact, humans do have gills as that term can mean the flesh between a person's jaw and ears, as well as the respiratory organs of a fish. Thus, "loaded to the gills" also makes good sense, in this case as a way of indicating that a person is filled up with booze and, therefore, quite simply drunk. When a person is filled up with food, the saturation point is at a similar level in the description, "stuffed to the eyeballs."

Someone who is "wet behind the ears" is lacking in experience much as a newborn animal, whose ears shield areas of the skin with the result that those areas are the last to dry after the birthing process. Several prominent figures, including President Barack Obama, have recently used a new phrase, "green behind the ears," without apparently intending to convey a figurative meaning any different from that of "wet behind the ears."

The expressions "don't get your tail in a knot" and "I'm freezing my tail off" notionally attribute a tail to a human. That's also the case with the saying "don't let your mouth overload your tail," which is used in the American south to caution against "running off at the mouth" by talking too much. Another warning "watch your tail" is much like "watch your back" and "watch your ass" in urging alertness, especially against something that might sneak up from behind and blindside you. A Jamaican proverb explains that things can quickly go wrong if this warning is ignored since "fire deh a moos-moos tail, him think a cool breeze," which translates as "fire can be brewing at the tail of a mouse and he thinks it's a refreshing zephyr."

Many facial expressions are exposed in our verbal expressions. A person may be described as "putting on a brave face," "putting on a long face" and "screwing up his face" as opposed to "keeping a straight face." Specific facial features are captured by "cocking an eyebrow," "furrowing the brow," "having a twinkle in the eye" and "keeping a stiff upper lip," thought to be a typically British characteristic.

The significance of facial expressions is brought out by the saying, "for news of the heart, ask the face." Sometimes identified as Cambodian in origin, sometimes as Guinean or simply West African, this saying recognizes that a form of body language, transmitted through the face, can be a reliable indicator of one's true emotions. A similar British saying recognizes that "the eyes are the window to the soul" and, therefore, that they disclose one's true nature. This was offered up by the narrator in Rosamund Lupton's best selling novel *Sister* as an excuse for limiting eye contact with her fiancé. As she put it: "We hadn't stared into each other's eyes because if eyes are the window to the soul, it would be a little rude and embarrassing to look in." You've "got to hand it to" her, she was certainly sensitive to privacy concerns, but at the expense of a bit of innocent intimacy.

"Don't cut off your nose to spite your face" is a saying that advises against harming yourself in attempting to harm someone else. The American entertainer Britney Spears, would have fallen headlong into this trap had she followed through on her threat to distribute free copies of a sex tape she had made with her one-time husband, Kevin Federline. Her motive was to prevent him from profiting from the sale of the tape. In the end, she decided that the best course was "to save face," including the personal embarrassment that would come from releasing the tape. She, therefore, refrained from the suicidal course of "slitting her own throat," having "come within an eyelash" or a "hair's breadth" of "cutting off her nose to spite her face."

Although there's often more than one way "to save face," the American comedian Steven Wright suggested that, "the best way [is] to keep the lower part shut," which is to say "clap your trap." You would then be unable to "put your foot in your mouth" because "a closed mouth gathers no foot." Not surprisingly, anyone with a persisting propensity for putting his foot in his mouth is often described as suffering from "foot-in-mouth disease" which, fortunately, has a mortality rate considerably lower than that of the foot and mouth disease infecting cattle that inspired the similar sounding description of the human condition.

Someone who exclaims, "I'll be gob smacked" is so shocked as to be dumbfounded. Consequently, nothing further is likely to come out of his mouth in the immediate term. While the word "gob" has gobs of meanings, the one it bears in this expression is "mouth" coming from the Gaelic term for that part of the face. The exclamatory expression "well, hush my mouth" indicates a more subdued level of shock or surprise.

Someone who "talks a good game" is "all mouth and no trousers," meaning "all talk and no action." The sense of these last two expressions is also conveyed, using the same format, by "all yak and no sack," "all bark and no bite," "all hammer and no nail," "all sizzle and no steak," "all froth and no beer" and, as a Texan might say, "all hat and no cattle."

"Living from hand to mouth" implies that everything at hand is consumed. It all goes to meeting immediate needs, leaving nothing to be "saved for a rainy day." If someone endures this state of poverty "with a stiff upper lip" and without "making a poor mouth of it," he may be prompted, despite his stoicism, to repeat the common complaint, that "there's too much month left at the end of the money." If his fortune turns, he may be able to secure enough cash "to make tucker," as they say in Australia, which means sufficient to cover all the food bills. But if he's a lazy lout from Newfoundland, a home to the Atlantic lobster, "his claws will never maintain his jaws."

Someone who's "born with a silver spoon in his mouth" is unlikely to be in difficult financial straits for he comes from a family that is wealthy and probably of high social standing "to boot." When a silver plated, or better still sterling silver, advantage is combined with a genetic inclination "to say the wrong thing at the wrong time," that happenstance may be put down to the fact that the person was "born with a silver foot in his mouth."

The tongue is often associated in our expressions with speech. Any words that come out of the mouth through "a slip of the tongue" are put down to pure accident. That's how a speaker will try to excuse a play on words when he immediately adds "no pun intended." This last expression has been explained by an experienced punster with a story of sending ten puns to his friends in the hope that at least one would be "music to the ears" and make them laugh. Alas, no pun in ten did.

"To hold your tongue" or "to bite your tongue" is to remain silent, while recognizing that this may be agonizingly difficult. Anyone who refuses to "hold his tongue" or "bite his tongue" and threatens to speak rudely might be admonished "to keep a civil tongue in his head." After all, anything scandalous, including inappropriate language, might "set tongues wagging."

Someone who breaks silence and proves to be a smooth talker could be described as "having a silver tongue" or as being "a silver tongued devil." Since silver is a valuable commodity, it might be assumed that this is a positive thing. But these expressions aren't always used in a complimentary way. They may carry the suggestion that the person to whom they're applied is a bit too glib, someone we might describe, uncharitably, as a "motormouth" or, more elegantly, as "inebriated with the exuberance of his own verbosity," borrowing British Prime Minister Benjamin Disraeli's description of his Liberal rival Sir William Gladstone.

"Running off at the mouth" and "talking [someone's] ear off" are other anatomically inclined indications of verbosity. They're frequently observed in North America. Someone who is guilty of these excesses might be described in Australia as "bashing the ear." The responsible party might then be branded as an "earbasher."

"Having the gift of the gab" is an alternative way of saying that someone has a considerable facility with speech. Legend has it that "the gift of the gab" is something you acquire after you've planted your lips, in the form of a kiss, on the Blarney Stone in Ireland. But that very origin suggests that the "gift of the gab," which sounds like some sort of blessing, isn't always a favorable endowment. It may simply be a cover for "a bit of blarney," which is to say deceptive nonsense.

In the bygone era of the phonograph record, someone who "talks a blue streak" or "talks nineteen to the dozen" was said to have been "vaccinated with a Victrola needle." For members of the younger generation, that expression is likely "to fall on deaf ears" or "to go in one ear and out the other" for lack of an appreciation of the mechanics of the old fashioned record player, which involved a special purpose needle tracing the grooves on a rotating vinyl disc. The recording company RCA Victor produced the required needles under its trade name Victrola.

The meaning of many of the expressions that feature the nose is "as plain as the nose on your face;" the meaning of others needs some explanation. "Putting your nose to the grindstone" means getting on, seriously and actively, with a task at hand, much like "putting your shoulder to the wheel." This can be explained by imagining a knife sharpener who brings his face, and, therefore, its most prominent feature, the nose, "within a whisker" of his grinding wheel. This would allow him to hold the knife blade at the correct proximity and angle to the wheel in order to come up with a sharp knife. Someone who isn't an experienced knife sharpener, however, may get into trouble by following this technique. "Case in point," the principal character in this old riddle: "What do you get when an army officer 'puts his nose to the grindstone'?" The answer, "not to put too fine a point on it," is "A sharp major."

If that riddle "hits the wrong note," there's another facetious play on the expression that goes like this; "Keep your eye on the ball, your ear to the ground, your nose to the grindstone. Now try to work in that position." You would be lucky indeed if you didn't "flip your wig," an action that's also known as "flipping your lid," in a sudden loss of composure.

If you were to seek instructions on how to get some place and you were told to just "follow your nose," you would probably know that you should go straight ahead or, perhaps, just "follow your guts," which is to say your instincts. Yet the nose can be misleading as it was for the woman in this limerick:

There once was a lady from Trent
Whose nose was most horribly bent

One day I suppose
She followed her nose
And nobody knows where she went

She might have been better off if she "couldn't see the nose in front of her face," but that would suggest, in a figurative sense, that she was missing the obvious, which could just as easily have led her astray. Of course, there is always the alternative of forgetting the nose and "following the heart," which allows the guiding force of passion to take over.

"To rack your brain" is "to put your thinking cap on" and try, with great effort, to remember something. The brain is a versatile organ that allows you "to push the envelope" and "think outside the box." "Thinking outside the box" is a recent expression that originated in the United States. The expression is used so frequently to refer to unconventional thinking, particularly in the business community, that it has become a cliché.

The expression alludes to a brainteaser, known as the Nine Dots Puzzle, which presents the challenge of connecting the dots that make up a box, as in the diagram below, by drawing four straight, continuous lines without lifting pen or pencil from paper.

A solution to the puzzle is shown on the following page.

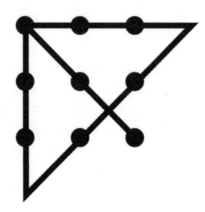

This solution involves "thinking outside the box" in the literal sense. It goes against the natural instinct to treat the limits of the box as a boundary within which the puzzle is to be solved.

Taco Bell, the fast food chain specializing in Mexican fare, capitalized on the public's familiarity with the expression in a recent advertising campaign urging consumers to "think outside the bun," an obvious dig at the ubiquitous hamburger, the "bread and butter" of competitors such as McDonalds. Other business enterprises, especially in the jewelry trade, have urged us to "think inside the box." "Thinking outside the box" may be the better course, however, for "you'll have a whole eternity to think inside the box," as many a wise person has observed. That's certainly a long time, in prospect, to be "buried in thought."

The single act of "licking your elbow" is sometimes used to signify the impossible, even though the video-sharing website YouTube has many examples of people licking one of their elbows. The phrase has recently become popular, in its Arabic form, through its use in reference to the near impossible odds against ousting Sudanese dictator, President Omar al-Bashir. The elbow isn't a destination but simply an inconvenient way station in a colloquial expression from the American south: "I had to go around my elbow to get to my thumb," meaning that I had to do something simple the hard way.

A "rule of thumb" is a rough and ready means of estimating something. The best explanation for this expression, "by any measure," is that it comes from the practice of wood workers using a thumb to make certain measurements. In other words, a manual rule or ruler was handily substituted for the usual wooden ruler. However, in the 1970s, a story began circulating to the effect that the expression came from an old common law rule that a man was allowed to beat his wife if he didn't use a stick any wider than his thumb. This became a modern feminist fiction through the ensuing couple of decades as the expression was used as evidence of society's historic tolerance of wife abuse. This theory about the origin of the expression would draw some credibility from the fact that the U.S. Commission on Civil Rights issued a report on wife abuse in 1982 with the title *Under the Rule of Thumb.*

There are a couple of fallacies in this latter day explanation for a "rule of thumb." For one thing, there is no etymological evidence to support the idea that a "rule of thumb" is related to wife abuse. For another, there was never any common law rule that, effectively, permitted husbands to beat their wives with a stick of a thumb's width. An eighteenth century English judge, Sir Francis Buller, was satirized in popular cartoons as responsible for that rule. However, it's never been established that this "Judge Thumb," to give him the name by which he was ridiculed, ever formulated such a rule, let alone applied it in an actual case. Of course, debunking the myths that have surrounded a "rule of thumb" shouldn't be used to deny the reality of domestic violence.

While a "rule of thumb" can be ruled out in a spousal abuse context, there is a rule of finger on the island of Sark, one of the Channel Islands. This dependency of the British Crown is home to about 600 souls. The rule of finger, to which the inhabitants are bound, recognizes that a husband is allowed to beat his wife subject to two limitations. He must use a stick no thicker than his little finger and he must not draw blood. This has been the rule in this tiny isolated corner of the U.K. for over 400 years.

Several expressions describe well understood gestures that evidence a person's feelings about, or reactions to, some other person or some situation or thing. "Giving a thumbs up," "keeping your fingers crossed," "thumbing your nose" or "cocking a snook" at someone or something," "giving [someone] the finger" and "patting [someone] on the back" all fall into this category. Each of these expressions describes a particular form of body language, thus capturing in words the visual signal conveyed by that form.

The expressions "giving a thumbs up" and "keeping your fingers crossed," and the gestures they describe, must be used with caution because of the different interpretations the gestures are given in different parts of the world. While putting thumbs up is generally an affirmative action, often a sign of approval, it can be an obscene insult in the Middle East and parts of West Africa and South America, much worse than "thumbing your nose" at someone and more like "giving [someone] the finger." While "keeping your fingers crossed" is generally meant to indicate a wish for good fortune, if you were to display crossed fingers to a friend in Turkey, this would evidence the breaking of the bond of friendship.

"A thumbs up" usually involves putting a single thumb in the vertical position. The popular view, which has not gone unchallenged, is that "giving a thumbs up" was originally something that spectators did at a Roman gladiatorial contest to express their conviction that the defeated combatant should be spared the penalty of death normally visited upon a loser, while "giving a thumbs down" indicated support for the imposition of the death penalty. The ancient Romans were clearly at the forefront in "giving [someone] the finger" for this "single digit salute" was well known to them as *digitus impudicus* or the "impudent finger," which carries the same implication as the gesture would today.

The British expression "to cock a snook" serves as an insult or a mark of disrespect. The gesture it describes involves putting thumb to nose, which suggests that a "snook" may be a "snout," and extending the fingers upwards and aligning them vertically with the target of derision, as in this diagram:

The amount of abuse dispensed is increased, dramatically, by wiggling the fingers and sticking out the tongue. Simply "snubbing your nose" is a half-cocked version of this more elaborate gesture. The full version is often called a "five-finger salute" in the United States.

"To pat [someone] on the back" is to compliment or encourage someone, whether by using that expression or the physical gesture it describes. But the expression can be turned against a self indulgent individual by portraying him as "breaking his arm patting himself on the back."

Other, largely unintentional body language may give something away about a person's condition, situation or attitude. In the American south, someone may develop "a hitch in his gitalong," meaning that he walks with a limp or, in a broader sense, that he has encountered an impediment to his plans. But, if someone has "a swagger in his step," that can be indicative of considerable confidence.

It sounds very serious when a person who is bankrupt is portrayed as having "gone belly up," a position that is commonly associated with being "dead in the water." It's as if a bankrupt could never be resuscitated and obtain a discharge from bankruptcy. The expression is, essentially, dysphemistic, portraying the state of affairs as worse than it usually is.

If you say that you "have no stomach for" something, it usually means that you simply can't deal with it. Beatrice Lillie, the English star of stage, screen and music hall, was once asked, in an interview, about belly dancing. This prompted her to say that she had "no stomach for that kind of thing," leaving everyone in a quandary as to whether her body or her mind wasn't up to it.

The imprecise word "guts" can mean the stomach and intestines, all the internal organs of the body or, as a slang term, determination. It's used in several expressions. If you were to "spill your guts" or "spew your guts," you would be confessing, telling all or revealing secret or personal information. This is clearly related to the Australian expression "to come one's guts" meaning to inform on someone, or "dob [someone] in," to the police or other authority.

In the U.S. military and in sports, "no guts, no glory" has been used to emphasize the fact that victory entails raw courage and determination. The Dodge Ram truck is advertised in North America as possessing both of these qualities through the simple tagline, "GutsGlory." Too much in the way of guts can cause trouble however. If someone boldly "jumps in with both feet" before thinking something through, he may be justifiably criticized as having "more guts than brains."

The English have a wonderful, if graphic, way of threatening punishment with the promise "I'll have your guts for garters." This alliterative expression has begun to fall into disuse, perhaps owing to the declining need for garters in light of the development of the elasticized, self-supporting sock or perhaps because it takes a good deal of intestinal fortitude to stomach the gruesome nature of the threat.

The political correctness movement is sometimes said, usually "tongue in cheek," to stand firmly against "sinistermanualistic" language. This language is of a kind that stigmatizes or could be offensive to a disadvantaged minority made up of those who are dominantly left-handed. Consequently, it would be wrong to describe the act of insulting someone in the guise of praising him as "paying [him] a left-handed compliment." This is especially so when "paying [him] a backhanded compliment" would serve the same purpose ambidextrously. It would also be inappropriate to say, even without a sinister motive, that someone "has two left hands" in order to draw attention to his awkwardness. Better to use the British expression "all fingers and thumbs."

If sinistermanualistic language is out, then it would seem to follow that it should be wrong to refer in a negative way to any left side extremities, the feet as well as the hands. Therefore, to describe someone as "having two left feet," to emphasize his clumsiness, would also fail to meet the high standards of political correctness to which some aspire. If you were to tell a person "put your best foot forward," this would avoid any awkwardness; it could be the left foot, it could be the right foot. If those who received this advice were to take it up, they could fairly be said to have "gotten off on the right foot." That would simply mean that they had made a good start, putting the correct foot forward, which could be the left or the right. If you were to say that they had "jumped in with both feet," in explaining their wholehearted involvement in an activity or a venture, there would likewise be no invidious distinction between the two feet. However, it would not be a good move to "jump in with both feet" in order to find out how deep a body of water might be. An African proverb wisely warns that "only a fool tests the depth of the water with both feet."

"To get a leg up" evokes an image of a frequent dog posture. It's not surprising, therefore, that a number of dog walking services have adopted the style name Get a Leg Up. But the leg underpinning the expression is not that of a dog but that of a human, in particular the leg of an equestrian who gets a boost, when he places a foot in the cupped hands of another, to help him get seated in his horse's saddle. That's what lies behind the figurative meaning of the expression, which is to give someone an advantage or a head start, often over the competition. One way you might "get a leg up" is by someone "giving a heads up," which would warn you of something coming your way for which you should be prepared.

Something that's expensive or overpriced "costs an arm and a leg," which uses a combination of metaphor and hyperbole to make the point. The expression is said to go back to an exchange between God and Adam, the first human in the biblical record of creation, which has been spiced up with more than a dash of modern day sexist humor. By this revised account, Adam was lonely as the one and only human being and asked God what could be done to provide him with some companionship. God replied, "I can make you a woman." "But what is woman?" asked Adam "in all innocence." God explained to Adam; "She will be beautiful, so much so that you won't be able to take your eyes off her; she'll clean house and do everything you ask of her; she'll wait on you hand and foot; she'll never spend your money without asking; she'll never have a headache when you're feeling amorous; she'll never tempt you with forbidden fruit." Naturally wary, Adam asked "what will it cost me?" to which God replied, "an arm and a leg." Adam thought for a moment and then asked God one final question, "what can I get for a rib?" "And the rest is history," as they say.

If this story was passed off to a gullible person as the biblical truth, it would amount to "pulling his leg," which is really a light-hearted way of saying "putting him on." In the U.K., a person who realizes that his leg is being pulled may be prompted to extend the following invitation, carrying the idiom one step further; "pull the other one, it's got bells on." The Australian equivalent is "pull the other one, it plays jingle bells," indicating in effect: I'm not that gullible, so "don't come the raw prawn with me." But someone who's prepared to admit to pulling another person's leg might change the idiom and say, in a Yankee manner of speaking, "just yanking your chain," which is often reduced to the short hand JYYC in text communications.

Several expressions involve similes that describe a body part in terms of an inanimate object, for example "a face like a can of worms," "a mind like a steel trap," "a mind like a sponge" and its opposite "a mind like a sieve," which means that you have to strain to think of something and, even then, may not be able to filter it out. "In a different vein," the saying "you can't get blood from a stone" stands firmly opposed to equating an essential element of the higher animals with an inanimate object.

Other expressions use a metaphor that envisages some element of an inanimate object as if it were a body part, for example "the legs of a table," "the lip of a cup" and "the eye of a needle." We know what each of these expressions means without first thinking in terms of a leg, a lip or an eye as part of a living body. The metaphor in each of the three expressions is, therefore, a dead metaphor. It's been used so often that it no longer involves a transferred image, which is the badge of a metaphor. I'll spare the reader from the debate about whether a dead metaphor is really a metaphor at all, for that debate is almost as futile as the one about whether a zombie is a person.

Many expressions include anatonyms, which are words for a part of the body used as a verb. "Thumb your nose at [someone or something]", "foot the bill," "shoulder responsibility," "face the music," "eye the target," "unable to stomach [something]" and "flesh [something] out" are some examples. It could be said, with appropriate apologies, that the Canadian author Robertson Davies declined to "flesh out" the title of his novel *What's Bred in the Bone*, which he drew from the saying "what's bred in the bone will come out in the flesh," signifying that "blood will tell."

The anatonym, "toe the line," is sometimes distorted to become "tow the line" through the substitution of a homophone for the word "toe." This hasn't changed the figurative sense in which the expression is used, which is to indicate conformity with a rule or standard. There's considerable dispute, however, as to the origin of "toe the line." The most plausible explanations for the expression are grounded in naval drill and sporting rules. At sea, enlisted sailors were required to line up on deck for inspection from time to time. To ensure that they formed up in a straight line, they all had to place their toes along a seam between the deck planks. The seams were prominent markers because they were sealed with pitch or tar. In the arena of sports, to ensure a fair contest in track competitions and boxing fights, the contestants had to place their feet, and therefore their toes, on or behind a starting line. Therefore, they had to "toe the line" before the starting gun or bell sounded.

When the names of body parts are used in expressions, the purpose may be to refer to the body as a whole in an indirect way. If an "extra pair of hands" is called for or if there is a cry on board ship for "all hands on deck," the need is really for the assistance of the individuals to whom the hands belong. Ogden Nash recognized that having "time on your hands" implicates more than just the hands when he wrote;

> Is time on my hands? Yes, it is on my hands and my face and my
> torso and my tendons of Achilles,
> And frankly, it gives me the willies.

If someone says he "hates the guts" of another person, he seems to be pretty anatomically specific about the subject matter of his distaste, but he really means that he has an abiding dislike of the whole person, "guts and all." When Mark Antony, in Shakespeare's play *Julius Caesar*, opened his eulogy of Caesar, by inviting his friends, Romans and countrymen to "lend me your ears," he was asking for the full attention of the members of his audience whose ears were but a part of their cognitive systems.

These expressions illustrate a little known figure of speech called a synecdoche, by which something is described in terms of one of its components. A synecdoche is like a metaphor since it involves an image that isn't to be taken literally. It only conveys part of the picture.

This kind of imagery is evident in the sayings "the hand that rocks the cradle rules the world" and "an army marches on its stomach." The first of these sayings comes from a poem by William Ross Wallace, published in 1865, that praises mothers as influential forces in the world. The second of the sayings calls attention to the importance of food to the over-all wellbeing and fighting fitness of soldiers. The collective noun "army" is used here to refer to the soldiers that make up an army, each of whom has a stomach that needs to be fed. The saying has been attributed to both Napoleon and Frederick the Great. For Napoleon, it would have represented a lesson learned from his Russian campaign of 1812, which failed badly due to inadequate provisioning along with severe winter weather, disease and defections.

Several of the expressions that use body language describe situations that are impossible, implausible or just plain wrong from a biological perspective, such as those expressions noted earlier in this chapter that refer to humans as if they had a tail. No one "has eyes in the back of his head," yet this expression is used to indicate that someone has the ability to observe everything that's going on around him. In this case, the figurative meaning is easy to figure out if it's recognized that the expression uses exaggeration for effect. Similarly, no one actually "has eyes bigger than his stomach," but that expression serves as a readily recognizable description of someone who takes more food than he can possibly eat. The mind doesn't have eyes, yet "in your mind's eye" is easily understood as a reference to your imagination.

Someone who has had a narrow escape or a close call has come through "by the skin of his teeth." But a tooth doesn't have skin and its protective layer of enamel could hardly be mistaken for epidermis. Being "long in the tooth" as a metaphor for advanced age is counterintuitive since teeth are worn down over time. But the expression makes "a lot of horse sense," for the receding gums of aging horses mean that, "for all appearances," their teeth are longer. The evidence of this is incontrovertible because it comes "straight from the horse's mouth." "Long in the tooth" is one of several idiomatic expressions based on features or actions involving animals that have no human counterparts. These include raising hackles, ruffling feathers and rattling dags, as we've seen in the previous chapter.

Someone who is upset or feeling slighted may be said "to have his nose out of joint" But the nose isn't articulated and it doesn't have bone in it. If something "tickles your funny bone," it appeals to your sense of humor. But the actual sensation that the expression describes comes from putting pressure on the ulna nerve in the elbow and the resulting effect is only funny in the sense of odd. At the elbow, the ulna nerve passes over the humerus, the bone in the upper arm. Therefore, there's an explanation, but only through the device of a lowly pun, as to why something that "tickles the funny bone" conjures up a humorous (humerus) thought.

When something "warms the cockles of the heart," it produces a very different sensation—a fuzzy feeling of gratification. Cockles, however, are a variety of mollusk. They don't figure as part of the heart. The only obvious connection is that they're both bivalves and, as such, share a common shape. If someone is envious, he might be said to be "eating his heart out," which is a physical impossibility and, in any event, would be fatal. The same thing could be said of "having your heart in your mouth," a symptom of alarm. "Having your heart in the right place," however, is normal and perfectly positive in its implications. A recent contestant on the reality TV show *American Idol* must not have entered the competition with "her heart in the right place" for she later said that she had became so excited that her "heart about fell out of [her] stomach."

While you might "pour your heart out" to someone, it's your spleen, which borders the stomach, that you would be venting if you were overtaken by a bout of anger, also known as "a fit of pique." The expression "vent your spleen" has its origin in early medicine, which attributed ill humor to that organ of the body, offering a convenient physiological excuse for bad temper. These days, if you vent about something, it's more likely to be said that you've "gotten it off your chest," suggesting that pent up emotions come from that equally improbable spot. Or could it be that the liver is the source of the problem, as suggested by the expression "having shit on your liver," a favored Australian way of explaining bad temper? This particular diagnosis of the cause is consistent with the fact that the word "bile," which is the name of a bitter fluid secreted by the liver, has long been used, in an alternative sense, to mean irritability.

Someone in motion who isn't blessed with acute observation skills may fall down in a dramatic fashion often portrayed as "head over heels." This also describes the intensity with which someone may fall in love. However, an abrupt physical fall is likely to propel someone heels over head rather than the reverse. "Spring forward, fall back" has the appearance of a saying about body movements. But it's actually a mnemonic reminder of the direction—forward or backward—in which clocks should be turned, by an hour, in the spring and the fall of the year. It is, therefore, an aid to "falling into step" with Daylight Saving Time, before the summer, and with Standard Time, before the winter.

On occasion, it's possible to substitute one body part for another without disturbing the meaning of an expression. You might "turn a blind eye" or "turn a deaf ear" to something and, in either case, you would be deliberately ignoring it. When someone is said to have "green fingers," it's the same as if he was described as having a "green thumb." Both expressions are used to indicate a talent for gardening. The difference is that "green fingers" has found favor in the U.K. and Australia while a "green thumb" has "found fertile ground" in the U.S. and Canada.

If you were adamant about some position you had taken, you might "dig in your heels" or "dig in your toes." If you wanted "to go out on a limb" with that position, you could "put your neck on the block" or "put your head on the block." Someone who witnessed your situation might come to your aid and "save your neck" or "save your skin." You might be happy if a rescuer "stuck his neck out" on your behalf. On the other hand, you might object to his uninvited intervention and react with the Irish request that he "wind his neck in," which is to say "mind his own business."

A formula for expressing a reaction to a particular situation or happening is that it's "better than" an attack on a particular part of the body. There are several colorful expressions that fit this mold, including "better than a poke in the eye with a burnt [or sharp] stick," "better than slap in the belly [or the face] with a wet fish," and "better than a kick in the ass with a frozen boot."

"Better than a kick in the teeth," "better than a smack in the eye" and "better than kick up the arse" are in the same style but they aren't quite as graphic since they omit any reference to the instrument responsible for the attack. A better-than expression is often used with the implication that the situation is only marginally better than the form of physical assault described in the expression.

The senses of smell, touch, taste, hearing and seeing involve the body's reactions to various external stimuli. Each of the five senses features in a number of expressions and sayings, although when the word "taste" is used, it's generally with the alternative meaning of a liking or partiality for something. The so-called sixth sense is recognized in "to have a gut feeling" about something.

"To smell a rat" is to sense deception while the "smell of blood" alerts one to the vulnerability of an opponent. "Take time to smell the roses" serves as a reminder to pause, from time to time, to enjoy life's pleasures while "wake up and smell the coffee" serves, much like "a java jolt," as an abrupt message to get realistic about an unpleasant situation.

The sense of smell is closely associated with the nose. It's not surprising, therefore, that the expression "follow your nose" has been commercialized in a way that alludes to that sense. It serves as the name of a children's board game that involves the matching of various aroma samples with corresponding images on the board. It's also the favorite call of Toucan Sam, the promotional character for the breakfast cereal Froot Loops, who has the ability to sniff out the delicious fruit flavors of this Kellogg's product from a great distance.

Someone who's "a soft touch" is an easy mark while someone who "has the Midas touch" stands to make money "hand over fist" and accumulate a lot of wealth from almost anything he tackles. King Midas, of Greek legend, found that his special power to turn things to gold, with a simple touch, was actually a curse. The most crushing evidence of this was his daughter becoming a golden statue when she fell into his arms. Not surprisingly, this moved him to ask the god Dionysus to revoke his magical power and undo everything he had done, accidentally or on purpose, with that power. "To have the Midas touch" ignores this aspect of the originating mythology for it carries no practical warning or moral judgment about the effortless accumulation of wealth. Midas, Inc., the international auto service chain best known for its mufflers, uses the slogan "trust the Midas touch." This too "flies in the face of" the mythology, for King Midas, understandably, lost faith in his touch.

The simple verbal aside "touch wood" or "knock on wood" is often used to reinforce an expectation. Of course, in this pragmatic modern world, few would put any real faith in the capacity of wood to make a wish come true. If someone says "touch wood" or "knock on wood," or pointedly carries out that action, it's usually simply to acknowledge that a little bit of luck will be needed for the realization of an expectation, a hope or a goal. That same acknowledgement might be made by the gesture of crossing fingers if no wood is handy.

"Hear, hear" is a contraction of "hear him, hear him." It's used as a way of expressing agreement with a speaker, particularly in a parliamentary setting where applause is forbidden. However, a great many people think the expression is actually "here, here," which sounds the same. That coincidence was used to advantage by Richard Brinsley Sheridan, the playwright and one-time member of the British Parliament. When plagued by constant interruptions of "hear, hear" from a lone member of the House of Commons, he departed from the prepared speech he was delivering in the House, posing the rhetorical question: "Where shall we find a more foolish knave than this or a more knavish fool than this?" The vocal member reacted in his usual way, but when he realized that he could be taken to have implicated himself in answer to the question, he "held his peace" for the rest of the speech.

A politician who wants to get a message heard selectively may engage in "dog whistle politics." That expression refers to the practice of appealing to voters with racist inclinations through policies that aren't overtly racist. These policies nonetheless carry a message that is likely to resonate with those voters but, like the high pitched tone of a whistle designed to give directions to a dog, can't be heard by others. There is never an apology for "dog whistle politics" from the politician who has adopted this form of political pandering, for that would "blow the whistle" on his tactic and his message would then be heard by all for what it really was.

Children, like politicians, generally want to "make their presence felt" by the noises they make, but if their vocalizations "get out of hand," they may be reminded that "children should be seen and not heard." A youngster could, however, take this saying and "turn it to his advantage." That's recognized in the Wellerism: "'Children should be seen and not heard,' as the boy said when he couldn't recite his lesson."

Someone who has no sense of hearing at all may be described, in inanimate terms, as "deaf as a post" or "deaf as a doornail," which is not surprising because both a post and a doornail are completely lifeless. In the case of the doornail, the expression "dead as a doornail" is an emphatic reminder of that fact. The same "accoustically challenged" individual, may also be described, in animate terms, as "deaf as an adder" or "deaf as a haddock." The adder expression echoes a biblical passage while the haddock expression has many possible sources. One fanciful explanation was offered by *The Gentleman's Magazine*, a London-based periodical that flourished through most of the eighteenth and nine-teenth centuries. By that account, originating with Cornish fishermen, the devil had a frustrating angling experience because a fish was con-stantly stealing his bait without getting caught. After a while, the devil became so annoyed that he put his mouth close to the water and yelled "Ha, dick," equating the fish with a stupid and irritating person, "I'll tackle thee yet." The noise broke the fish's ear drums, making him stone deaf and, ever since, the fish has been known as Ha dick or haddock. Of course, the story itself is really a cod, which in British terminology means a hoax as well as "a fish of a different stripe."

"To see the light" is to have a stroke of understanding and "to see the light at the end of the tunnel" is to see signs of hope that difficult times or some lengthy task or process may soon be over. However, having "tunnel vision" doesn't really help in bringing something into full view. It's actually an impediment to human perception since it signifies narrow mindedness or, scientifically speaking, a loss of peripheral vision such as might be brought on by an advanced case of glaucoma. Robert Lowell, the American poet, wrote that "if we see light at the end of the tunnel, it's the light of the oncoming train," from which there would usually be no escape for anyone in the tunnel. Thus, he turned an optimistic expression of impending relief or satisfaction into a fatalistic representation of impending doom. We can only speculate that, at the time, he was in a depressive phase of the bipolar disorder from which he suffered.

"Seeing is believing" recognizes that if you see something with your own eyes, you're likely to believe in its existence or qualities however unexpected that existence or those qualities might be. The saying has tremendous potential in product advertising. This has been exploited by many manufacturers, most prominently by Elizabeth Arden, for its cosmetic lines, and by Nintendo, for 3DS, its three-dimensional portable game console. The English poet Ralph Hodgson turned the saying around when he observed that "some things have got to be believed to be seen." He may have had "in his mind's eye" the Loch Ness Monster and other apparitions such as the three G's; ghosts, ghouls and gremlins.

Someone who is "seeing challenged," either for failure to focus or because of a visual impairment, may be described, in an extreme case, as "blind as a bat" or "blind as a mole." It's been said that those who believe that bats are blind just can't see the truth. Most large species of bats can, in fact, see better than humans, although smaller bats that hunt by night rely to a large extent on "seeing" with their ears through echolocation, a sort of sonar system. Although it's a much less common expression, "blind as a mole" is a better way of describing an inability to see since the vision of moles has become extremely limited as a result of their subterranean existence.

When bodily functions, or malfunctions, are the subject matter of expressions, those expressions are often of the slang variety. For example, "shit or get off the pot" directs someone "in no uncertain terms" to get on with a job or else "give it up as a bad job." Crass as the expression may sound, its use can always be forgiven, as with other rough slang, by simply saying "pardon the French," a language thought to be more *risqué* in its terms and expressions than English.

The act of vomiting, especially as it follows excessive drinking, has been variously described, in somewhat milder slang expressions, as "tossing your cookies," "laughing at the carpet," "barfing up your boots," "driving the porcelain bus," which envisages someone clinging to the toilet as if it were a steering wheel, and "yawning in technicolor." The last of these expressions was, no doubt, inspired by the mainline expression "dreaming in technicolor." Perhaps the cleverest and best disguised expression for this wretched condition is "talking to Ralph on the big white phone." This imaginative description comes out of the subculture of American college students. "Ralph" is an onomatopoeic representation of the act of retching and the "big white phone" is a metaphor for a toilet. The expression is certainly "close to the knuckle," as the Brits would say, since it borders the limits of decency. If, despite the disguise, the expression were to "leave a bad taste in the mouth" of a California Valley Girl, she would probably say, in a supercilious tone, "gag me with a spoon."

15

FOOD FOR THOUGHT

Eat, drink and be merry, for tomorrow ye diet.

William Gilmore Beymer, American author

Not surprisingly, food is often "front of mind," for we can't be sustained without it. That makes it fruitful fodder for our language. This chapter examines the smorgasbord of food images in expressions and sayings that are drawn from fruits, vegetables, meat, fish and eggs, cooked and baked dishes and, more broadly, from the three main meals of the day and typical snacks in between.

Buddha is credited with the saying "we are what we think." But when our thoughts turn to food, we're reminded, in a modern twist on the Buddhist philosophy, that "you are what you eat." This enigmatic saying has been called a "bromide," which does double duty in this situation since it's a term for a trite phrase as well as for something you would consume for its sedative properties.

What the saying is really getting at, somewhat inelegantly, is that the nutritional value of what you eat will be reflected in the condition of your body. As such, it's a motivational saying, intended to encourage good eating habits. It's clearly a product of our modern world where there is widespread concern about obesity and the kinds and quantities of the food we consume, which contribute to "oversizing" the population in a virtual epidemic of "globesity." When it comes to food, most of us seem to have "taken to heart" Oscar Wilde's claim, in the form of a perverted proverb, that "nothing succeeds like excess," while ignoring the proverb "after the feast the reckoning."

There's really nothing new about the suggestion that we eat sensibly for the Greek philosopher Socrates is credited with the long standing proverb, "eat to live, don't live to eat." Even the Epicureans, who favored good eating as well as the other pleasures of life, embraced moderation. In one of his many aphorisms, the Greek philosopher Epicurus noted that "a man is wealthy in proportion to the things he can do without."

Certainly, food is not "the be-all and the end-all" of human existence for "man does not live by bread alone," according to a biblical proverb, yet "bread is the staff of life," which also has biblical origins. "Bread" is used here as a symbol for food. It serves as a very different metaphor in "cast your bread upon the waters and after many days you will find it again" for most food would be pretty soggy and uninteresting after submersion. In this last proverb, also from the Bible, "bread" likely stands for anything of value. Although the proper interpretation of the proverb is unsettled and has been the subject of many sermons, the most widely accepted view is that if you give in a generous spirit, it will eventually come back to you for "whatever a man sews that will he also reap."

The proverb is often reduced to the bare injunction, "cast your bread upon the waters." As such, it proved to be a verbal trap for an unwary radio announcer who was running out of time to conclude a religious program. His hurried parting words were: "And be sure to tune in next week when the topic will be cast your broad upon the waters. This is the National Breadcasting Corporation." This now famous Spoonerism was among the broadcasting *faux pas* collected by Kermit Schafer in the first of his *Pardon my Blooper* records of the 1950s and 1960s. According to Schafer, another announcer misspoke, even more drastically, when he signed off with these words: "This is the Dominion network of the Canadian Broadcorping Castration."

For a Cockney, a loaf of bread is synonymous with a head. Thus, for him, the expression "use your head," meaning think about something carefully, translates to "use your loaf of bread" in rhyming slang. That's invariably shortened to "use your loaf." "Half a loaf is better than no bread" expresses a roughly similar notion to "a bird in the hand is worth two in the bush." Since the word "loaf" can also describe casual idling, this has led to a perversion of the traditional proverb to "half a loaf is better than no time off." In Trinidad, someone who engages in this kind of a "loaf" might be described, in terms of another food, as "liming around." That covers any kind of "hanging out," when you may be simply "shooting the breeze" or else "chewing the fat," an expression that may have originated as Cockney rhyming slang for "chat" or as a logical analogy to the prolonged movement of the jaw when trying to masticate tough fat.

Loaves of bread were always sold uncut until the late 1920s when Otto Rohwedder of Missouri, an inventor and engineer, developed an automatic machine, for commercial use, that could slice and wrap a loaf of bread. This significant invention ultimately gave birth to the expression "the greatest thing since sliced bread," which, of course, "invites the question:" What was the greatest thing before sliced bread?

In his book *Playing with Words: Humour in the English Language*, Barry Blake has reinterpreted this "slice of history," using it as the basis for this parody on the overblown style of a voice-over in a TV documentary:

Looking at this humble cottage behind me it is hard to believe that we are standing in front of the birthplace of a man who would change forever the way we live. After him life would never be the same again.

Raymond Baker left school at the age of 15 and took a job in a sawmill, and it was there that he conceived of the idea of sliced bread, when, eating his lunch at his workbench, he dropped his roll into the path of a circular saw. Now it is hard to believe today that up to the middle of the last century people bought bread in one solid mass and had to cut it themselves with a breadknife, a process which invariably resulted in a pile of crumbs and, if the operator wasn't careful, occasionally a splatter of blood or occasionally a small piece of finger.

The expression "the greatest thing since sliced bread" is used, often with a hint of cutting sarcasm, to praise a recent invention or a new development of some kind. It's no wonder that some sarcasm may creep in when the expression is used today, for it sets a pretty low threshold for measuring greatness. Many things have happened since the 1920s that far outstrip sliced bread in their positive impact on our lives. The comedienne Ellen DeGeneres has suggested that we replace the expression with "the greatest thing since pre-made margaritas."

What we're portrayed as eating in our idiomatic expressions isn't always confined to conventional foods. We may be compelled;

"to eat our hearts out," if we're consumed with envy;

"to eat someone's dust," if we fall far behind in a competitive situation;

"to eat our words" or "to eat our hats," if something we've promised doesn't come about.

We may also be forced "to eat crow," a worthy substitute for "eating our words" or "our hats," if we're wrong about something. It's best to admit that we're wrong sooner rather than later for, in the words of an American country saying, "the easiest way to eat crow is while it's still warm, 'cause the colder it gets the harder it is to swallow." This fact is probably better understood in South Australia than elsewhere. The inhabitants of that state are known, not always respectfully, as "croweaters" because the early settlers had to settle for crow as part of their diet in the absence of a plentiful supply of red meat.

For lawyers, "eat what you kill" has a figurative meaning of reaping the full financial rewards from the business they generate rather than sharing those rewards with the other members of their firm. The expression brings to mind roadkill, suggesting that those lawyers who participate in this system of rewards are "feeding off the misfortune" of their clients and that they have had a hand in bringing about that misfortune. Not a pretty picture!

We must surely recognize, however, that "one man's meat is another man's poison." This saying inspired George S. Kaufman's famous spoof "one man's Mede is another man's Persian." A later commentator, perhaps with the famous playwright's double pun in mind, wrote "one man's meat is another man's poison and, by the same token, one man's joke is another man's snooze." In fact, there are any number of witty lines that have been built from the template "one man's _____ is another man's _____," including:

one man's meat is another man's cholesterol;
one man's fish is another man's *poisson*;
one man's bait is another man's sushi;
one man's corn is another man's bourbon.

Hunger may push us to the limits so that we're tempted to eat what we'd normally reject as totally unappetizing. Thus someone may be so hungry he "could eat a horse," "could eat the leg off a low flying duck" or "could eat a buttered monkey." Apparently, a bit of buttering up can make almost anything edible; witness the exclamatory expression, "well butter my butt and call me a biscuit," sometimes used in the rural American heartland to register surprise. The disposition of a clam is, obviously, improved by butter for an individual may be described as "happy as a clam in butter sauce."

A sauce generally adds relish to food, although "hunger is the best sauce." A sauce doesn't play favorites, for "what's sauce for the goose is sauce for the gander." The word "goose" is routinely used to describe a particular variety of fowl although it's technically the term for a female of that variety, while "gander" is the term for a male. Thus the saying logically signifies, in human terms, that what's good for a woman is good for a man. It could be viewed, therefore, as promoting male equality. Accordingly, if a wife can "play around" outside a marriage, a husband should be free to do the same thing. But it's the reverse that's more likely to be offered as an example of the practical application of the saying. These days, the saying is often used, without reference to equality of the sexes, as meaning that what's acceptable for one person is acceptable for another.

The Australian colloquial expression "a fair suck of the sauce bottle," meaning "a fair go," was originally taken to refer to the bottle from which a sauce is dispensed. But, under the influence of the

Americanism "getting into the sauce," it came to conjure up visions of a liquor bottle, wrapped in a brown paper bag, that's shared around among down-and-out drinkers. With the increase in the cost of liquor, however, these drinkers are now, more likely, to be "on the turps," as they also say Downunder.

Children are often described as "full of beans" if they are exuberant and in high spirits. But if an adult is described as "full of beans," it usually means that he's "full of hot air." That may remind us of this childish ditty:

> Beans, beans, the musical fruit:
> The more you eat the more you toot!
> The more you toot the better you feel,
> So let's have beans for every meal!

While this indicates that there's some ultimate redeeming value to beans, in the form of a feeling of relief, which commends their consumption, the expression "not worth a hill of beans" suggests that beans are virtually worthless.

In Australia, it's the whole meal, not just the beans, that gets the blame for flatulence, for "to drop one's lunch" means "to pass wind." In an imitation of the sound associated with that action, someone may "blow a raspberry," by inserting the tongue between the lips and exhaling. This largely British and Australian expression comes from rhyming slang, which associates raspberries with tarts. In the U.S., the equivalent expression is the more respectable "give a Bronx cheer," which evidences the same physical action involving the tongue and lips.

A Chinese proverb that's over two millennia old provides "food for thought" about larger issues under the guise of offering advice for achieving a continuous source of nourishment for the body. It advises, "give a man a fish, feed him for a day; teach him to fish, feed him for a lifetime," which lauds the benefits of giving someone the tools to become self-sufficient. This proverb has, not surprisingly, become the credo of several international development agencies. Since development aid is often more effective in the hands of women than men, it's sometimes said, "give a man money and watch his harem grow, give a woman money and you've empowered a whole community."

The many frivolous variations on the ancient proverb include:

Give a man a fish and you feed him for a day; teach a man to fish and you get rid of him for the whole weekend;

Give a man a fish and you feed him for a day; teach him to use the Net and he won't bother you for weeks;

Teach a man to fish and you've fed him for a lifetime unless, of course, he doesn't like sushi, then you also need to teach him how to cook.

All of these perverted proverbs ignore the metaphorical sense of the original proverb.

Another Chinese proverb warns, in the supposed words of Confucius himself, that "man who eat crackers in bed wake up feeling crummy," a prediction that needs to be "taken with a grain of salt." The expression, "that's the way the cookie crumbles" is particularly prevalent in North America. It's sometimes put in Dog Latin as *sic biscuitus desintegrat* or, in more respectable Latin, as *sic friatur crustum dulce*. The reminder of the vulnerability of the cookie tells us much the same thing as *c'est la vie* (that's life) and "that's the way the ball bounces." There's more than a hint of resignation in all of these expressions that "bad things happen," so it's not worth becoming too upset about it. In order to make it clear that it's not just cookies, amongst foods, that can leave you badly off, these additional phrases have been coined; "that's the way the gravy stains" and "that's the way the potato mashes."

Crackers and cookies are usually a snack; it's hard to make a meal of them. For a between meal snack, doughnuts are also favored, especially in North America. The U.S. spelling is often "donuts" even though these bakery goods are made of dough and have no connection with the first note in a musical scale. Their popularity as a relatively inexpensive treat made them a natural to be set up against dollars in the expression "dollars to doughnuts." This is a pseudo-betting proposition to indicate that a person has considerable confidence in a particular outcome, so much so that he'd be willing to be bet short odds on it. But inflation has shifted the odds dramatically in a dollars-to-doughnuts wager. A doughnut now costs around a dollar in the U.S. and Canada and a Krispy Kreme, the *crème de la crème* of the doughnut world, commands a price of around three dollars in Australia and in excess of a pound in the U.K. Better, therefore, to say that you would "bet your bottom dollar" on something happening if you think it's an absolute certainty or, in the U.K., better to express a willingness to offer "a pound to a penny" that it will happen. These are essentially inflation proof alternatives.

A poetic saying elevates the doughnut from a mere betting chip to something of a spiritual beacon:

As you go through life
Make this your goal;
Watch the doughnut
Not the hole.

These lines were, largely, incorporated into "The Donut Song" of the 1970s, which was sung by the "larger than life" singer-actor Burl Ives. The point of the saying is that you should concentrate on, and be thankful for, the good things that you have rather than dwelling on, and worrying about, what you don't have.

Someone who "makes a meal of something," to use an idiomatic turn of phrase, is directing more time and attention to it than is really justified. But "to have someone for breakfast" is not so single-minded. It might bring to mind any one of three quite different scenarios. If it were Hannibal Lector, or any other cannibalistic serial killer, who was "having someone for breakfast," the word picture portrayed would be pretty gruesome. On the other hand, if you or I were "having someone for breakfast," it might indicate that we were simply being hospitable by sharing the first meal of the day. We might expect "a bread-and-butter letter," after the fact, to thank us for our hospitality. But if "having someone for breakfast" were used as an idiomatic expression, it would carry the notion of having someone at a considerable disadvantage or defeating someone with ease. That's "a far cry from" a welcoming invitation to "break fast" by breaking bread together at the beginning of the day. We can only conclude that the image that's intended to be etched upon the mind by the expression "to have someone for breakfast" can only be determined by the situation at hand for, as the saying goes, "circumstances alter cases."

If someone is "out to lunch," in a figurative sense, he could be completely "crackers" or, more generously, out of touch with the realities of a particular situation or harboring an eccentric or unusual view about the situation. Not surprisingly, the expression is derived from the notion of getting away from work in order to enjoy a midday meal, liquid or otherwise, after which it's "back to the salt mines." For many, work is the hard reality of life. As Oscar Wilde said, turning around a long standing saying of the temperance movement, "work is the curse of the drinking classes."

Of course, "there's no such thing as a free lunch." This saying seems to "put paid to" the idea that anyone might ever enjoy a meal, or anything else for that matter, without someone having "to foot the bill." The concept that some consideration or *quid pro quo* will be required is also implicit in "to sing for your supper," meaning to earn a benefit by providing a service, This expression comes from the nursery rhyme "Little Tommy Tucker" and recounts what Tommy had to do in order to be fed. Another rhyme, "after dinner rest a while, after supper walk a mile," reflects the more substantial nature of the formal evening meal. It's with that meal in mind that Australians and Canadians are apt to say that someone is "done like dinner" if his "goose is cooked." Both culinary expressions suggest ultimate defeat.

The North American expression "easy as duck soup" suggests that duck soup is likely to be a straightforward appetizer with which to begin a meal. That's not the reality, however, for duck soup is simply a murky term for a mud puddle, which can collect rainwater easily. Groucho Marx had his own recipe for "duck soup," which was also the title of a Marx Brothers movie: "Take two turkeys, one goose, four cabbages, but no duck, and mix them together. After one taste, you'll duck soup for the rest of your life."

Unmistakable national traits are commonly associated, in expressions, with national dishes or varieties of produce. Thus something may be "as American as apple pie," "as Canadian as maple syrup," "as Australian as meat pies," "as English as fish and chips," "as Scottish as haggis" or "as Kiwi as kiwifruit."

Although something typically American is often described as "American as apple pie," apples are an introduced fruit in the United States and were used as ingredients in pie or tart making in Europe well before settlers from that continent populated the Americas. But the dessert was to become a symbol of American comfort, prosperity and pride. It even played a large role in persuading servicemen from the initially reluctant U.S. to take up arms against the Axis powers in the Second World War. Asked why he was joining the battle, a soldier would often reply, "for mom and apple pie." "For God and country" was "put on the back burner."

It takes a British saying to address the way apple pie should be eaten, with the suggestion that "apple pie without cheese is like a hug [or a kiss] without a squeeze." This equation ignores those who prefer their pie à la mode. Take-offs on the saying include "apple pie without cheese is like a cold without a sneeze" and "apple pie without cheese is like the birds without the bees."

Mince pies, unlike apple pies, remain distinctively British, but they aren't always for consumption as they can serve as a stand-in for "eyes" in rhyming slang. Therefore, those who are conversant with that manner of speaking might dote on "the apples of their mince pies."

In Canada, the food product most often singled out as typically Canadian is maple syrup. The expression "as Canadian as maple syrup" draws legitimacy from the fact that Canada is, by far, the largest producer in the world of this variety of syrup. The national flag also features the maple tree, from which the syrup is produced, through a representation of that tree's distinctive leaf.

The expression "as Australian as meat pies" is sometimes expanded to include, as additional Australian symbols, kangaroos and Holdens, the locally produced General Motors vehicles that once blanketed the country. Meat pies are more commonly associated with Britain than Australia, but other Australian foods that might be more distinctive, such as Vegemite (a brown paste spread sometimes confused with England's own Marmite), Pavlova (a meringue), Lamingtons (sponge cakes covered with chocolate icing and coconut) and Tim Tams (chocolate coated biscuits through which coffee or hot chocolate can be sucked up in a so-called Tim Tam Slam) just don't have the same international recognition.

Something that's quintessentially English may be described as being "as English as fish and chips" or, somewhat less commonly, "as English as Yorkshire pudding." But nowadays the Englishman's favorite meal is chicken tikka masala, which has surpassed fish and chips and roast beef and Yorkshire pudding in popularity.

"As Scottish as haggis" is a natural. That particular dish is peculiar to the Scots while for others, it's just plain peculiar. It receives almost reverential treatment, aided and abetted by the poet Robbie Burns, who praised it in his famous "Address to a Haggis," which is repeated around the world on January 25, the anniversary of his birthday, wherever a haggis is piped in at a Burns dinner. The opening verse, as adapted for the modern English tongue, goes like this:

Fair full your honest, jolly face,
Great chieftain of the sausage race!
Above them all you take your place,
Stomach, tripe or intestines:
Well you are worthy of a grace
As long as my arm.

You would think that the Scots would bristle at an expression that compares things distinctively Scottish to "a lot of tripe," but not so.

It also seems natural, "at first blush," that Kiwis, to use the birdlike nickname for New Zealanders, should be identified in their special characteristics by the fruit that also bears the name "kiwi." Not well known, at least among members of the younger generation, is the fact that what's now the kiwi fruit is really the Chinese gooseberry, relabeled in New Zealand in the 1950s, for export marketing purposes, without the consent of the Chinese. So an alien fruit, wrongfully appropriated, has become a mark of the distinctive traits of the country's citizens. Yet New Zealand can't even claim to be the world's largest producer of the fruit. That distinction belongs to Italy.

"Taking a leaf from the book of" New Zealand, Canada has unilaterally re-branded "rapeseed oil," in nationalistic fashion, as "Canola oil." The justification offered for the change is that Canada produces this vegetable product from a new, genetically modified variety of the rapeseed plant and to call it what it is, namely "GM rapeseed oil," would severely limit the market for the product. "As Canadian as Canola," whatever it has going for it, has never managed to capture the public imagination, perhaps because of its rapacious ancestry.

Although humans and food would seem to have little in common, there are many similes that describe an individual's conduct or characteristics in terms of a particular food, to wit "busy as popcorn on a skillet," "nutty as a fruitcake," "cool as a cucumber," "keen as mustard," "slow as molasses in January" and "full as a goog [an egg]." Most people know about the hyperactivity of corn when it's popped and the certifiable nuttiness of fruitcake. But just how eager is mustard, how cool is a cucumber, how slow is molasses in the midst of a northern winter and how full is an egg?

"Keen as mustard" signifies considerable enthusiasm. It's a somewhat archaic British expression. Mustard may be viewed as "keen" in the sense of sharp as it adds zest to food, but it's not "keen" in the sense of eager. Therefore, that stimulating explanation doesn't really "cut the mustard." It remains quite mystifying why the keenness of mustard should be used as a yardstick to measure someone's enthusiasm. The expression makes about as much sense as "mean as custard," the popular Spoonerism to which it gave birth.

A possible answer to the question "how cool is a cucumber?" is that it's considerably cooler than the ambient air when it lies in a farmer's field. However, the expression "cool as a cucumber" doesn't use "cool" in that sense. Rather, it uses the word in the sense of unperturbed, yet a cucumber doesn't demonstrate that characteristic any better than any other vegetable. The acceptance of the expression, therefore, owes more to its alliterative quality than to the helpfulness of any image it might logically portray.

As to the speed of molasses, Bostonians who "have an eye for" their city's history, would attest to the fact that it can travel at up to 30 miles an hour (48 kilometers an hour). This is the speed at which it was clocked in Boston's Great Molasses Flood on a relatively balmy, 43 degree (six degree Celsius) day in January of 1919. On that occasion, 14,000 tons of treacle (hardly a trickle) escaped into the streets, doing extensive damage to many structures, killing 21 people and injuring another 150 in its fast moving escape from a storage tank. The moral: Molasses isn't always as slow, or as harmless, as the expression would suggest.

When an Australian is completely satiated with food or drink, he may be described as "full as a goog." The word "goog" comes from "goo-gie," a term that Scottish children commonly used for an egg. While an egg might seem to have no more room inside to accommodate any further matter, egg producers know better. There's invariably an air cell at one end of an egg, the size of which helps to determine the grade of the egg and, therefore, its market value for the producer.

It takes some skill to extract all of the matter from an egg by sucking it out. Grandmothers who had lost their teeth in the pre-denture era acquired that skill because they ate a lot of raw or lightly boiled eggs, a readily available source of soft food that wasn't likely to get their gums worked up and "gum up the works," to put it in chiastic terms. It would be wise, therefore, to pay heed to the saying, "don't teach your grandmother to suck eggs" or this expanded poetic rendition:

Teach not thy parent's mother to extract
The embryo juices of the bird by suction
The good old lady can that feat enact,
Quite irrespective of your kind instruction.

The saying recognizes, broadly speaking, that a veteran at any kind of endeavor will have acquired skill at it and, "sure as eggs is eggs," a novice shouldn't be offering advice to the veteran.

The toothless are actually favored in a perverse and frustrating sort of way for "the Gods send nuts to those who have no teeth," as a person who has recently lost her hearing might say upon learning that she had won season's tickets to the symphony in a draw. A skeptical literalist might ask who "in his right mind" would want to consume nuts anyway since "you are what you eat."

Although sucking eggs involved an admirable talent on the part of grandmothers, the demand "go suck eggs" developed as a slang form of derision in North America. That expression comes from the behavior of unwanted henhouse intruders, the skunk and the weasel, who are wont to come at night "under cover of darkness" and suck out the contents of any eggs they find. At least "that's what they say," to add some "weasel words" to the narrative. The stoat, also known as the ermine, behaves in the same fashion as the weasel but, otherwise, the two species are readily distinguishable for, in the words of a punishingly bad joke (repeated here with suitable apologies), "one is weasily recognized and the other is stoatally different." However, it's worth noting, while temporarily mired at this low level of humor, that "stoat" and "weasel" do have certain similarities, for there's an "a" in each and an "n" in neither.

A person can always remove the yolk and albumen from an egg by blowing, although one shouldn't try to "suck and blow at the same time" as these are two inconsistent actions, like whistling and chewing gum. The delicate process of blowing out an egg, often carried out as a preliminary to decorating the egg, requires that the shell be first punctured with a pin, at both ends, to allow for air to be blown in and the contents of the egg to escape. The shell is left more or less intact. Since this extraction process can be quite successful in gathering the prime ingredient for cooked egg dishes, it can't really be said, without qualification, that "you can't make an omelet without breaking eggs." Yet this saying is used to describe any situation in which it's hard to accomplish something without some destructive side effects.

In the popular board game *Clue*, Colonel Mustard is recorded as observing, "you can't make an omelet without breaking a few eggs; every cook will tell you that." This line punctuates the scene of one of the murders the players are called upon to solve, the victim being the resident cook. Mrs. Peacock, another of the characters in the game, responds, prophetically, to the Colonel, "but look what happened to the cook."

The Egg Farmers of Canada, an egg marketing agency, incorporates the directive "get cracking" in its logo. Operation Omelet, one of the agency's advertising campaigns, naturally encourages consumers to "get cracking" on cooking up this venerable egg dish. Egg marketers have balked, however, at using the slogan "eggs are hard to beat" for fear that it might be taken literally. It's the possibility of just such an interpretation that prompted the facetious comment: "You can't beat a pickled egg."

It's often important to preserve eggs from destructive cracking, say when they're to be kept fresh for later use in making an omelet or baking a cake. It's not surprising, therefore, that "walking on eggs," in its idiomatic sense, involves an exercise of extreme caution in one's words or actions so as to avoid causing damage or grief to anyone. Over time, the expression has become "walking on eggshells," although that could easily be taken to describe a situation in which the damage had already been done. Nonetheless, this most recent version of the expression is used to describe the same prudent behavior as the original. It's also been incorporated into this apt description, from the province of Nova Scotia, of a young woman in high heels, namely "a high stepper walking on eggshells."

"You can't have your cake and eat it" only makes sense if it's reversed to read "you can't eat your cake and have it," which is close to an early version of the saying. The fact is that you can, literally, have your cake and eat it if you follow that sequence. I have anecdotal evidence to support this conclusion; my wife and I had our wedding cake in the freezer for years and eventually ate it. The metaphorical meaning of the saying "you can't have your cake and eat it" is, in essence, "you can't have it both ways." But that only matches the literal logic of the saying if it's restored to "you can't eat your cake and have it."

We may be told that "the proof of the pudding is in the eating." "Proof" is used here in the old sense of "test" just as the verb "proves" in "the exception proves the rule" means "tests." The saying "the proof of the pudding is in the eating" carries a fairly obvious meaning for someone who knows the early meaning of "proof." It stands for the proposition that you can't judge the quality of something without trying it out. But, in common parlance, the saying is often reduced to "the proof is in the pudding," which makes little sense. It's not surprising that this version has prompted some wit to focus on another meaning of "proof" and come up with the perverted proverb, "the proof of the pudding depends on how much brandy is in it." "When all is said and done," however, the "proof of the pudding" may actually be in the serving rather than the eating. Evidence of that comes in the form of a parental response to a child's question: "What's for dessert?" A traditional answer was "wait-and-see pudding."

It's also hard to make sense of "easy as pie" because it too omits any reference to the crucial element of eating. This elliptical expression is a contraction of "easy as eating pie," for which the "proof," in the modern sense of establishing truth or accuracy, is the easy comfort that comes with the consumption of that dish. The comfort of eating anything is "aided and abetted" by washing it down with liquid refreshment. Indeed, food and drink are closely associated as helpmates in the saying "eat, drink and be merry." Time, then, to pass on to drink, as taken with food or alone, lest it be soon forgotten.

16

DRINK AS AN AFTERTHOUGHT

When the wine is in, the wit is out.

14th century English proverb, favoured
by temperance societies in later centuries

And so to the dénouement with its concluding toasts. This final chapter focuses on the sustenance that drinks and drinking provide to expressions and sayings. In particular, it looks at the contribution of alcoholic beverages and that of the less potent alternatives, water, milk, tea, coffee and fruit drinks.

A toast takes place when people participate in a traditional ritual of drinking to honor someone or something or to wish someone good luck or good health. The drink involved is usually wine or some other alcoholic beverage. The person proposing the toast will often use one of several set expressions for this kind of occasion while lifting his glass, and inviting any others around him to do the same and join him in drinking to the person or thing to be toasted. There are many set expressions that are regularly used in "raising a toast." The expressions themselves are also called toasts. Perhaps the strangest of these is "here's mud in your eye" for it seems to foretell a misfortune that could result in losing sight of the way ahead. An earlier, more expansive version, "here's mud in your eye while I look over your lovely sweetheart," reveals a possible self-serving motive for someone raising this particular toast.

It's much easier to understand why "here's looking at you" became a popular toast. In a scene from the 1942 film *Casablanca*, the central character Rick Blaine, played by Humphrey Bogart, toasts his ex-lover

Ilse Lund, played by Ingrid Bergman, with the words "Here's looking at you, kid." This is consistently ranked as one of the most memorable lines in American cinematic history, making it one of the best known toasts of all time. The toast probably originated from the old practice of drinking from glass bottomed tankards, which allowed a tippler to see an approaching enemy when his tankard was in the "bottoms up" position. That same position, assumed in the course of a friendly toast, would, therefore, enable the toaster to look directly at the toastee.

The Irish, who aren't known for their succinct way with words, often use this much lengthier toast:

> May you have food and rainment
> A soft pillow for your head
> May you be many years in heaven
> Before the devil knows you're dead.

The economical Scots prefer the short, inclusive toast "here's tae us," but when pressed will add:

> Wa's like us?
> Damn few
> And they're a' deid
> Mair's the pity!

Another old Scottish favorite is "lang may your lum reek," which translates as "long may your chimney smoke." The success of this toast probably contributed to the City of Edinburgh becoming known, in its former coal burning days, as "Auld Reekie."

The noun "toast" is also used to denote the person or persons to whom a toast is directed. This is the way in which it's used in the expression "the toast of the town." Someone who is said to be "the toast of the town" is widely popular and admired as would be the case if he were honored by frequent toasts throughout the community. But if it's said of someone "he's toast," it doesn't mean that he's the object of affection; rather he's finished, or at least in big trouble, as if he were another kind of toast that has been "burnt to a crisp." If you "have [someone] on toast" it means, in a British manner of speaking, that you have him in a vulnerable position with the result that he may soon "become toast."

"I'll drink to that" was originally the form in which someone would express his agreement to join in a toast proposed by another. It's now used, more broadly, as an interjection to signify complete accord with something that's just been said. The American entertainer Dean Martin took the expression back to its alcoholic roots, in the 1960s and 1970s, when he used it repeatedly, on his TV variety show, while he appeared well on the way to inebriation. For him, it became something of a signature line that reinforced his image as a heavy drinker, an image that he actively cultivated as part of his comedy routine. "Bottoms up" and "down the hatch" are the favored verbal accompaniments to actually carrying through with the intention of "drinking to that."

There is no shortage of expressions that can be applied to someone who is drunk. "The Drinker's Dictionary," published by Benjamin Franklin in his *Pennsylvania Gazette* column in 1737, contained 220 synonyms for "drunk" that were current at the time. The expressions that are in use today to describe someone who is intoxicated, many of them euphemistic, include "three sheets to the wind," "under the table," "well into his cups," "feeling no pain," "high as a kite," "drunk as a lord," "drunk as a skunk," "half in the bag," "tight as a tick," "into the sauce" and "loaded to the gills." There are two main ways of getting to any of these states, you can drink with fellow imbibers, often sharing toasts along the way, or you can "drink with the flies," as they say in Australia and New Zealand, on an otherwise lonely binge.

It's assumed by the expression "driven to drink" that one can be pushed to "hit the bottle" as a last refuge from frustration or annoyance. The movie actor W.C. Fields wasn't at all fazed by being "driven to drink," for he said that he just worried about being driven home. On another occasion, he lamented: "A woman drove me to drink and I didn't even have the decency to thank her."

The effects of particular kinds of alcoholic drinks are brought out by the proverbs "he that drinks beer, thinks beer," alerting us to the addictive nature of beer, and "there is truth in wine" (*in vino veritas*), identifying the juice of the grape as a sort of truth serum. Then there's the perverted proverb that speculates upon the beneficial, after-dinner effects of a liqueur, with its suggestion that "absinth makes the tart grow fonder." Finally, as to the loosening effects of liquor generally, who can forget Ogden Nash's "Reflection on Ice-Breaking," a fine example of an epigram:

Candy
Is dandy
But liquor
Is quicker.

"There is no accounting for taste" when it comes to drink for the world is full of people "with champagne taste on a beer belly." On the other hand, there are those who disdain champagne from which they "get no kick," as proclaimed in a song from Cole Porter's 1934 Broadway hit *Anything Goes*. The book for the musical, which is full of zany humor, has a holier-than-thou widow reject any strong drink with the lifetime teetotaler's mantra, "liquor has never passed my lips," at which point the wealthy lush who's courting her asks, hopefully, "you know a short-cut?" Well, there wasn't a short-cut in the 1930s, but there are several in the twenty-first century, including the use of body orifices besides the mouth and the dangerous practice of "vodka eyeballing," as its known in student circles, which involves pouring vodka into the eye for an instant high.

The relation of the earth to the sun determines when "the sun is over the yardarm." When that happens in the course of a day, it's permissible to "hoist a glass," but not sooner. For those properly informed about the location of the yardarm, which hangs from a ship's mast suspending a square sail, the sun will have reached this point, as viewed from the deck of a ship in the North Atlantic, at around 11:00 a.m. That's when the first tots of rum for the day were issued to sailors in the British Navy in a rationing scheme designed to ensure that a ship's crew didn't become too groggy on grog. Most poor sods, particularly those who are landlubbers, think that the sun doesn't reach the yardarm until much later in the day and that they have to hold off from imbibing until 5:00 p.m. That's when "happy hour" usually begins. Others have adopted the more liberal attitude that they can take a drink whenever they're so inclined because the sun is bound to be "over the yardarm" somewhere in the world at any given moment. If they start drinking early, they can be "three sheets to the wind," in other nautical terms, before the sun reaches the yardarm in their own time zone.

"Water is the only drink for a wise man" was the considered opinion of the writer and back-to-nature philosopher Henry David Thoreau. He would, no doubt, have agreed that while "bread is the staff of life," strong drink is a crutch to make one's way through life. The actor and sometime philosopher W.C. Fields took a position opposed to that of Thoreau, swearing off water completely with this reasoning: "I never drink water because of the disgusting things that fish do in it."

A drink that proved to be a much more potent potable than alcohol is brought to mind by the modern expression "drinking the Kool-Aid." It's used to indicate, in a critical way, an unquestioning adherence to a particular belief or philosophy. The expression is quite tasteless, as others have observed, because it draws upon the horrifying circumstances in which over 900 men, women and children died in the Jonestown Massacre in November of 1978. The victims were followers of the American cult leader Jim Jones who had led them to Guyana to establish a commune in what became known as Jonestown. In the face of serious allegations about his activities and a threatened investigation, Jones assembled his followers and ordered them to commit suicide by swallowing Kool-Aid, which was laced with cyanide. Most complied willingly, but others, including many children, received involuntary injections of the fatal poison. The expression adverts to the response and the fate of the willing participants, providing a ghastly reminder of a terrible human tragedy.

Using an interrogatory expression that pre-dates Jonestown, a host might ask his guest "what's your poison?" in a light hearted attempt to find out what the guest would like to drink. This informal expression is somewhat diluted in its humor now that "drinking the Kool-Aid," with its background in the events of Jonestown, has entered our lexicon.

On a more upbeat note, the expression "the milk of human kindness" signifies compassion and caring for others. The expression has inevitably surfaced in the headings of news items about mothers sharing their breast milk with other mothers who can't produce enough for their own infants. There are limits, however, to how far "the milk of human kindness" will go, for "feeding a snake with milk will not change its poisonous character," an Indian proverb.

A person who is particularly caring is sometimes described as "overflowing with the milk of human kindness." Yet it was an excess of human kindness that prompted Shakespeare's Lady Macbeth to say of her husband, in the first recorded use of the expression:

Yet do I fear thy nature;
It is too full o' th' milk of human kindness
To catch the nearest way...

The "nearest way," of which Lady Macbeth spoke, was the way to the throne of Scotland then occupied by King Duncan. The three witches, those "black and midnight hags," had saluted Macbeth as the future king, but his wife wonders aloud, in this passage, whether he is mean enough to do what he has to do in order to claim the throne.

Tea is praised in this modern saying, attributed to British politician, Sir William Gladstone: "If you are cold, tea will warm you; if you are too heated, it will cool you; if you are depressed, it will cheer you; if you are excited, it will calm you." It's "not everyone's cup of tea," but it certainly carries a variety of benefits for those who "take a cuppa." Coffee, by comparison, gets a less enthusiastic endorsement in a Dutch proverb which proclaims that "coffee has two virtues; it is warm and wet," effectively "damning it with faint praise." One might be easily led to conclude that, in the healthy competition between tea and coffee, tea has it "in the bag," especially for anyone who's tired of the "daily grind."

The saying "if life hands you lemons, make lemonade" provides some final "food for thought." It's telling us, not surprisingly, that if "bad things happen," we should try to "make the best of it." The word "lemons" also has an informal meaning of defective goods. That's what inspired the title of Canadian consumer advocate Phil Edmonston's annual *Lemon-Aid* guides with their exposés of vehicle defects, model by model.

In one variation, it's been said that "if life hands you lemons, make a whiskey sour." Another variation "flies in the face of" the real message of the saying by suggesting that "if life hands you lemons, make lemonade and then throw it in the face of the person who handed you the lemons." That's more consistent with President John F. Kennedy's reminder of "the wonderful law of the Boston Irish political jungle: 'Don't get mad, get even.'"

Life can also saddle you with other fruits, bearing different lessons or opportunities. It's been observed that "if life gives you melons, you're probably dyslexic." Singer-songwriter Jimmy Buffet, of Margaritaville fame, has proposed: "If life gives you limes, make margaritas," out of that sour fruit, which brings us to this final toast:

Here's to you my reader friend
Who made it to the bitter end
May you well and truly savor
The fruits of all your labor
For language can be really fun
"When all is said and done."

ENDNOTES

INTRODUCTION

Page 2   And so, "without further ado," I end this introduction…Knowles, Elizabeth (ed.), *Little Oxford Dictionary of Proverbs* (Oxford: Oxford University Press, 2009), at p. 27.

CHAPTER 1

Page 6   "Fuddle duddle" found its way… *Canadian Oxford Dictionary* (Don Mills, Ontario: Oxford University Press, 2001), at p. 502. In a bracketed aside, the dictionary's editors note that the meanings the dictionary provides reflect what the PM claimed he said in Parliament when he was accused of using the 'f' word.

Page 7   While this is not an established expression… *The Sydney Morning Herald*, issue of June 25, 2009.

Page 8   A recent study reported by the magazine *Science*… See, Williams, Sarah C.P., "Sexually Rejected Flies Turn to Booze" (March 15, 2012), at http://news.sciencemag.org/sciencenow/2012/03/sexually-rejected-flies-turn-to.html.

Page 9   Still other alliterative expressions embody pairs of words…Burchfield, R.W. (ed.), *The New Fowler's Modern English Usage*, 3rd ed. (Oxford: Clarendon Press, 1996), at p. 712.

CHAPTER 2

Page 13 Oscar Wilde applied this recipe...See Act 3 of *Lady Windermere's Fan* (London: Penguin Books, 1995), at p. 56.

Page 13 This line was part of a routine...See Morecambe, Eric and Ernie Wise, *The Morecambe & Wise Jokebook* (London: Arthur Barker, 1979), at p. 22.

Page 15 The headline: "Rum maker's pact with Virgin Islands...*The Globe & Mail*, issue of October 7, 2009.

Page 15 That initiative prompted this February, 2010 headline...*The Globe & Mail*, issue of February 23, 2010.

Page 15 The headline: "Teammates Stand Behind Keeper...*Toronto Star*, issue of June 13, 2010.

Page 15 The caption: "So I screwed up...*Toronto Star*, issue of May 24, 2011.

Page 15 A British tabloid, the *Daily Mail*,...*Daily Mail*, issue of October 31, 2013.

Page 17 The prolific Scottish writer Alexander McCall Smith proved to be a master at this...*Bertie Plays the Blues: A 44 Scotland Street Novel* (Toronto: Vintage Canada, 2013), at p. 204.

Page 19 In *The Saint Goes On*, Templar adds...*The Saint Goes On* (New York: Triangle Books, 1940), at p. 60.

Page 19 But the translators who prepared...Genesis 4:1.

Page 21 The Walrus in Lewis Carroll's poem...The poem is included in Amis, Kingsley (ed.) *The New Oxford Book of Light Verse* (Oxford: Oxford University Press, 1978), at p. 128.

Page 22 The English mystery writer Simon Brett has taken it to an even lower level... See *The Hanging in the Hotel* (London: Pan Books, 2004), at p. 160.

Page 22 An Ontario judge declined to enforce that judgment...In *Yaiguaje v. Chevron Corporation*, 2013 ONSC 2527, reported at http://www.canlii.org, see esp. at para. 111. An appeal from the trial judge's stay of the enforcement action was allowed by the Ontario Court of Appeal, see *Yaiguaje v. Chevron Corporation*, 2013 ONCA 758, reported at http://www.canlii.org.

Page 26 But even a declared intention to be ironic...The poem is entitled "Ironist" and appears in Bennett, Bruce, *Not Wanting To Write Like Everyone Else* (Brockport, N.Y.: State Street Press, 1987). The poem is reprinted here by permission of Bruce Bennett.

Page 26 It's pretty clear that Dorothy Parker...Dorothy Parker's poem, entitled "Comment," is reprinted in Dorothy Parker. *Complete Poems* (London: Penguin Books, 2010), at p. 46. It is reprinted here by permission of Penguin, a division of Penguin Group (USA) LLC, and Gerald Duckworth & Co. Ltd.

Page 29 In his novel *Farewell, My Lovely*, he provided this description...*Farewell, My Lovely* (New York: Vintage Books, 1992), at p. 4.

CHAPTER 3

Page 33   The expression, therefore, builds on a misunderstanding...See *Merriam-Webster's Dictionary of English Usage: The Complete Guide to Problems of Confused or Disputed Usage* (Springfield, Mass.: Merriam-Webster, 1994), at p. 486.

Page 35   In the best of the Spooner tradition, the poet Ogden Nash...From his poem "Everybody's Mind to Me a Kingdom Is," reprinted in *Candy is Dandy: The Best of Ogden Nash* (London: Methuen London, 1985), at p. 264. The poem is reprinted here by permission of Curtis Brown Ltd. and Carlton Publishing Group.

Page 36   This sentence was penned by Gordon Gibson...See his *Thirty Million Musketeers: One Canada, For All Canadians* (Toronto: Key Porter Books, 1995), at p. 63.

Page 37   If a particular rule is more often broken than not...*Hamlet*, I, iv, 14.

Page 40   The British economist John Maynard Keynes was plagued by economics students...See Humphries, John, *Lost for Words: The Mangling and Manipulating of the English Language* (London: Hodder & Stoughton, 2004), at pp. 85-86.

CHAPTER 4

Page 44   Like the expression "pushing up daisies," the folk balled, *Clementine*...The ballad is included in Harmon, William (ed.), *The Oxford Book of American Light Verse* (Oxford: Oxford University Press, 1979), at p. 108.

Page 44   Much better to be described as "pushing up daisies,"...See *Genesis*, 3:19 for the expression "from earth to earth, from dust to dust."

Page 44   Substitutes for the verb "to die"...For the Shakespearian expression, see *Hamlet*, III, i, 68.

Page 48   "By the way," or BTW, it joins at least two other ubiquitous acronyms... These last two acronyms have been "banished" for overuse following an informal survey by Lake Superior State University, of Sault Ste. Marie, Michigan, see http://www.lssu.edu/banished.

Page 48   "Netspeak," the Internet slang that is often used in computer-mediated communication...See Crystal, David, *Language and the Internet*, 2nd ed. (Cambridge: Cambridge University Press, 2006), at pp. 89–92.

Page 49   The *Parents Shouldn't Text* Website records this unfortunate message... For this posting (January 1, 2011), see http://www.parentsshouldnttext.com/155/moms-dont-understand-lol.

Page 50   These graphic illustrations of expressions are part of a long tradition... See Mieder, Wolfgang, *Proverbs Are Never Out of Season* (New York: Oxford University Press, 1993), at pp. 58–65.

CHAPTER 5

Page 55   No wonder it's said that "England and America are two countries divided…The quotation attributed to Shaw doesn't appear in any of his published works but Wilde used the following line in *The Canterville Ghost* (Cambridge, Mass.: Candlewick Press, 1997), at p. 12: "We have really everything in common with America nowadays, except, of course, language."

Page 56   *The Sydney Morning Herald* reported…Gibson, Jano, "Fair dinkum! Aussie lingo sparks security scare," *The Sydney Morning Herald*, issue of August 10, 2007.

Page 57   In his book *Let Stalk Strine*, Professor Lauder…*Let Stalk Strine* (Sydney: Ure Smith, 1965), see at p. 17 for Lauder's discussion of the expression "flesh in the pen."

Page 58   In a subsequent book, *Nose Stone Unturned*…*Nose Stone Unturned* (Sydney: Lansdowne Press, 1982), at pp. 107–111.

Page 59   The expression is generally thought to have originated with Yogi Berra…A number of Yogi Berra quotes, including the two noted in this paragraph of the text, are collected in Berra, Yogi, *The Yogi Book: I Really Didn't Say Everything I Said* (New York: Workman, 1998), see esp. at pp. 9 & 30.

CHAPTER 6

Page 64   The online *Urban Dictionary* describes him…www.urbandictionary.com/define.php?term=good+time+charlie.

Page 65   In his book *Graffiti Lives, O.K.*…*Graffiti Lives, O.K.* (London: Unwin Paperbacks, 1979), at p. 52.

Page 67   Sir Edmund would probably "roll over in his grave"…The Service poem is included in *The Complete Poems of Robert Service* (New York: Dodd, Mead, 1940), at p. 228.

CHAPTER 7

Page 73   He wrote that phrase for Hamlet…*Hamlet*, I, iv, 14.

Page 73   "At one fell swoop," which the Bard of Avon used…See *Macbeth*, IV, iii, 219, for the expression "at one fell swoop."

Page 74   In another one of Shakespeare's plays…*King John*, IV, ii, 9.

Page 74   But when the Dutch humanist Erasmus…This error is described in O'Conner, Patricia and Stewart Kellerman, *Origins of the Specious* (New York: Random House, 2009), at pp. 126-129.

Page 75   According to newspaper reports, the victims of crime were asked…Howden, Daniel, "Zimbabwe Cash Crisis Sees Victims Drive Accused to Trial," *The Independent*, issue of May 5, 2010.

Page 77   But it did become labeled as "jump the couch,"...See the on-line *Macmillan Dictionary* at http://www.macmillandictionary.com/buzzword/ entries/jump-the-couch.html as to this expression and the 2005 honors that it received.

Page 78   "You ain't heard nothin' yet" also became famous...The full story is related in Geduld, Harry M., *The Birth of the Talkies: From Edison to Jolson* (Bloomington, Ind.: Indiana University Press, 1975), at pp. 180–185.

Page 80   An Australian newspaper, *The Age*, used the expression...*The Age*, issue of September 12, 2003.

Page 81   He ultimately "let everyone in on" the censored joke...*P.S. Jack Paar: An Entertainment* (New York: Doubleday, 1983), at pp. 114–131.

Page 82   After Nike's shares had had a good run...*The Globe & Mail*, issue of January 11, 2014.

Page 83   The terminology of computer and electronic technology...Crystal, David, *Language and the Internet*, 2nd ed. (Cambridge: Cambridge University Press, 2006), at p. 21.

Page 83   However, the immediate inspiration for the use of the word...A video clip of this sketch can be seen on YouTube at http://www.youtube.com/ watch?v=anwy2MPT5RE

Page 84   The Lake Superior State University, in Sault Ste. Marie, Michigan, publishes an annual list...The annual lists can be found at http://www.lssu.edu/ banished.

Page 85   The expression, therefore, refers...See htpp://www.urbandictionary.com/ define.php?term=birds%20of%20a%20feather.

Page 85   If some act is described as a case of "the blind leading the blind,"...*Matthew*, 15:14 and *Luke*, 6:39.

CHAPTER 8

Page 87   A saying may also be described as "an old saw"...Thurber's skepticism about "an old saw" was actually the moral that he drew from his story of a tortoise and a hare. Upon learning of Aesop's fable in which a tortoise outdistances a hare, Thurber's tortoise challenges a hare to a race believing that "slow and steady wins the race," which was the moral of the ancient fable and had, by then, become an old saw. But the outcome of the modern day race was a decisive victory for the hare. See Thurber, James, *Fables for Our Time and Famous Poems Illustrated* (New York: Harper Collins, 1983), at p. 61.

Page 88   The biblical proverb "the truth will set you free" embodies a personification...*John*, 8: 32.

Pages 91–92   He recorded some of his favorite exchanges...*Kids Say the Darndest Things* (Woodstock, Ill.: Dramatic Publishing, 2004), see esp. at p. 32.

Page 92   Another of Linkletter's young interviewees...For the exchange on the grass-is-greener saying, see *Kids Say the Darndest Things* (Woodstock, Ill.: Dramatic Publishing, 2004), at p. 32.

Page 92   A primary school teacher is reported to have fed her six year old charges...See http://www.alphadictionary.com/fun/kids_in_school.html.

CHAPTER 9

Page 97   "Handsome is as handsome does" dates back...The saying appears in "The Wife of Bath's Tale," one of Chaucer's *Canterbury Tales*, in the form "To do the gentil dedes that he can; Tak hym for the grettest gentil man;" see Chaucer, Geoffrey, *Canterbury Tales* (New York: Alfred A Knopf), at p. 187 (lines 1115-1116).

Page 98   Some epigrams aren't particularly poetic...The Oscar Wilde line comes from Act 1 of his play *Lady Windermere's Fan* (London: Penguin Books, 1995), at p. 17.

Page 98   In fact, Wilde was so famous for...The poem, entitled "Oscar Wilde" is reprinted in Dorothy Parker. *Complete Poems* (London: Penguin Books, 2010), at p. 111. The poem is reprinted here by permission of Penguin, a division of Penguin Group (USA) LLC, and Gerald Duckworth & Co. Ltd.

Page 99   Professor Wolfgang Mieder, a prominent proverb expert, has collected a number...Mieder, Wolfgang and Anna Litovkina, *Twisted Wisdom: Modern Anti-Proverbs* (Hobart, Tas.: De Proverbio.com, 2002), see at pp. 73–77 for the early-to-bed twisted wisdom. See also Mieder, Wolfgang, *Proverbs Are Never Out of Season: Popular Wisdom in the Modern Age* (New York: Oxford University Press, 1993), at pp. 123–125 for additional examples of that wisdom.

Page 99   Recent scientific research has established...See "Gene that makes people 'early to bed and early to rise' demystified," at http://www.eurekalert.org/pub_releases/2007-01/cp-gtm010807.php.

Page 99   The American humorist James Thurber...This perverted proverb served as the moral of Thurber's modern day fable titled "The Shrike and the Chipmunks;" see Thurber, James, *The Thurber Carnival* (New York: Random House, 1994), at pp. 326–327.

Page 99   Several sayings without the benefit of internal rhymes...*The Complete Plays of Gilbert and Sullivan* (New York: W.W. Norton, 1976), at pp. 239–240.

Page 101   Or it may even have come from Borneo...These lines are from Swift's poem "The Revolution at Market Hill," which is included in Rogers, Pat (ed.), *Jonathan Swift: The Complete Poems* (New Haven and London: Yale University Press, 1982), see at pp. 396-398, esp. lines 75–82.

Page 102   However, the authoritative *Fowler's Modern English Usage*...Burchfield, R.W. (ed.), *The New Fowler's Modern English Usage*, 3rd ed. (Oxford: Clarendon Press, 1996), at p. 617.

Page 102   In his book *Parkinson's Law or the Pursuit of Progress ... Parkinson's Law or the Pursuit of Progress* (London: John Murray, 1958).

Page 103   Murphy's Law is to the effect that "if anything can go wrong, it will"... See Bloch, Arthur, *The Complete Murphy's Law: A Definitive Collection*, rev. ed. (Los Angeles: Price Stern Sloan, 1991).

Page 103   Jon Henley, writing in the *Guardian* newspaper ... "Accidents will Happen," *The Guardian*, issue of January 5, 2009.

Page 104   His contribution came through his popular 1968 book... *The Peter Principle: Why Things Always Go Wrong* (New York: William Morrow, 1969), see esp. at pp. viii and 25.

Page 104   The principle is elaborated in Adams 1996 book... *The Dilbert Principle: A Cubicle's-Eye View of Bosses, Meetings, Management, Fads and Other Workplace Afflictions* (New York: HarperCollins, 1996), see esp. at p. 12–14.

Page 109   But one cartoonist has given us a different story... The cartoon is reprinted by permission of www.cartoonstock.com.

CHAPTER 10

Page 109   If this point is easily missed, it's because of the archaic and cryptic structure... *The Proverbs and Epigrams of John Heywood (A.D. 1562)*, reprinted 1867 (London: The Spenser Society, 1867), at p. 140.

Page 110   That reality was neatly captured by Ambrose Bierce... See his *Devil's Dictionary* (New York: Dover Publications, 1958), at p. 15 (The Dover edition of the Dictionary is a republication of the original work, published in 1911).

Page 111   According to Mark Kurlansky... *The Big Oyster: History on the Half Shell* (New York: Ballantine Books, 2006), at p. 205.

Page 111   Ogden Nash declared in verse that he fancied the life of an oyster... In his poem "The Oyster," reprinted in *Candy is Dandy: The Best of Ogden Nash* (London: Methuen London, 1985), at p. 16. The poem is reprinted here by permission of Curtis Brown Ltd. and Carlton Publishing Group.

Page 113   Recent studies support the proposition... Media reports of a couple of these studies can be found at http://www.siasat.com/english/news/germs-can-be-good-study and at http://www.dailymail.co.uk/news/article-139469/why-eating-dirt-good-stomach-act-shield-stomach.html.

Page 113   This prompted Dr. Edward de Bono, the father of lateral thinking... See Jury, Louise, "De Bono's Marmite Plan for Peace in the Middle Yeast," *The Independent*, issue of December 19, 1999.

Page 113   The current acceptance of the saying "a woman's place is in the home"... See "Is a Woman's Place in the Home? 1 in 4 Say No" at http://www.reuters.com/article/2010/03/07/us-women-poll-idUSTRE6261ES20100307.

Page 114   The 1992 self-help book by John Gray...*Men are from Mars, Women are from Venus: A Practical Guide for Improving Communications and Getting What You Want in Your Relationships* (New York: HarperCollins, 1992).

Page 114   Professor John Pentland Mahaffy, who served as provost of Trinity College...See Grothe, Mardy, *Viva la repartee: clever comebacks and witty retorts from history's greatest wits and wordsmiths* (New York: HarperCollins, 2005), at p. 34.

Page 115   Another old saying, "the cock may crow...As reported by Quote Investigator, see http://quoteinvestigator.com/2013/04/14/hen-lays.

Page 119   That might be implied by this epitaph...See McPhee, Nancy, *The Second Book of Insults* (Toronto: Van Nostrand Reinhold, 1981), at p. 104.

Page 120   "Sometimes you have to be cruel to be kind,"...*Hamlet*, III, iv, 176.

Page 121   The Bible records these words of Jesus...*Matthew*, 19: 24.

Page 121   As Bill Bryson points out...*The Mother Tongue: English and How it Got That Way* (New York: HarperCollins, 1990), at p. 80.

Page 122   "The child is father of [to] the man,"...The poem is included in *William Wordsworth: Poems Selected by Seamus Heaney* (London: Faber & Faber, 2011), at p. 98.

Page 122   The later English poet-priest Gerard Manley Hopkins...Hopkins poem, entitled "Triolet," is reprinted in Amis, Kingsley (ed.) *The New Oxford Book of Light Verse* (Oxford: Oxford University Press, 1978), at p. 162.

Page 123   Others were collected by Tom Weller...*Minims or Man is the Only Animal that Wears Bow Ties* (Boston: Houghton Mifflin, 1982).

CHAPTER 11

Page 125   In his *Canterbury Tales*, from the fourteenth century...The first saying appears in "The Tale of Melibee" in the form "whil that iren hoot, men sholden smyte" and the second saying appears in "The Clerk's Prologue" in the form "every thing hath tyme;" see Chaucer, Geoffrey, *Canterbury Tales* (New York: Alfred A Knopf), at p. 394 (line1131) and p. 221 (line 6).

Page 126   Two centuries later, William Shakespeare...See, for the first saying, *Hamlet*, IV, iii, 9; for the second saying, *Hamlet*, V, i, 286; for the third saying, *Hamlet*, 1, iii, 75; for the fourth saying, *Hamlet*, 1, iii, 75, and for the fifth saying, *The Merchant of Venice*, II, vi, 69.

Page 126   The original saying concludes the final verse...Reprinted in Amis, Kingsley (ed.), *The New Oxford Book of Light Verse* (Oxford; Oxford University Press, 1978), at p. 46.

Page 127   This last proverb is drawn from the Bible...*Luke*, 6:31.

Page 129   It became particularly well known...Mitford, Nancy (ed.), *Noblesse Oblige* (Harmondsworth, Middlesex: Penguin Books, 1959).

Page 129   The motto of the state of Maryland... See Safire, William, *Watching My Language: Adventures in the Word Trade* (New York: Random House, 1997), at pp. 37–38.

Page 131   In the second half of the twentieth century... See Augustine, Norman R., *Augustine's Laws*, 6th ed. (Preston, Va.: American Institute of Aeronautics and Astronautics, 1997), at p. 24.

Page 132   It appeared as a headline over a newspaper article... *The Globe and Mail*, issue of November 20, 2008.

Page 133   The word "pinta" became so well known... *Collins English Dictionary*, 11th ed. (Glasgow: HarperCollins, 2012).

Page 134   It's been described as... See Geary, James, *The World in a Phrase: the Brief History of the Aphorism* (New York: Bloomsbury, 2005), at p. 21.

Page 135   Naturally, the astute restaurateur will be anxious to make sure... The cartoon following is by Anthony Jenkins and appeared the *The Globe & Mail*, issue of November 17, 2008. It is reprinted here by permission of The Canadian Press.

CHAPTER 12

Page 137   Another American politician, who will go unnamed, had no such regrets... See White, Michael, "Americans Find 169 Languages," *The Guardian*, issue of April 30, 1985.

Page 138   A journalist is reported to have sent a letter... See Mount, Harry, *Carpe Diem... Carpe Diem: Put a Little Latin in your Life* (New York: Hyperion Books, 2007), at p. 242.

Page 138   Imagine Ogden Nash, after composing the first line... His poem is included in *Bed Riddance: A Posy for the Indisposed* (Boston & Toronto: Little Brown, 1969), at p. 14. The poem is reprinted here by permission of Curtis Brown, Ltd. and Carlton Publishing Group.

Page 139   A Latin word or expression is often used... For the quotation from Poohbah, see *The Complete Plays of Gilbert and Sullivan* (New York: W.W. Norton, 1976), at p. 337 & 344.

Page 140   A couple of sharply contrasting interpretations are brought out... This cartoon is reprinted by permission of Doug Pike.

Page 141   The most famous is Robert Herrick's... Herrick's poem is included in *Poems of Robert Herrick* (New York: Thomas Y. Cromwell, 1967), at p. 45.

Page 141   There's also some question about what Descartes may have been thinking... The Descartes clerihew was the winning entry, submitted by Steve Fogland, in a contest entitled "Do You Clerihew?" initiated in the May 1983 issue of *Games* magazine, at p. 59. The winning entry appeared in the September 1983 issue of the magazine, at p. 60. It is reprinted here by permission of Games Publications, a part of Kappa Publishing Group, Inc.

Page 143　This was the period of her life of which Cleopatra spoke...*Antony and Cleopatra*, I, v, 77.

Page 148　*Mens sana in corpore sano*...The translation by Alexander McCall Smith comes through one of his characters in *The Dog Who Came in from the Cold* (Edinburgh: Polygon, 2010), see at p. 1.

Page 149　*Sine die*...The biblical warning is raised in *Romans*, 6:23.

Page 150　In their book *Liberated Latin*...*Liberated Latin* (Garden City, N.Y.: Doubleday, 1951).

Page 153　Writing in *The Guardian* newspaper..."The Battle Over Pro Bono," *The Guardian*, issue of October 8, 2002.

Page 153　The move against legal Latin has its fervent critics...*Lawyers' Latin: A Vade-Mecum*, new ed. (London: Robert Hale, 2006), at p. 15.

Page 156　That earlier proceeding is recounted in "The Devil and Daniel Webster,"...See Benét, Stephen Vincent, *The Devil and Daniel Webster* (New York: Farrar & Rhinehart, 1937).

Page 157　The poem describes the crushing of cheese, garlic and green herbs... See Bryson, Bill, *Made in America: An Informal History of the English Language in the United States* (New York: William Morrow, 1994), at p. 24.

Page 158　There's a strong hint that the motto is Dog Latin...See Simpson, D.P. (ed.), *Cassells New Latin-English, English-Latin Dictionary*, 5th ed. (London: Cassell, 1968), at p. 266.

CHAPTER 13

Page 159　Several of the earliest examples...Most of Aesop's fables referred to in this chapter are collected in Pinkney, Jerry, *Aesop's Fables* (New York: SeaStar Books, 2000) and in Gibbs, Laura, *Aesop's Fables* (New York: Oxford University Press, 2002, rev. 2008).

Page 161　In Thurber's fable, titled "The Unicorn in the Garden,"...See Thurber, James, *The Thurber Carnival* (New York: Random House, 1994), at pp. 340-342.

Page 161　In another, early fable, a huntsman...The fable of "A Hunts-man and a Currier" is included in l'Estrange, Sir Roger, *Fables of Aesop and the Eminent Mythologists with Morals and Reflections*, 2d ed., corrected and amended (London: R. Sare, B. Took et al., 1692), where it appears under the heading "The Fables of Astemius," at p. 269.

Page 162　The celebrated American poet Carl Sandburg used this...For these illustrations from the poem, see Harmon, William, *The Oxford Book of American Light Verse* (Oxford; Oxford University Press, 1979), at p. 310 (the complete poem is published in Sandburg, Carl, *The People, Yes* [New York: Harcourt Brace, 1936]).

Page 162   One is reminded of a famous line...From his poem "To a Mouse," collected in *A Night with Robert Burns: The Greatest Poems*, arr. by O'Hagan, Andrew (Toronto: McClelland & Stewart, 2009), at pp. 181-182.

Page 163   A famous poem is the source of the expression...The lines from the poem that are quoted in this paragraph of the text are lines 115-116. 135-138; see *Samuel Taylor Coleridge: The Complete Poems* (London: Penguin Books, 1997), at pp. 150 and 151.

Page 163   No such guilt was felt by the cinema snack vendor...A video clip of this sketch can be seen on YouTube at http://www.watch.com/watch?v=2_u7vGiMO0u.

Page 165   The current scientific consensus is that on extended flights...For a description of the behavior noted in the text, see Michener, Charles D., *The Social Behavior of Bees: A Comparative Study* (Cambridge, Mass.: The Belnap Press, 1974), at pp. 148-151, 159-177.

Page 166   This reproductive fact has even influenced the expressions that rabbits themselves use...The cartoon is reprinted by permission of www.CartoonStock.com

Page 167   The degree of haste involved is captured in another rabbit cartoon...This cartoon by David Pope, a.k.a. Heinrich Hinze, is reprinted from *Aussie English for Beginners: Book Three* (Canberra, National Museum of Australia, 2004) courtesy National Museum of Australia.

Page 168   This tactic is one that managers urge...See Jacobs, Andrew, "Chirps and Cheers: China's Crickets Clash," *New York Times*, issue of November 5, 2011.

Page 171   The British newspaper, *The Daily Telegraph*, carried the story...*The Daily Telegraph*, issue of May 18, 1980.

Page 172   Other helpful hints for worldly success...The first two of the "be-like" examples are built upon samples offered up by Richard Lederer in *Lederer on Language* (Portland, Ore.: Marion Street Press, 2013), at pp.142–143.

Page 173   It was questioned by Ogden Nash...The poem is reprinted in *Candy is Dandy: The Best of Ogden Nash* (London: Methuen, 1985), at p. 253 and is reprinted here by permission of Curtis Brown Ltd. and Carlton Publishing Group.

Page 173   Sir Winston Churchill compared the two companions...As recounted by Martin Gilbert in *Never Despair: Winston S. Churchill 1945–1965* (Toronto: Stoddard Publishing, 1988), at p. 304.

Page 174   However, it's reinforced by these lines...Swift's poem is included in Rogers, Pat (ed.), *Jonathon Swift: The Complete Poems* (New Haven and London: Yale University Press, 1982), see at 113–114, esp. at lines 31–32, 53–54 & 62–63.

Page 175   It's used in American political terminology...Safire, William, *Safire's Political Dictionary* (Oxford: Oxford University Press, 1993), at pp. 302–303.

Page 177   A pig needs to be aware of the person... This poem is included in Harmon, William, *The Oxford Book of American Light Verse* (Oxford; Oxford University Press, 1979), at p. 181.

Page 181   This kind of image is comfortably captured by *Canberra Times* cartoonist David Pope... The cartoon by David Pope, a.k.a. Heinrich Hinze, is reprinted from *Aussie English for Beginners: Book Three* (Canberra, National Museum of Australia, 2004) courtesy National Museum of Australia.

Page 183   It's what happens when you set the cat amongst the possums... This cartoon by David Pope, a.k.a. Heinrich Hinze, is reprinted from *Aussie English for Beginners: Book Three* (Canberra, National Museum of Australia, 2004) courtesy National Museum of Australia.

Page 187   This response carries an ominous suggestion... *Book of Genesis*, 4: 9.

Page 189   In a 2009 survey in the U.K.... See "Damp Squid: The top 10 misquoted phrases in Britain," *The Telegraph*, issue of February 24, 2009.

Page 192   Apparently, Sir Winston Churchill wasn't particularly moved... This Churchillian observation is noted by Dr. Mardy Grothe in his book *Viva la repartee: clever comebacks and witty retorts from history's greatest wits and wordsmiths* (New York: HarperCollins, 2005), at p. 186.

Page 193   In 2009, the Global Language Monitor, a Texas-based organization... See http://www.languagemonitor.com/tag/politically-correct.

Page 193   In an effort to correct the incorrect, some schools in Oxfordshire... See Blair, Alexandra, "Why Black Sheep are Banned and Humpty Can't be Cracked" in *The Times*, issue of March 7, 2006.

CHAPTER 14

Page 196   Consider the crow who can learn the technique... See the report of a recent study published in the scientific journal *PLOS One* at www.plosone.org/article/info%3Adoi%2F102Fjournal.pone.0026887. The fable "The Crow and the Pitcher" is included in Pinkney, Jerry, *Aesop's Fables* (New York: SeaStar Books, 2000), at p. 72.

Page 199   This was offered up by the narrator in Rosamund Lupton's best selling novel *Sister*... (London: Little Brown, 2011), at p. 137.

Page 205   There are a couple of fallacies in this latter day explanation... See O'Conner, Patricia T. and Stewart Kellerman, *Origins of the Specious: Myths and Misconceptions of the English Language* (New York: Random House, 2009), at pp. 123-126.

Page 206   While "keeping your fingers crossed" is generally meant... See Geary, James, *I is an Other: The Secret Life of Metaphor and How It Shapes the Way We See the World* (New York: HarperCollins, 2011), at p. 107.

Page 206   The popular view, which has not gone unchallenged...For a serious challenge to the popular view, see Morris, Desmond, *Gestures: Their Origins and Distribution* (London: Jonathon Cape, 1979), esp. at p. 186–193.

Page 206   The ancient Romans were clearly at the forefront...See Axtell, Roger E., *Gestures: The DO's and TABOOS of Body Language Around the World* (New York: John Wiley & Sons, 1991), at p. 34.

Page 207   Beatrice Lillie, the English star of stage, screen and music hall, was once asked, in an interview,...The interview is recounted by Bill Bryson in *Made in America: An Informal History of the English Language in the United States* (New York: William Morrow, 1994), at p. 320.

Page 208   The political correctness movement is sometimes said...See Beard, Henry and Christopher Cerf, *The Official Politically Correct Dictionary and Handbook* (New York: Villard Books, 1993), at p. 67.

Page 211   Ogden Nash recognized that having "time on your hands"...These are the opening lines of Nash's poem "Thoughts Thought While Waiting for a Pronouncement from a Doctor, an Editor, a Big Executive, the Department of Internal Revenue or Any other Momentous Pronouncer," which is included in *Bed Riddance: A Posy for the Indisposed* (Boston: Little Brown, 1969), at p. 38. The excerpt from this Nash poem is reprinted here by permission of Curtis Brown, Ltd. and Carlton Publishing Group.

Page 212   When Mark Antony, in Shakespeare's play...*Julius Caesar*, III, ii, 73.

Page 212   The first of these sayings comes from a poem by William Ross Wallace...The poem is reproduced in Felleman, Hazel (ed.), *Poems That Live Forever* (Garden City, N.Y.: Doubleday, 1965), at p. 149.

Page 217   The adder expression echoes a biblical passage...*Psalms* 58:4 refers to "the deaf adder that stops its ears."

Page 217   One fanciful explanation was offered up by *The Gentleman's Magazine*...The Magazine's account was reproduced in *The New York Times*, issue of June 29, 1901.

Page 218   Robert Lowell, the American poet, wrote that...These are the concluding lines of the poem "Since 1939," which is included in Lowell, Robert, *Day by Day* (New York: Farrar, Straus and Giroux, 1977), at p. 30–31.

CHAPTER 15

Page 222   Certainly, food is not "the be-all and the end-all"...The biblical proverb "man does not live by bread alone" can be found, with slight variations, in *Deuteronomy*, 8:2-3, *Matthew*, 4:4 and *Luke*, 4:4. For a biblical reference to bread as the staff of life, see *Ecclesiastes*, 11:1–2.

Page 222   Although the proper interpretation of the proverb is unsettled...See *Galations*, 6:7 for the proverb "whatever a man sews that will he also reap."

Page 222   According to Schafer, another announcer misspoke...In his book *Blooper Tube: The Best of 25 Years of Bloopers Including the History of Bloopers* (New York: Crown Publishers, 1979), Schafer attributes a similar sign-off to a BBC announcer, who is reported to have said: "This is BBC, the British Broadcorping Castration" (see at p. 113).

Page 223   In his book *Playing with Words*...Blake, Barry, *Playing with Words: Humour in the English Language* (London: Equinox, 2007), at p.18. The excerpt from Blake's book is reprinted by permission of Equinox Publishing, Ltd.

Page 223   The comedienne Ellen DeGeneres has suggested that we replace the suggestion...The suggestion was made in the course of the monologue for the January 15, 2014 episode of the Ellen DeGeneres Show, which can be viewed at http://www.ellentv.com/episodes/the-american-idol-judges-and-ryan-seacrest/.

Page 231   The opening verse, as adapted for the English tongue...This translated version is provided by the venerable Alexandria Burns Club; see http://www.robertburns.org.uk/Assets/Poems_Songs/toahaggis.htm.

CHAPTER 16

Page 240   Finally, as to the loosening effects of liquor...This poem is reprinted, not surprisingly, in *Candy is Dandy: The Best of Ogden Nash* (London: Methuen London, 1985), at p. 3 and is reprinted here by permission of Curtis Brown, Ltd. and Carlton Publishing Group.

Page 241   "Water is the only drink for a wise man"...Thoreau, Henry David, *Walden* (Philadelphia, Pa.: Running Press, 1990) (reprint of the 1st ed. 1854), at p. 131.

Page 242   Yet it was an excess of human kindness...*Macbeth*, I, v, 16–18.

BIBLIOGRAPHY

Ammer, Christine, *The American Heritage Dictionary of Idioms*, 2d ed. (Boston/New York: Houghton Mifflin Harcourt, 2013)

Ammer, Christine, *It's Raining Cats and Dogs... and Other Beastly Expressions* (New York: Paragon House, 1989)

Australian Slang (Camberwell, Vic.: Penguin, 2008)

Ayto, John (ed.), *Oxford Dictionary of English Idioms*, 3rd ed. (Oxford: Oxford University Press, 2009)

Bernard, Jim, *Words Gone Wild: Fun and Games for Language Lovers* (New York: Skyhorse, 2010)

Blake, Barry, *Playing with Words: Humour in the English Language* (London: Equinox 2007)

Butterfield, Jeremy, *Damp Squid: The English Language Laid Bare* (Oxford, Oxford University Press, 2008)

Casselman, Bill, *Canadian Sayings: 1,200 Folk Sayings Used by Canadians* (Toronto: McArthur & Co., 1999)

Davies, Christopher, *Divided by a Common Language: A Guide to British and American Expressions* (Boston: Houghton Mifflin, 2005)

Dent, Susie, *Larpers and Schroomers: the language report* (Oxford: Oxford University Press, 2004)

Farkas, Anna (ed.), *The Oxford Dictionary of Catchphrases* (Oxford: Oxford University Press, 2002)

Geary, James, *The World in a Phrase: A Brief History of the Aphorism* (New York: Bloomsbury, 2005)

Gooden, Philip and Peter Lewis, *Idiomantics: The Weird World of Popular Phrases* (London: Bloomsbury, 2012)

Grothe, Mardy, *I never metaphor I didn't like: a comprehensive compilation of history's analogies, metaphors, and similes* (New York: HarperCollins, 2008)

Grothe, Mardy, *Ifferisms: an anthology of aphorisms that begin with the word 'if'* (New York: HarperCollins, 2009)

Grothe, Mardy, *Never Let a Fool Kiss You or a Kiss Fool You: Chiasmus and the World of Chiastic Quotations* (New York: Penguin Books, 2012)

Grothe, Mardy, *Oxymoronica: paradoxical wit and wisdom from history's greatest wordsmiths* (New York: HarperCollins, 2004)

Grothe, Mardy, *Vive la repartee: clever comebacks and witty retorts from history's great wits and wordsmiths* (New York: HarperCollins, 2005)

Hendrickson, Robert, *QPB Encyclopedia of Word and Phrase Origins* (New York: Facts on File Inc., 2004)

Holder, R.W., *Oxford Dictionary of Euphemisms: How Not to Say What You Mean*, 4th ed. (Oxford: Oxford University Press, 2007)

Hole, Georgia, *The Real McCoy: The True Stories Behind Our Everyday Phrases* (Oxford: Oxford University Press, 2005)

Humphries, John, *Lost for Words: The Mangling and Manipulating of the English Language* (London: Hodder & Stoughton, 2004).

Jack, Albert, *Red Herrings & White Elephants: The Origins of the Phrases We Use Every Day* (New York: HarperCollins, 2004 and London: Metro Publishing, 2004)

Jack, Albert, *Shaggy Dogs and Black Sheep: The Origins of Even More Phrases We Use Every Day* (London: Penguin Books, 2005)

Keyes, Ralph, *The Quote Verifier: Who Said What, Where and When* (New York: St. Martin's Griffin, 2006)

Knowles, Elizabeth, ed., *The Little Oxford Dictionary of Proverbs* (Oxford: Oxford University Press, 2009)

Lakoff, George and Johnson, Mark, *Metaphors We Live By* (Chicago: University of Chicago Press, 2003)

Lederer, Richard, *Lederer on Language* (Portland, Oregon: Marion Street Press, 2013).

Makin, Tom, *Brief Encounters: From Einstein to Elvis* (Bloomington, Indiana: AuthorHouse, 2008)

Manser, Martin, *The Facts on File Dictionary of Proverbs*, 2nd ed. (New York: Facts on File, 2007)

Martin, Gary, "The Phrase Finder" Website, at http://www.phrases.org.uk

Metcalf, Fred (ed.), *Dictionary of Modern Humorous Quotations*, 3d rev. ed. (London: Penguin Books, 2009)

Mieder, Wolfgang, *Proverbs Are Never out of Season* (New York: Oxford University Press, 1993).

Mieder, Wolfgang and Anna Litovkina, *Twisted Wisdom: Modern Anti-Proverbs* (Hobart, Tas.: De Proverbio.com,, 2002)

Mieder, Wolfgans and Stewart A. Kingsbury, *A Dictionary of Wellerisms* (New York: Oxford University Press, 1994)

Mount, Harry, *Carpe Diem: Put a Little Latin in Your Life* (New York: Hyperion, 2007)

O'Conner, Patricia T. and Stewart Kellerman, *Origins of the Specious: Myths and Misconceptions of the English Language* (New York: Random House, 2009)

Oliver, Harry, *Flying Pigs and Nosey Parkers: Origins of Words and Phrases We Use Every Day* (London: Metro Publishing, 2009) (published in the U.S. as *Flying by the Seat of Your Pants: Surprising Origins of Everyday Expressions* (New York: Penguin, 2011)).

Oliver, Harry, *March Hares and Monkeys' Uncles: Origins of Words and Phrases We Use Every Day* (London: Metro Publishing, 2005)

Oliver, Harry, *Bees Knees and Barmy Armies: Origins of the Words and Phrases We Use Every Day* (London: Metro Publishing, 2008).

Pollack, John, *The Pun Also Rises: How the Humble Pun Revolutionized Language, Changed History and Made Wordplay More Than Some Antics* (New York: Bantam Books, 2011)

Price, Steven D., *Endangered Phrases: Intriguing Idioms Dangerously Close to Extinction* (New York: Skyhorse Publishing, 2011)

Quinion, Michael, "World Wide Words" Website at http:/www.worldwidewords.org

Quinion, Michael, *Why is Q Always Followed by U? Word-Perfect Answers to the Most-Asked Questions About Language* (London: Penguin, 2009)

Ratcliffe, Susan, *Oxford Treasury of Sayings & Quotations*, 4th ed. (Oxford, Oxford University Press, 2011)

Rees, Nigel, *Cassell's Dictionary of Catchphrases*, 2d ed. (London: Weidenfield & Nicolson, 2005).

Rees, Nigel, *Cassell's Dictionary of Word and Phrase Origins*, new ed. (London: Cassell, 2002)

Rees, Nigel, *The Politically Correct Phrasebook, what they say you can't say in the 1990's* (London: Bloomsbury Publishing, 1993)

Rhodes, Chloe, *A Certain "Je Ne Sais Quoi": The Origin of Foreign Words Used in English* (Pleasantville, N.Y./Montreal: Readers Digest Trade Publishing, 2010 and London: Michael O'Mara Books, 2009)

Richler, Howard, *Can I Have a Word With You?* (Vancouver: Ronsdale Press, 2007)

Safire, William, *Safire's Political Dictionary* (New York: Random House, 1978)

Shapiro, Fred R. (ed.), *The Yale Book of Quotations* (New Haven, Conn: Yale University Press, 2006)

Speake, Jennifer (ed.), *Oxford Dictionary of Proverbs*, 5th ed. (Oxford: Oxford University Press, 2008)

Spears, Richard A., *American Idioms Dictionary*, 4th ed. (New York: McGraw-Hill, 2007)

Udang, Laurence, *The Last Word: The English Language: Opinions and Prejudices* (Detroit: OmniData, 2008)

Wilkes, G.A., *Stunned Mullets & Two-pot Screamers: A Dictionary of Australian Colloquialisms*, 5th ed. (South Melbourne, Vic.: Oxford University Press, 2008)

Zullo, Allan & Gene Cheek, *Butter my Butt and Call me a Biscuit* (Kansas City, Andrews McMeel Publishing; 2009)

INDEX